AF600361

THE CATHOLIC UNIVERSITY OF AMERICA
CANON LAW STUDIES
No. 166

THE DISMISSAL OF RELIGIOUS IN TEMPORARY VOWS

AN HISTORICAL CONSPECTUS AND COMMENTARY

by

REV. FRANCIS JOSEPH O'NEILL, C.SS.R., J.C.L.
Priest of the Saint Louis Province

A DISSERTATION

Submitted to the Faculty of Canon Law of the Catholic University of America in Partial Fulfillment of the Requirements for the Degree of Doctor of Canon Law

THE CATHOLIC UNIVERSITY OF AMERICA PRESS
WASHINGTON, D. C.
1942

Imprimi Potest:

FRANCISCUS J. FAGEN, C.SS.R.,
Superior Provincialis.

Sancti Ludovici, die 25 maii, 1942.

Nihil Obstat:

HIERONYMUS D. HANNAN, A.M., LL.B., S.T.D., J.C.D.,
Censor Deputatus.

Washingtonii, die 3 iunii, 1942.

Imprimatur:

✠ MICHAEL J. CURLEY, D.D.,
Archiepiscopus Baltimoriensis-Washingtoniensis.

Baltimorae, die 3 iunii, 1942.

Printed by
THE PAULIST PRESS
New York, N. Y.
61

AD

SANCTUM ALPHONSUM

DOCTOREM ZELANTISSIMUM

TABLE OF CONTENTS

PART II—CANONICAL COMMENTARY

CHAPTER I

CHAPTER II

CHAPTER III

CHAPTER IV

CHAPTER V

FOREWORD

THE purpose of the historical synopsis of this dissertation is to trace the Church legislation on the religious vows of Congregations, paying special regard to the legislation on temporary vows, and on dismissal of religious in such vows. In introducing the historical treatise to the reader one can perhaps find no words more appropriate and to the point than those contained in Cardinal Gasquet's introduction to Augustine's third volume of his Commentary:

> . . . Hitherto legislation in regard to religious has been in what may be called "a fluid state." It was mostly based upon special Pontifical Constitutions and deductions from the same, and had not hitherto been gathered together and coordinated officially. The marvelous growth of religious bodies and the variety, especially in modern time, of their scope and purpose, had rendered it difficult, to say the least, to set out the ecclesiastical law applicable to them.
>
> After the Council of Trent, the advent of Congregations of Clerks Regular made necessary great changes in the old monastic legislation, and these again opened the way for other Congregations of simple vows, perpetual or temporary, which have proved useful and even necessary to meet the needs of the Church in modern times.[1]

The main part of the historical synopsis will undertake to follow in the best way possible the evolution of law found in this "fluid state." The new discipline of the Code in which the Institutes of simple vows have obtained a certain juridic parity with the old religious Orders and enjoy the rights and names of the older religious institutions presuppose an evolution of law through several centuries.[2] During this period the new Congregations, especially those of women religious, were only slowly and almost furtively approved. At first they met with opposition. Many reasons were advanced

[1] Augustine, *A Commentary on the New Code of Canon Law* (8 vols., Vol. III, 4. ed., St. Louis: B. Herder, 1929), III, iii-iv (henceforth cited as *Commentary*).

[2] La Puma, "Evoluzione del diritto dei religiose da Pio IX a Pio XI"—*Acta Congressus Iuridici Internationalis* (5 vols., Vol. IV, Romae: Libraria Pont. Instituti Utriusque Iuris, 1937), 195.

against their existence and approval. Then came successively periods of toleration, permission, praise, and, finally, immediately before the New Code and at the time of the New Code, a period which saw their full official approval.[3]

During this period the Sacred Congregation of Bishops and Regulars began to modify profoundly the old law of the regulars. On some points unity of discipline was possible; on many points, however, because of differences in purpose, vows and constitution, the legislation of the regulars would not fit the new Congregations. The result was a gradual formation of a *schema* of legislation to fit the new Congregations—it was a period of trial. The Sacred Congregation of Bishops and Regulars proceeded wisely and cautiously. In such a difficult situation it at first allowed, for experiment, certain provisions which it had later to forbid or change. There thus arose apparent and even real contradictions of legislation on the same matter. The legislation was built up by means of constitutions, decrees, answers to doubts, and animadversions upon constitutions of Congregations submitted to it for approval. There arose a jurisprudence built up on conclusions drawn from the decrees, constitutions, etc. During this whole period the legislation as well as the jurisprudence deriving from it never had its juridical character expressly or accurately defined. Nor was there ever given in this period an example or model for the constitution of a congregation which embraced an orderly collection of previous legislation on this matter. The first idea for such an orderly collection came in 1897 when a Commission was appointed to draw up rules to be followed in the approbation of religious Institutes. These rules were not promulgated but were found worked into the constitution *Conditae a Christo* of Pope Leo XIII. In 1901, these rules had evolved and become the *Normae*. Only in 1901, then, did a full schema (found in the *Normae*) supplant the very general *Methodus* of approving new Congregations given by Cardinal Bizzarri in 1862.[4]

[3] Larraona, "Commentarium Codicis in partem secundam libri II codicis quae est: De Religiosis"—*Commentarium pro Religiosis,* I (1920), 45 (the article henceforth will be cited as "De Religiosis" and the periodical as *CpR*).

[4] Larraona, "De Religiosis"—*CpR,* I (1920), 135-136; 140, note (25); Battandier, *Guide Canonique Pour Les Constitutions Des Instituts À Voeux*

The reason for this original opposition cannot be fully understood without a previous knowledge of the mind of the law at that time on the essentials of the religious state. For several centuries, at least, all religious took solemn vows. Many claimed that solemn vows were of the essence of the religious state. As a consequence, the new idea of religious with simple vows clashed with the accepted ideas of the time. It was a practically foreseen result that great opposition would be manifested to the innovation. A lengthy treatment of the period leading up to the appearance of religious in simple vows would be out of place in this dissertation; what is in place is a short preliminary treatment of the previous Church legislation on religious vows with this purpose in view: to give the legal setting of religious vows when in the late sixteenth century the Constitution *Ascendente Domino* of Pope Gregory XIII appeared. Only with such a setting is there a satisfactory explanation of the opposition to the simple vows sanctioned by Pope Gregory XIII.

In short, the plan of the historical synopsis will be to offer a short preliminary treatment of early Church legislation which will furnish an understanding of the status of religious vows in the late sixteenth century, to view the result of this piece of legislation in regard to congregations of men and women religious in simple vows, and to follow the formation of the law which was invoked to fit the needs of the new Congregations.

To do this is not easy. Much that has been written on this period has been inaccurate and false.[5] In many other questions the sources of law are easily obtainable. Such is not the case here. The principal decrees of the Popes and of the Sacred Congregation of Bishops and Regulars which were used in the codification of the New Code are found in the *Codicis Iuris Canonici Fontes.* But these are only the better known and the more general decrees. The *Acta* of the Sacred Congregation of Bishops and Regulars containing all the

Simples (6. ed., Paris: Gabalda, 1923), n. 16, p. 7, cf. also p. XXXI (henceforth cited as *Guide Canonique*. The sixth edition is cited whenever a different edition is not specifically indicated).

[5] Cf. on this point: Creusen, "Esquisse Historique: Les instituts religieux à voeux simples"—*Revue des Communautés Religieuses,* XV (1939), 52 (henceforth cited *RCR*).

acts, decrees, responses, etc., of that Congregation are to be found in full only in the archives of that Congregation; they have never been edited in full.[6] Partial collections of the decrees, animadversions, answers to doubts, and approbations of rules are to be found only in private collections, in periodicals, and in canonical and theological reviews.[7]

The purpose of the canonical commentary is to present as clearly as possible the meaning of canons 647 and 648 and of the other canons in their relation to them; to evaluate and arrive, when possible, at a conclusion on disputed points; and, finally, to furnish some ideas or conclusions hitherto not considered and to elaborate and clarify the conclusions which have already been drawn by authors on the subject. In endeavoring to reach new conclusions, the chief purpose and intent has been to give a more complete listing of causes which may rightfully be accepted as sufficing for the act of dismissal. Although some authors consider the listing of such causes as useless,[8] inasmuch as the Code has left the decision as to the sufficiency of the causes to the prudence and judgment of the superiors, still it seems that a particularization of a general cause is always useful, although it must be granted that it is still left to the prudence and judgment of the superiors to decide when even these particularized causes are sufficient for the act of dismissal. In an effort to furnish a full list of these causes the writer consulted as

[6] Wernz, *Ius Decretalium* (ed. altera, 5 vols., Romae, 1905-1914), I, p. 381, n. 271, note (42); Maroto, *Institutiones Iuris Canonici,* I (3. ed., Romae: apud Commentarium pro Religiosis, 1921), 94 (henceforth cited *Institutiones*).

[7] The chief of the private collections found useful are listed here. Bizzarri, *Collectanea in usum Secret. S. C. Episcoporum et Regularium* (3. ed., Romae, 1885). This work contains in an appendix a work by the same author: *Acta S. Congregationis Super Statu Regularium* (Romae, 1862). The former will be cited: *Coll. S. C. Ep. et Reg.*; the latter will not be abbreviated. Lucidi, *De Visitatione Sacrorum Liminum* (3. ed., purgata et aucta per R. J. Schneider, S.J., 3 vols., Romae, 1883), cited as *De Visitatione. Analecta Iuris Pontificii* in vols. XI, XII, XIII and XIV, contains decrees of the Sacred Congregation of Bishops and Regulars which had until then been unedited. The various other periodicals and reviews from which the decrees and acts of the Congregation are taken will be indicated in the footnotes.

[8] Coronata, *Institutiones Iuris Canonici* (5 vols., Vol. I, 2 ed., Taurini [Italia]; Marietti, 1939), I, 869; (henceforth cited *Institutiones*).

many authors and as many Rules and Constitutions as were available for his use. Particularly helpful was the collection of Rules and Constitutions presented to the Canon Law Library of the Catholic University of America by the local unit of the Catholic Students' Mission Crusade. Most of the Rules and Constitutions merely report the exact wording of the Code. Of the number listed in the bibliography less than ten furnish any material at all to guide a superior in making his decision. In view of these considerations it was assumed that a listing in full of the various causes which suffice for the act of dismissal would prove to be of canonical value.

In regard to the bibliography, the listing of so many articles of Goyeneche, Larraona and Maroto under the very general headings of "Consultatio" and "Annotatio" could not be avoided. As the *consultationes* are cases sent in to the *Commentarium pro Religiosis et Missionariis* for solution, a listing of them in their complete wording would make the bibliography unnecessarily lengthy. However the exclusion of these articles would leave the bibliography incomplete. The only solution was to include them under the general titles "Consultatio" and "Annotatio".

The writer wishes publicly to acknowledge the help given him by the Canon Law faculty as well as by the staff of the University library. He wishes to thank especially his former Provincial, Rev. Thomas M. Palmer, C.SS.R., for the opportunity given him to pursue the course of graduate study in Canon Law and to his present Provincial, Very Rev. Francis J. Fagen, C.SS.R., for the opportunity to complete his studies. He wishes also to acknowledge the help he received from so many of his confrères, relatives and friends; especially to Rev. Francis J. Bieter, C.SS.R., J.C.D., does he give grateful acknowledgment for his many helpful suggestions. In short, he wishes to give acknowledgment and thanks to all who have helped him in any way in the preparation of this thesis.

Part One

Historical Synopsis

CHAPTER I

RELIGIOUS VOWS IN THE EARLY CHURCH

Article 1. The Vows Themselves

The religious state denotes a fixed and permanent manner of life in common by means of which the faithful, besides observing the common precepts, bind themselves to the observance of the evangelical counsels by the vows of obedience, chastity, and poverty.[1] The vows by which the religious bind themselves are called *religious vows* as opposed to those which are termed *secular vows*. Religious vows, according to our present day usage, are those vows which are concerned with the evangelical counsels and which are taken as public vows in a religious Institute approved by the Church, whereas all other vows are secular vows.[2]

It will be desirable, in order to avoid confusion, to define *public* and *private* vows as well as *solemn* and *simple* vows. Since the terms *solemn* and *simple* came into use so late in the Church, and since the exact conditions in which a solemn vow is taken were not definitively stated until the mid-thirteenth century, it was easy to make the error of confusing these two classifications of vows. A *solemn* vow is a vow which the Church recognizes as such.[3] Lucidi records a reply of the Sacred Penitentiary as to the requisites of a solemn vow: A *solemn* vow is one which the Church accepts as such and which (in view of the ordinary law and apart from the case of pontifical dispensation) deprives the person who vows perpetually

[1] Canon 487.

[2] Molitor, *Religiosi Iuris Capita Selecta* (Ratisbonae, 1909), p. 180; Maroto, "Consultationes"—*CpR,* V (1924), 351.

[3] Canon 1308, §2.

and immutably of the power to contract matrimony and of the power to acquire dominion over things.[4] *Simple* vows are those which are recognized by the Church as not being solemn because they lack the requirements of a solemn vow. A *public* vow is one which is accepted in the name of the Church by a legitimate ecclesiastical superior. It is taken in the public forum of the Church with the intervention and the acceptance of the Church. A *private* vow is any other type of vow, *i. e.*, one which is taken without the intervention and acceptance of the Church.[5] However, since it was not until the Council of Chalcedon (451) that the Church took a hand in the approbation of a religious Institute by committing it to the care of the bishop of the city,[6] one must until that date (451) omit the one portion of the definition: "approved by the Church." In those days religious vows were the vows of poverty, chastity and obedience which were taken in order to live a religious life in common with others.

Religious life can be traced back to the very early ages of the Church. In Apostolic times both men and women practiced the evangelical virtues of poverty, chastity and obedience.[7] These virgins and ascetics, as they were named, practiced perfect continence and voluntary poverty, but whether or not they bound themselves to

[4] S. C. Poenit. *Ep. Lemovicensi,* 1820—*apud* Lucidi, *De Visitatione Sacrorum Liminum,* II, p. 265, n. 298 (to be cited henceforth as *De Visitatione*). Cf. Pirhing, *Ius Canonicum Novo Methodo Explicatum* (ed. novissima iuxta exemplar Dilingae, 1721), in Decret., Lib. III, tit. 34, n. 1.

[5] Canon 1308, § 1; Molitor, *Religiosi Iuris Capita Selecta,* p. 180; Maroto, "Consultationes"—*CpR,* V (1924), 351.

[6] C. 4—Mansi, *Sacrorum Conciliorum Nova et Amplissima Collectio* (53 vols. in 59, Parisiis, 1901-1927), VII, 359 (hereafter cited as Mansi). Cf., Orth, *The Approbation of Religious Institutes,* The Catholic University of America Canon Law Studies, n. 71 (Washington, D. C.: Catholic University of America, 1931), pp. 14 ff.

[7] Schäfer, *Compendium De Religiosis Ad Norman Codicis Iuris Canonici* (3. ed. Roma: S. A. L. E. R., 1940), p. 18 (henceforth cited as *De Religiosis*); Heimbucher, *Die Orden und Kongregationen der katholischen Kirche* (3. ed., 2 vols., Paderborn: Ferd. Schöningh, 1933-1934), I, 61; Frey, *The Act of Religious Profession,* The Catholic University of America Canon Law Studies, n. 63 (Washington, D. C.: Catholic University of America, 1931), p. 8 ff. (henceforth cited as *Religious Profession*).

these counsels by vow is not certain. Some authors maintain that from the very beginning of the Church there were formal vows as we now understand them; *i. e.*, as defined in canon 1307, § 1: "a deliberate and free promise made to God concerning something good which is possible of accomplishment and of higher moral excellence than its opposite and which must be fulfilled by reason of the virtue of religion."[8] From the available evidence it seems that up to the middle of the second century the *virgines* bound themselves only by a *propositum*,[9] *i. e.*, by a determination to do or to omit something that pertained to divine worship. No obligation was assumed in a *propositum* nor was any promise made. It was equivalent to our present day good resolution, and induced no obligation in conscience to carry out the work proposed.[10] It seems from the writing of the Fathers that evidence pointing to the existence of a vow can be found in the middle of the second century.[11] Although there was external solemnity connected with the taking of these vows, as may be seen in St. Ambrose's description,[12] it cannot be said with certainty that these vows were public, *i. e.*, that they were taken in the public forum of the Church with the intervention and acceptance of the Church

[8] Cf. S. C. Ep. et Reg., *Bergomen.*, 14 sept. 1841—*apud* Lucidi, *De Visitatione*, II, p. 264; n. 297; Wilpert, *Die gottgeweihten Jungfrauen in den ersten drei Jahrhunderten* (Freiburg im Breisgau, 1892), p. 7; Heimbucher, *op. cit.*, I, 64; Weckesser, "Das feierliche Keuschheitsgelübde in der alten Kirche"—*Archiv für katholisches Kirchenrecht*, LXXVI (1896), 89 (he says that solemn vows are as old as the Church), (this periodical will hereafter be cited *AKKR*).

[9] Frey, *Religious Profession*, p. 10.

[10] Suarez, *Opera Omnia*, Vol. XIV, pp. 750-751, *De Virtute et Statu Religionis* (Parisiis, 1859), tract. VI, proem.; Ferraris, *Prompta Bibliotheca Canonica, Juridica, Moralis, Theologica necnon Ascetica Polemica, Rubristica, Historica* (Parisiis, 1860-1863), VII, sub. v. "Votum," art. 1, n. 1; Kirchberg, *De Voti Natura, Obligatione, Honestate Commentatio Theologica* (Aschendorf, 1897), p. 1.

[11] Frey, *op. cit.*, p. 10; Schiewietz, "Das Mönchtum der ersten drei Jahrhunderte"—*AKKR*, LXXVIII (1898), 20; Steiger, "De propagatione et diffusione vitae religiosae"—*Periodica de re Canonica et Morali*, XIII (1924), 40-41 (hereafter referred to as *Periodica*).

[12] *De Virginibus*, Lib. III, cap. 1—Migne, *Patrologiae Cursus Completus, Series Latina* (221 vols., Parisiis, 1844-1864), XVI, 219 (henceforth cited as *MPL*).

as prescribed in canon 1308, § 1.[13] Only from fourth century documents can there be drawn any certainty as to public vows. In short, it is sure that the vows of the virgins were distinct in form; *i. e.*, some were external and others were internal (*soli Deo notae*); [14] but before the fourth century there is no certain evidence that there were public vows as distinct from private vows.

No matter what be the outcome of the dispute on these vows, they were (among the virgins and ascetics) concerned with chastity alone. And even if they had vows and took them even publicly, since they did not vow all the three counsels together, they did not strictly constitute the religious status as defined above.

The virgins and ascetics, as it were, gave a preview of the religious state as it was to be developed through the institution of monasticism. In the third century, especially in the deserts of Egypt, many of the faithful began to practice the eremitical life. Their numbers grew so great that they began to join together into groups or societies under leaders like St. Paul the Anchorite (234-347), St. Anthony (251-356), and St. Pachomius (292-345). Rules or regulations became necessary for discipline and good order. It is to these rules that one must go to inquire about the religious vows of that period.

Of those mentioned, St. Anthony left no rule,[15] but under his guidance his disciples faithfully observed the evangelical counsels. However, it was their own love and desire of poverty, chastity and obedience and their determination to persevere that bound them together—there were no vows.[16] St. Pachomius was the real founder of the cenobitical life. He wrote the first rule for a monastic com-

[13] Koch, "Virgines Christi"—*Texte und Untersuchungen zur Geschichte der alt-christlichen Literatur,* XXXI (1907), 63 ff. and 75 ff.; Pourrat, *La Spiritualité Chrétienne,* I (Paris, 1918), 64—compare his use of the words *engager* and *engagement* with *vouer* on pp. 64, 264 and 389.

[14] Wernz-Vidal, *Ius Canonicum,* V (*Ius Matrimoniale,* 2 ed., Romae: apud Aedes Universitatis Gregorianae, 1928), 349; Wernz, *Ius Decretalium,* III, pars II, 233.

[15] Heimbucher, *Orden und Kongregationen,* I, 69; Maroto, "Studia canonica" *CpRM,* XVIII (1937), 31 (In 1935 this periodical changed its name to *Commentarium pro Religiosis et Missionariis;* it will, in issues dating from 1935, be cited *CpRM*).

[16] Frey, *Religious Profession,* p. 12; Thomassinus, *Vetus et Nova Ecclesiae Disciplinae* (10 toms., Magontiaci, 1787), pars I, Lib. III, cap. 48, n. 3.

munity. In the forty-ninth chapter of that rule is described the profession made by those who embrace the monastic life—no mention is made of an explicit vow.[17] Schenute, whose birth is placed in the uncertain range of eighteen years (332-350) and who died in 451 or 452, used St. Pachomius' rule as a basis, but made some changes. The candidates had to declare their determination to strive after perfection and to bind themselves to it by a promise or by an oath. This oath was made orally according to a certain written formula.[18]

St. Basil (329-379) wrote his rule about the year 361. It was written in two forms: one a shorter form called *Regulae Brevius Tractatae,* and one a longer form called *Regulae Fusius Tractatae.* In the latter rule, in the fifteenth chapter, St. Basil orders that, after a time of probation, the candidate be admitted to a profession of chastity. The rule enjoined on him obedience and poverty as is mentioned in several places.[19] On the foundation of this rule St. Basil brought the institution of monasticism to its greatest perfection in the Eastern Church. He is called the "Patriarch of Monasticism in the East" and his rule spread throughout the East, constituting there the basis of monasticism, so that even to the present day it is the rule even of the Eastern schismatic monks. In the East, then, the rule of St. Basil is the one which embodied the religious vows. This rule spread to the West in a few places, only to be supplanted by the rule of St. Benedict.[20]

17 *Regula S. Pachomii—MPL,* XXIII, 70; Frey, *op. cit.*, p. 14; Heimbucher, *op. cit.*, I, 77-85, esp. pp. 79-80.

18 Piontek (*De Indulto Exclaustrationis necnon de Indulto Saecularizationis,* The Catholic University of America Canon Law Studies, n. 29 [Washington, D. C.: Catholic University of America, 1925], pp. 19-20), says: ". . . In formula hac habebatur quoque explicita mentio verbi 'voveo' . . . in normis Schenuti habemus . . . prima vestigia votorum professionis explicitae."; Ott ("Schenute"—*Catholic Encyclopedia,* XIII, 527) gives the English formula of the vow.

19 Migne, *Patrologiae Cursus Completus, Series Graeca* (161 vols., Parisiis, 1856-1866), XXXI, 905; 1051 (hereafter cited *MPG*). Cf. Frey, *op. cit.*, pp. 15-16; Heimbucher, *op. cit.*, I, 92. Piontek (*op. cit.*, p. 23) says: " . . . Regula S. Basilii postulat professionem *votorum* explicitam verbis prolatam et quidem post interrogationem. Quae emissio votorum debet esse libera atque coram communitatis Superioribus facta."

20 Heimbucher, *op. cit.*, I, 93, ff; Wernz, *Ius Decretalium,* III, 268; Ver-

In the West, St. Benedict (c. 480—c. 553) embodied religious vows in his rule. In Chapter 58 of the rule he demanded verbal vows and a written document bearing witness that the required vows had been taken.[21] Explicitly the monk vowed: stability, conversion of morals, and obedience. With conversion of morals he implicitly vowed to strive for higher perfection, and with obedience he implicitly vowed chastity [22] and poverty.[23]

As St. Basil in the East, so did St. Benedict in the West merit the title of "Patriarch of Monasticism." His rule, containing the three vows and embodying all that was necessary to constitute the religious state, was accepted by almost all the monasteries of the West. From Italy it went to England with St. Augustine, and thence to Germany with St. Boniface. St. Placidus introduced it into Sicily and St. Maurus into France. Two hundred years after St. Benedict's death, his rule was observed throughout the entire West—all monasteries followed it—it had gradually supplanted all other rules—it was *the rule*.[24]

Thus the religious state continued in this form, with slight changes, until the canons regular began to take vows and until the rise of the mendicants. These slight changes were occasioned by the various reforms. Since each monastery under the Benedictine rule was a separate and distinct entity, it was not surprising that they should group together into many congregations or new orders. These different divisions had for their purpose not only the restoration of the ancient rule, but also a more perfect unity and a more compact social order. The tenth century saw the rise of the Congregation of Cluny under St. Odo; the eleventh saw the rise of the Camaldolese under St. Romuald, the Vallambrosians under St. John Gualbertus, and

meersch, *De Religiosis Institutis et Personis* (2 vols., Vol. I, 2. ed., 1907; Vol. II, 4. ed., 1909, Brugis), I, 32, 33 (hereafter cited as *De Religiosis*).

[21] Butler, *Sancti Benedicti Regula Monasteriorum* (3. ed., Friburgi-Brisgoviae, 1935), Caput LVIII, pp. 105-110.

[22] *MPL*, LXVI, 824; contained in Caput IV, no. 63 of the rule—*MPL*, LXVI, 334.

[23] Contained in Caput XXXIII of the rule—*MPL*, LXVI, 551-564.

[24] Heimbucher, *op. cit.*, I, 168-177; Wernz, *op. cit.*, III, pars II, 269; Pourrat, *La Spiritualité Chrétienne*, I, 417; Suarez, *De Statu Perfectionis et Religionis*, Trac. IX, Lib. II, c. 2, n. 7; Vermeersch, *op. cit.*, p. 33.

the Carthusians under St. Bruno. There were others, but these were the more prominent ones. They all followed the rule of St. Benedict, and hence had the same three vows of poverty, chastity, and obedience, which were set down at the beginning of this dissertation as conditions essential for constituting the religious state—but they all had their own customs and constitutions which marked them as new and distinct orders.[25]

ARTICLE 2. THE NATURE OF THESE VOWS

The question to be treated now is admittedly a well-nigh insoluble one. It is the following: Were these religious vows solemn or simple? A variety of opinions, all held by reputable authors, confronts a student of the question. It will be helpful to see whether a definite decision can be reached on the question whether religious vows were solemn or simple up to the year 1123, and then to consider the situation existing in the Church legislation on religious vows in the late sixteenth century at the time of the Constitution *Ascendente Domino.*

The first explicit use of the term *simple vow* is found in Gratian.[26] In reviewing the ancient legislation on vows, Gratian rightly concluded that there were two kinds of vows of perpetual chastity: the one which invalidates a subsequent marriage [27] and the other which renders the subsequent marriage illicit but not invalid.[28] This distinction between simple vows and other vows of perfect chastity was taken up by Bernard of Pavia (d. 1216), taught in the schools,[29]

[25] Wernz-Vidal, *Ius Canonicum,* III, 33-34; Heimbucher, *op. cit.,* I, 177 ff., 315 ff.

[26] *Dictum Gratiani* ad c. 8, D. XXVII: "Hic distinguendum est, quod voventium alii sunt simpliciter voventes, de quibus Augustinus et Theodorus locuti sunt, alii sunt, quibus post votum accedit benedictio consecrationis, vel propositum religionis, de quibus Ieronimus et Nicolaus et Calixtus scripserunt."

[27] C. 8, D. XXVII; c. 1-40, C. XXVII, q. 1—*Dictum Gratiani* ad c. 40: "His omnibus auctoritatibus voventes prohibentur contrahere matrimonia, et quidam eorum, si contraxerint, separari iubentur."

[28] C. 2, 3, 4, 5, D. XXVII; c. 41-43, C. XXVII, q. 1—*Dictum Gratiani* ad c. 43: "Quod autem voventes premissis auctoritatibus iubentur ab invicem discedere, quorum vero coniugia auctoritate Augustini et Theodori solvendi non sunt in capitulo de ordinatione clericorum evidenter ostenditur."

[29] Vermeersch, *De Religiosis,* II, (12).

officially adopted by Popes Celestine III and Boniface VIII [30] and handed down to the present day as connoting the difference between *solemn* and *simple* vows.

Though a review of the ancient legislation shows that the vow of chastity which is now called solemn existed *in fact* in the early centuries, but is found *in name* only at the time of Gratian, there is no certainty at all about the exact date when *in fact* there came into being this distinction; [31] nor can there be any certainty at all as to whether religious vows were all solemn or all simple up to the time of the I Lateran Council in 1123. It is due to a tendency to confuse solemn with public and simple with private vows that authors were led to varied opinions on the status of religious vows in the early centuries.[32] What lends even more difficulty to the task of deciding this question is the inaccuracy of the terminology of the early Councils relative to whether the vow merely prohibited or also invalidated a subsequent marriage.[33] The writings of the Fathers also reveal conflicting testimony. In short, there was no uniformity in legislation concerning the effect of religious vows on subsequent attempted marriages. Hence, nobody can argue *conclusively* that the religious vows previous to 1123 were uniformly of the kind which from Gratian's time were called solemn; nor can one argue conversely that none of them was *solemn* but all were *simple*. It is the writer's opinion that Suarez is right in concluding that, since the religious communities had been placed under the guidance of the local ordinaries, these ordinaries could have legislated that for their territory

[30] C. 3, 6, X, *Qui clerici vel voventes,* IV, 6; c. un., *de voto et voti redemptione,* III, 15 in VI°; c. 5, *de regularibus,* III, 14, in VI°.

[31] Goyeneche, "De votis simplicibus"—*Acta Congressus Iuridici Internationalis . . . Romae 1934* (5 vols., Romae: Libraria Pont. Instituti Utriusque Iuris, 1935-1937), IV, 303.

[32] Cf. Wernz, *Ius Decretalium,* III, pars II, p. 228, note 23. This author lists the various opinions, current in the different centuries, on the nature of a simple vow, how it was confused with a private vow, and how a solemn vow was confused with a public vow.

[33] Council of Agde (506), c. 61—Mansi, VIII, 335; Synod of Epaon (517), c. 30—Mansi, VIII, 562-563. These Councils declared the union *illicit* and at the same time demanded the separation of the parties. Such a separation is usually demanded only when the marriage is invalid. Cf. Wernz, *Ius Decretalium,* IV, 347; Wernz-Vidal, *Ius Canonicum,* V, 167.

such a vow was a diriment impediment.[34] It was easily possible, then, for differences to arise in local legislation with regard to the nullifying or impeding character of the impediment of religious profession. The question concerning the solemnity of religious vows before 1123 has been ably considered and the arguments of both sides have been well reviewed and weighed by Suarez.[35]

The first evidence of any universal legislation which contained at least an implicit declaration that certain vows did invalidate a subsequent marriage dates from the year 1123 at the I General Lateran Council.[36] The II General Lateran Council in 1139 cleared up any doubts there might have been concerning the twenty-first canon of the I Lateran Council.[37] The writers and commentators after Gratian took up this distinction of solemn and simple vows, wrote about it, argued it, and more and more it came to be the accepted and received opinion that the solemn vow of chastity, at least the one annexed to religious profession, annulled a subsequent marriage.[38] Further declarations by the Popes took away any doubt in this matter. Alexander III (1159-1161) declared that a solemn vow taken in a religious order was a diriment impediment to marriage and that a

[34] Gasparri says that it is the more probable opinion that the bishops have the power by their office to make marriage impediments, but that for the sake of uniformity the power has been reserved to himself by the Pope—Gasparri, *De Matrimonio* (3. ed., 2 vols., Parisiis, 1904), I. 179.

[35] *De Statu Perfectionis et Religionis,* Tr. VII, Lib. IX, C. 21; cf. also Ballay, "Quaestiones quaedam de votis simplicibus"—*AKKR,* XVII (1867), 1-42; Frey, *Religious Profession,* 31-39; Devoti, *Institutionum Canonicarum Libri Quattuor* (ed. prima Romana post quintum, 3 vols., Romae, 1825), II, 220.

[36] C. 21: ". . . monachis . . . matrimonia penitus interdicimus; contracta quoque matrimonia ab huiusmodi . . . disiungi . . . iudicamus."—Mansi, XXI, 286.

[37] C. 7: ". . . statuimus quatenus . . . monachi, atque conversi professi qui . . . uxores sibi copulare praesumpserint, separentur. Huiusmodi namque copulationem . . . matrimonium non esse censemus." In Canon 8 the same ruling was extended to religious women: "Idipsum quoque de sanctimonialibus feminis si . . . nubere attentaverint, observari decernimus"—Mansi, XXI, 527-528; c. 40, C. XXVII, q. 1.

[38] Cf. Wernz-Vidal, *Ius Canonicum,* V, 353; Bernard of Pavia in c. 6, X, *qui clerici vel voventes,* IV, 6; Peter Lombard, *Liber Quartus Sententiarum,* d. 38.

simple vow was a prohibitive impediment.[39] Celestine III (1191-1198) and Innocent III (1198-1216) [40] reiterated and reaffirmed the declaration of Alexander III so that Gratian's distinction was "canonized" by these declarations.

All the doubtful matters were not as yet cleared up however. Just what vows besides those taken in religion and on the reception of Holy Orders were solemn, or were there any solemn vows besides these? Boniface VIII (1294-1303) settled this matter when he restricted the classification of solemn vows to such vows as were taken at the reception of Holy Orders or by an express or tacit profession *in a religious order approved by the Holy See.*[41]

As has been seen, the Benedictine rule in the West and the Basilian rule in the East were the rules followed almost universally—they had been approved. There was also the rule of St. Augustine under which the members at first did not take vows.[42] The rule was collected from the writings of St. Augustine in 700 and those following it were called Canons Regular in contradistinction to the Canons Secular; under this rule the members took solemn vows at least from 1059.[43] All following this rule were approved, *e. g.*, the Premonstratensians in 1126; the Trinitarians in 1198. These three rules were solemnly approved by the IV General Lateran Council.[44]

St. Francis of Assisi at the time of the council had verbal approbation of his Institute from Innocent III, who had it recognized as one of the approved rules, though it was not formally approved until 1223 by Honorius III.[45] The *Mendicants* now arose. The Domini-

[39] C. 3, X, *qui clerici vel voventes matrimonium contrahere possunt,* IV, 6; cf. also c. 4 and 5 in the same place.

[40] C. 6, 7, X, *qui clerici vel voventes matrimonium contrahere possunt,* IV, 6.

[41] C. un., *de voto et voti redemptione,* III, 15, in VI°.

[42] Heimbucher, *Orden und Kongregationen,* I, 125.

[43] Heimbucher, *op. cit.,* I, 397-398; Steiger, "De propagatione et diffusione vitae religiosae"—*Periodica,* XIII (1924), 89; Maroto, "Regulae et Particulares Constitutiones Singularum Religionum ex Jure Decretalium usque ad Codicem"—*Acta Congressus Iuridici Internationalis,* IV, 220-221, 228 sq.; cf. also *CpRM,* XVIII (1937), 31-32; 99 sq.

[44] C. 13—Mansi, XXII, 1002; c. 9, X, *de religiosis domibus ut episcopo sunt subiectae,* III, 36.

[45] Orth, *Approbation of Religious Institutes,* p. 33, note 96.

cans, a foundation based on the rule of St. Augustine, were approved in 1216, the Carmelites in 1226, and the Hermits of St. Augustine in 1256. But many more organizations sprung up in defiance of the law of the IV General Lateran Council (1215) with no ecclesiastical approbation—and some of these (especially the Waldensian and Albigensian groups) were distinctly heretical.[46]

The violations of the IV General Lateran Council as to the founding of new orders caused the Fathers of the II General Council of Lyons (1274) to repeat, emphasize and extend the law. In this law Gregory X declared that the meaning of the II Council of Lyons was this: the founding of any new order or the joining of such was forbidden in the future. He placed under perpetual prohibition those new orders which had been founded without pontifical approbation since the IV General Lateran Council. As to the orders approved by the Holy See since then, he forbade them to receive new candidates, to acquire a new foundation, to sell any foundation they had, to preach, to hear confessions or to exercise the parochial rights with regard to Christian burial. Anyone disobeying these prescriptions was excommunicated. He ruled that these last prohibitions did not pertain to the orders of the Dominicans or Franciscans in view of their evident utility nor to the orders of the Hermits of St. Augustine or the Carmelites, for he wished these orders to remain. To the members of the prohibited orders he gave general permission so that the individual religious could transfer to one of the approved orders, but he forbade, in the absence of any special permission of the Holy See, the transfer from one order to another or from one convent to another.[47]

The Council of Trent reiterated this law.[48] Therefore any order to be approved in the future had to follow one of the rules approved before 1215, *i. e.*, the Benedictine, Basilian, Augustinian or Franciscan. All other orders, even if they were approved by the bishop or by the Holy See between 1215 and 1274, were condemned to a slow death, for the law prohibited the reception of new members; the Dominicans, Carmelites and Hermits of St. Augustine were excepted.

[46] Orth, *op. cit.*, 28-32; Wernz, *Ius Decretalium*, III, pars II, 271-273.
[47] C. 23—Mansi, XXIV, 96; c. un., *de religiosis domibus*, III, 17, in VI°.
[48] Sess. XXV, *de matr.*, c. 9.

A comparison of the law of Boniface VIII with the canons of the IV General Lateran and of the II General Council of Lyons gives us this conclusion: the only religious Institutes then allowed in the Church were those which followed one of the four rules approved before 1215. Because these rules made provision only for solemn vows, each and every order then existing, and every order to be founded in the future had to profess solemn vows, unless in the approbation of the new Institute the Pope decided otherwise.

CHAPTER II

THE BEGINNINGS OF SIMPLE RELIGIOUS VOWS

ARTICLE 1. THE IDEAS ON RELIGIOUS VOWS

FROM Boniface VIII onward it was clear that solemn vows were those and only those which were taken by clerics in major orders or religious who were professed in an approved order. As a consequence, for almost three centuries *all* religious vows were *certainly* solemn. As has been seen, however, the tradition of solemn vows goes back much further than that though there can be no certainty as to the solemnity of *all* religious vows before Boniface VIII.

An effort will now be made to show how the opinions of that period reflected the tradition of solemn vows. There is needed here solely a statement of fact, first, as to the controverted opinions, secondly, as to the men who held them, and thirdly, as to the dates of these men. These facts will be sufficient for the purpose of this article, namely, to present a brief historical background. Against this background one can see much better the legal situation and sense more clearly the attitude in regard to the solemnity of religious vows existing at that time when there appeared on the scene simple vows which for the first time were certainly regarded as religious vows.

This tradition of solemn vows was so strong that there arose in this period the opinion that solemn vows were essential to the religious state. Those who held this opinion claimed that St. Thomas was on their side, but in none of the places cited can it be shown definitely that he held this opinion,[1] Suarez states that this opinion had many eminent men to support it: Hostiensis (d. 1271), Ancharano (1330-1416), Parnormitanus (1386-1453), Felinus (1444-1503), Thomas Cajetan (1469-1534), Rebuffus (1487-1557), Domi-

[1] St. Thomas, *Summa Theologica* (in *Opera Omnia,* 24 tomes, Parmae, 1852-1869), IIa IIae, q. 184, a. 5; IIa IIae, q. 188, a. 7, *in corpore* et ad 2; IIa IIae, q. 189, a. 2, ad 1.

nic de Soto (1494-1560), Navarrus (Martin de Azpilcueta) (1493-1586), and many of the Summists.[2] Their argument, in general, was that the religious state was constituted only by the three substantial vows made in a religious profession. They based their reason for this statement on the texts of the law.[3] Hence, vows taken at religious profession were necessarily solemn.[4] Therefore without solemn vows the religious state could not subsist properly and substantially. Thus the solemnity of the vows was of the essence of the religious state, the word "essence" in this case being understood as signifying whatever was indispensably necessary to constitute that state.[5]

Another opinion of the time shows how strongly rooted was this idea of the necessity of solemn vows for the constitution of the religious state. It was a corollary, in a way, of the theory held by those requiring the solemnity of vows for the essence of the religious state. At this period (1200-1500) many authors held that the Pope could not dispense from solemn vows. They said that the Pope could not dispense from the substantial element of the vows; *i. e.,* their solemnity, since it connoted the *traditio* of oneself to God, which *traditio* implied the presence of a bond and of a relationship that was regulated by the divine law itself and therefore could not be relaxed by means of a dispensation.[6] For the better understanding of this opinion it will be necessary to explain the teaching of these authors on the nature of the solemnity of vows. The one school of thought (the Thomists in general) held that by a solemn vow man was given over wholly to God just as by consecration a

[2] Dominic de Soto, *De Iustitia,* q. 1, art. 1 et 3; Navarrus, *De Regularibus Commentaria Quattour* (in *Opera Omnia,* 6 vols., Venetiis, 1618), Commentarium I, nn. 18, 24, 25; Felinus, *Commentaria in V. Libros Decretalium* (3 vols., Venetiis, 1570), in c. 10, X, *de constitutionibus,* I, 2; in c. 11, X, *de iureiurando,* II, 24. Confer Suarez, *De statu perfectionis et religionis,* Tr. VII, Lib. II, c. 14, n. 1.

[3] C. 22, X, *de regularibus et transeuntibus ad religionem,* III, 31; c. 21, *de sententia excommunicationis,* V, 11, in VI°; c. 4, *de regularibus et transeuntibus ad religionem,* III, 14, in VI°; c. 1, *de religiosis domibus ut episcopo sint subiectae,* III, 11, in Clem.

[4] C. un., *de voto et voti redemptione,* III, 15, in VI°.

[5] Suarez, *De statu perfectionis et religionis,* Tr. VII, Lib. II, c. 14, n. 1.

[6] Suarez, *De statu perfectionis et religionis,* Tr. VII, Lib. VI, c. 16, n. 8.

chalice was dedicated entirely to God. A thing once given irrevocably to one person could not validly be given to another person. Therefore a religious who gave himself over to God by the *traditio* of himself which was contained in his vows could not validly give himself to another in marriage.[7] St. Thomas argued that the Pope could not make a thing which had been permanently in its essence consecrated to the service of God cease to be consecrated to Him. He also cited Innocent III, who stated that the giving up of property and the keeping of chastity were so attached to the monastic rule that contrary to it not even the Pope could dispense or bestow any permission.[8] If he could not dispense for acts contrary to the vow, *a fortiori* he could not dispense by taking away the vow entirely.[9]

The Thomists of this period in general and also many others followed St. Thomas in this opinion. It had been held by some authors before him, too.[10] Many hold that the Pope could not dispense from

[7] St. Thomas, *Commentarium in Librum IV Sententiarum,* dist. 38, q. 1, art. 2, q. 3, ad 2, et art. 3, q. 3; *Quaestiones quodlibetales,* quodl. III, art. 18; quodl. X, art. 11, ad 1; also probably in *Summa Theologica* IIa IIae, q. 8, art. 11. The Thomists in general as well as others held this: St. Bonaventure (1221-1274), Richardus de Mediavilla (d. 1307), Durandus de S. Porciano (d. 1334), Capreolus (d. 1432), Ioannes Turrecremata (1388-1468), Dominicus de Soto (1494-1560), Petrus de Aragon (d. 1595), Valentia (1551-1603) and others listed in Suarez, *De statu perfectionis et religionis,* Tr. VII, Lib. II, c. 7, n. 2.

[8] "Abdicatio proprietatis, sicut et custodia castitatis, adeo est annexa regulae monachali, ut contra eam nec Summus Pontifex possit licentiam indulgere"—c. 6, X, *de statu monachorum,* III, 35.

[9] ". . . Papam non posse facere quod ille, qui est professus religionem, non sit religiosus, licet quidam iuristae ignoranter contrarium dicant."—IIa IIae, q. 28, art. 11. St. Thomas here departed from the opinion he had formerly held in *Commentarium in IV Sententiarum,* dist. 38, q. 1, art. 4, q. 1, ad 5. Cf. on this Prümmer, "Kann der Papst in den feierlichen Ordensgelübden dispensieren?"—*Jahrbuch für Philosophie und spekulative Theologie,* XXII (1908), 55-56.

[10] Dominicus de Soto, *Dominici Soto Segobiensis in quartum (quem vocant) Sententiarum Tomus Secundus* (2 toms., Venetiis, 1575) in lib. 4, dist. 38, q. 2, ad 2; *Glossa* in c. 6, X, *de statu monachorum,* III, 35; St. Albertus Magnus, *Commentarium in quartum librum Sententiarum,* dist. 38, art. 16; Suarez lists for this opinion also: Capreolus (d. 1432); St. Bonaventure (1221-1274); Tabiena (d. 1521); Alphonsus Tostatus (1400-1455).

religious vows. By this they implied that the only religious vows of the time were solemn vows. Some, viewing not only the Church's legislation on the necessity of taking such vows in a religious Institute, but considering also the law that all vows in religion were solemn, concluded that solemn vows were essential to the religious state, so much so that they declared that the simple vows mentioned by Gratian were not religious vows.[11]

These views did not go unchallenged, for there were many opponents.[12] It is not the intention of the writer to delve deeply into these problems; for a full consideration of the question the reader is referred to the places cited in Suarez. The background furnished by the first chapter (concerning the uncertainty as to the solemnity of religious vows before 1123) and this article will give one a clearer and more definite understanding of the feeling of the time on the solemnity of vows. When, in 1583, Gregory XIII issued his Constitution *Quanto fructuosius* on the Jesuit simple vows it was recognized as probable that solemn vows had been taken in religious orders since the fifth century and as certain that for three centuries *all* religious vows had been solemn. At the end of the sixteenth century there existed a strongly defended view that solemn vows were essential to the religious state and that, as a consequence, no community, the members of which lived with only simple vows, could be a religious Institute. There also existed the strongly defended opinion that the Pope could not dispense from religious vows as they were then accepted and understood.

Article 2. The Jesuit Simple Vows

With the conclusions of the preceding article in mind one can much more easily understand what a startling change of legislation came about with the approval of the Jesuit rule. Pope Julius III

[11] Cf. on this Suarez, *De statu perfectionis et religionis,* Tr. VII, Lib. II, c. 14, n. 2 sq.

[12] Some of the opponents were: the Glossators, Scotus (1266-1308), Joannes Andreas (c. 1270-1348), Paludanus (d. 1342), Hostiensis (d. 1271), Parnormitanus (1386-1453); Salmanticenses, *Cursus Theologiae Moralis,* Tr. XV, *de statu religioso,* Cap. I, p. 3, n. 30. For further details, confer Suarez, *De statu perfectionis et religionis,* Tr. VII, Lib. II, c. 10, n. 4.

approved the first formula of the Institute on September 27, 1543.[13] On June 5, 1546, Pope Paul III approved the plan of simple vows for the coadjutors. These coadjutors were *spiritual* and *temporal*. St. Ignatius had taken great pains to have himself educated, and he and all his first associates obtained master's degrees. When the Society was formed with its members taking solemn vows, they decided that only those should become members of the Society who had proved their intellectual ability by means of successfully undergoing searching examinations. This necessarily limited their numbers. So they admitted priests as *coadjutores spirituales,* who as fellow laborers would preach, hear confessions, and the like. Until they were deemed ready to teach or had obtained a degree they, as well as the *scholastics,* took only simple vows. The *temporal* coadjutors were lay brothers. They were never admitted to solemn vows.[14] These simple vows were perpetual on the part of the religious but temporary on the part of the Society.[15]

As to poverty there was an innovation. Those who took solemn vows renounced all ownership as did the members of the other Orders, but those who were not yet in solemn vows could still hold property, but not at their own free disposition. They had to renounce their property before taking solemn vows, and even earlier if the Superior commanded it. Without the superior's permission

[13] *Institutum Societatis Jesu* (ed. Florentiae, 3 vols., 1892-1893), I, 10 (henceforth cited *Institutum S.J.*); *Bullarum Diplomatum et Privilegiorum Sanctorum Romanorum Pontificum Taurinensis Editio* (25 vols., Augustae Taurinorum, 1857-1872), VI, 303-306 (henceforth cited as *Bull. Rom.*).

[14] *Institutum* S.J. I, 12; II, 2, 15, 20, 21, 90, 91; *Examen,* c. I, n. 9, 10; C. IV, n. 41; C. VI, n. 1, 2, 3, 8; *Constitutio,* Pars V, c. IV, n. 1, 2, 3; *Declarationes* A et B, in C. IV; Pastor, *The History of the Popes from the Close of the Middle Ages* (29 vols., St. Louis: Herder, 1906-1938), XII, 33-37; XVII, 278-279 (hereafter cited as *History of the Popes*).

[15] "Quod dicitur, iuxta Bullas et Constitutiones, intelligendum est, quod Coadjutores emittunt huiusmodi simplicia vota, cum tacita quadam, quod ad perpetuitatem attinet, conditione, quae haec est: si Societas eos tenere volet. Quamvis enim illi, quod in ipsis est, se obligent, in perpetuum suae devotionis et stabilitatis gratia; liberum tamen erit Societati eos dimittere"—*Institutum S.J.,* II, 92; *i.e., Constitutio,* Pars V, C. IV; et *Declaratio* B in C. IV.

no one could make use of anything or dispose of anything by loan or alienation.[16]

Members of the Society could be dismissed if it was found that life in the Society was not their vocation or if the common good of the Society demanded their departure. The more the Society owed a member because he had labored well for it, or because his talents and God-given gifts endowed him with ability to help the Society, the less easily could he be dismissed. The Scholastics and Coadjutors with public simple vows could be dismissed, but not as readily as the novices in the first or second year of their probation. In certain cases, but only for the gravest crimes, could those who were professed with solemn vows be dismissed.[17] St. Ignatius' idea and plan behind the simple vows is seen very clearly in the ruling that if one is not fit for studies he can be engaged by the Society in those duties for which he seemed fitted; but if he was found to be entirely unfitted for the intellectual duties required in his state he could be dismissed even if he had been admitted to simple vows in the Scholasticate.[18] The General Chapter and the *Praepositus Generalis* himself could effect the dismissal. Others also could receive this power, *e. g.*, the provincials and the local rectors, whenever it was thought expedient to bestow this power upon them.[19] When the religious in simple vows was dismissed he was freed from his vows *ipso facto* and there was no need for a dispensation. But, if there was time to do so, the superiors were to obtain a dispensation from the vows for their subjects rather than to use their power of dismissing them in order to gain the same effect. If the dismissed religious was in

[16] *Institutum S.J., Examen,* C. I, n. 4; C. IV, n. 4; *Constitutio,* Pars IV, C. II, n. 5; *Declaratio* E, in C. IV.

[17] *Institutum S.J., Examen,* C. I, n. 4; *Constitutio,* Pars IV, C. II, n. 5; C. X, n. 1; Pars VI, C. II, n. 3; C. X, n. 4; Pars IX, C. III, n. 18; C. IV, n. 7.

[18] *Institutum S.J., Constitutio,* Pars IV, C. VI, n. 15, *Declaratio* N; *Examen,* C. V, n. 6; C. VII, n. 1. This was reaffirmed two centuries later by Benedict XIV, *Opera Omnia* (17 vols., Prati, 1839-1847), Vol. XI, *De Synodo Dioecesana,* Lib. XIII, C. XI, n. 22 sq.

[19] *Institutum S.J., Constitutio,* Pars II, C. I, n. 1; Pars IX, C. III, N. 1, *Declaratio* B; C. VI, n. 2; Pars X, n. 8.

solemn vows he was not freed from his vows in the act of being dismissed.[20]

Keeping in mind the ideas of the time on religious vows one can easily see what a novelty these simple religious vows were. A still greater departure from the traditional practice was implied in the fact that the very act of dismissal was recognized to be the equivalent of a dispensation from these vows. This question will be more fully considered in the following article. Naturally the untraditional usage evoked considerable opposition. When the Constitutions were being examined, many Cardinals, especially Cardinal Guidiccioni (d. 1549), one of the three Cardinals appointed to examine them, were thoroughly adverse to the Society on the general principle of opposition to the foundation of new orders. They pointed out the great number of religious orders then in existence and they recalled the decrees of the IV Lateran and the II Lyons Councils. Cardinal Guidiccioni finally declared that an *exception* should be made in this case.[21] In France twenty theologians, when they were requested by the French Parliament to give a decision on the Jesuit "rules and statutes," issued on December 1, 1554, what was practically a complete condemnation of them and stated that all the deviations from the older orders in the Constitutions of the Society were to be held blameworthy. Already the difficulty against simple vows had arisen. Not only the vows themselves, but also the changes made necessary by them ran counter to a long tradition.[22] In Spain it was objected that the members of the Society were not obliged to choir service. This was indeed a novelty, since all the orders at that time had the choral obligation. Further objections were brought against the Society for its lack of the usual penances and austerities.[23] Pope St.

[20] *Institutum S.J., Examen,* C. VII, n. 1, 2; *Constitutio,* Pars II, C. IV, n. 3, 4; Pars V, C. IV, *Declaratio* B.

[21] Pastor, *History of the Popes,* XII, 34; De Cugnac, *La Défense des Jésuites* (Lille, 1880), pp. 3-4.

[22] Pastor, *History of the Popes,* XIII, 206.

[23] Brucker *La Compagnie de Jésus* (Paris, 1919), pp. 120-121. "Saint Ignace, nous l'avons vu, a introduit dans la vie religieuse quelques points si nouveaux pour son temps, qu'on ne s'étonne pas de les voir peu goûtés, spécialment des religieux accoutumés à des observances différentes."—*ibid.,* p. 192.

Pius V, even though he was friendly to the Society, did not approve its provision of ordaining priests with simple vows, even though the Society agreed to support them if they were dismissed. Consequently he included the Jesuits in his decree of October 14, 1568, which demanded that religious have solemn vows before they be raised to the priesthood.[24] Gregory XIII later exempted them from this law on February 28, 1573.[25]

Article 3. The Dispute on Religious Simple Vows

The most fundamental objection against the new Society concerned the cardinal point of the simple vows. Could one be a religious and have only simple vows? The answer was found in the Constitution *Quanto fructuosius* of February 1, 1583,[26] and the Constitution *Ascendente Domino* of May 25, 1584.

The reason behind the short interval between these two decrees was the great difficulty there was in accepting the doctrine of simple religious vows. The difficulty was occasioned by the case of a young Jesuit of simple vows who had left the Society and thereupon married. After an attempt was made to induce the fugitive to return, he was given a salutary penance and then was dismissed. The case offered the occasion for Diego Peredo, a lector of theology at Avila, to teach that by simple vows the novices of the Society did not become members of the Jesuit Order. In the light of this assumption Peredo taught (1) that those who are in simple vows bring no harm to the Society by their departure; (2) that any bishop can dispense from the vow; (3) that the Jesuits have no privilege which reserves the dispensation of these vows to the Society or to the Pope, and (4) that the Pope cannot give the Jesuits the faculty to annul the

Cf. Pastor, *History of the Popes*, XVII, 280; Astrain, *Historia de la Compañia de Jésus* (7 vols., Madrid, 1902-1925), III, 290-291.

[24] Const. *Romanus Pontifex—Fontes*, n. 129; Pastor, *op. cit.*, XVII, 280-282.

[25] Brucker, *op. cit.*, p. 155; Benedict XIV, *De Synodo Dioecesana*, Lib. XIII, C. XI, n. 24.

[26] Note that the date on the original *Constitutio* is 1582. That is because it was dated *Anno Incarnationis*. The year accordingly began on March 25th. According to our reckoning from January 1st, then, the year is 1583. Cf. Astrain, *op. cit.*, III, 271.

vows of these religious for the reason that the Jesuits have no power over them.

The General, Claude Aquaviva (1543-1615), saw the latent danger in this, namely, the denial that a good number of the Jesuits were truly religious. He presented the case to the Pope and the result was the Constitution *Quanto fructuosius*. After explaining the reason for the simple vows and stating that, in regard to the manner of living in general, and in regard to obedience in particular, there was no difference between the members in solemn vows and those in simple vows, the Pope stated that all the Jesuits, even those in only simple vows, were and always had been religious and that they should be considered and called such.[27]

Peredo's answer was that the Pope was speaking here as a *doctor particularis*, and not as the head of the Church; that the Pope intended to enact a particular law and that in doing so he could err; and, finally, that because of false information the Pope did in fact err. There were, Peredo said, three errors in the narrative part of the Constitution *Quanto fructuosius:* (1) that the members were incorporated into the Society by simple vows; (2) that they ceased to be novices; (3) that they were bound to obedience equally with those in solemn vows.

The Jesuits summarized Peredo's fifteen points and presented them to the Pope who in turn handed them over in March, 1584, to theologians for their judgment. They gave the decision that the statements were false and temerarious. In a letter to the Nuncio of Spain which arrived in April, the Pope ordered that if Peredo wished to dispute the point he was to come to Rome; if he wished to remain silent then he should publish the condemnation of his propositions and repair the harm done by his teaching. Peredo answered that he had but defended the doctrine of St. Thomas as it had been defended by many great theologians, and that in fact he was a friend of the Jesuits. He submitted to the decision and asked only that his propositions be reexamined by other doctors in theology.

In order to have the matter fully settled, Aquaviva, the Jesuit General, asked the Pope to declare minutely the nature and the extent of the simple vows in the Society in order to do away with all

[27] Const. *Quanto fructuosius*, 1 febr. 1583, §§ 2, 3, 5—*Fontes*, 150.

contrary criticism. The Pope did so in the Constitution *Ascendente Domino* of May 25, 1584. In it Gregory XIII cited the many approbations the Society had received, gave a succinct and complete schema of the purpose and makeup of the society, and went into detail about the simple vows—in short, he gave a sketch of the constitutions.[28] He then cited Peredo's propositions and recounted them one by one, stating that he spoke *ex cathedra* in the *Quanto fructuosius*. He labelled propositions such as Peredo's as *false* and *temerarious*.[29] In the same Constitution he blamed Peredo for interpreting the *Quanto fructuosius* according to previous law. He stated again that all the rules and privileges remained in force, that he healed any defects of law or fact in them, and that the simple vows of the Society by institution of the Holy See were truly substantial vows of religion, and that those with the said simple vows were truly and properly religious.[30] Gregory XIII concluded with placing a *latae sententiae* excommunication and the penalty of ineligibility for all offices and benefices, reserved to the Holy See, upon all those who sought openly to perpetuate the dispute, or who directly or indirectly impugned or contradicted anything stated in his Constitution. Any doubts regarding it were to be referred to the Holy See, to the General of the Jesuits, or to a delegate appointed by either of them for this.[31] This Constitution was promulgated on July 16, 1584, by the affixing of it to the doors of St. Peter's, of St.

[28] *Fontes,* n. 153. The sketch here mentioned is contained in §§ 1-17 of this papal constitution.

[29] § 18: " . . . non defuit temeraria quorumdam audacia, qui post declarationem, decretum, praeceptum, et interdictum nostrum huiusmodi . . . ipsa Apostolica decreta, ac praecepta, publice, et ex cathedra, ausu temerario impugnare, mentemque nostram perverse interpretari non erubescunt . . . " etc.—*Fontes,* n. 153; cf. also § 23 of the Constitution.

[30] §§ 17-21: " . . . statuimus, atque decernimus, tria vota huiusmodi etsi simplicia, ex huius Sedis institutione, ac nostra etiam declaratione et confirmatione esse vere substantialia Religionis vota . . . et . . . omnes, et quoscumque, qui in ipsam Societatem admissi, . . . tria vota substantialia praedicta, tametsi simplicia emiserint, aut emittent in futurum, vere, et proprie religiosos fuisse, et esse, ac fore, et ubique semper, et ab omnibus censeri, et nominari debere . . . " —*Fontes,* n. 153.

[31] § 24—*Fontes,* n. 153.

John Lateran's, of the Apostolic Chancellery, and in the *Campo de' Fiori.*

Peredo answered that the Constitution had not been promulgated in the proper form and therefore had no force. He was silenced and punished by his superiors. After the death of Gregory XIII on April 10, 1585, Peredo, hoping for a favorable hearing from Sixtus V whose attitude towards the Jesuits was less favorable than that of his predecessor, decided to go to Rome and to present his case. He arrived in 1587 and his doctrine was given a reexamination by the Sacred Office of the Inquisition. They reviewed the matter, declared that he was wrong in his opinion, but absolved him from blame and removed the censures, *because the matter was much in doubt and he was following approved authors.* The sentence was pronounced January 24, 1590.[32]

Another dispute was to be settled before the matter could be considered as closed. On December 13, 1589, there was scheduled to be defended in the University of Salamanca the following thesis:

> Status vero religiosorum, qui et in statu perfectionis sunt, simpliciter et absolute comparatur ad statum episcopalem, sicut disciplina ad magisterium. Est enim religiosus status disciplina et exercitum perveniendi ad perfectionis charitatis. Unde necessarium est, quod per tria vota essentialia, voluntariae scilicet paupertatis, perpetuae continentiae atque obedientiae, religiosi abstrahantur a rebus mundanis ut libere Deo vacare possint, et in his substantia religionis consistit, dummodo solemni voto firmentur, quod fit per solam professionem in religione approbata.

The Nuncio at the request of the Jesuits forbade the thesis to be defended as it manifestly ran counter to the Constitution *Ascendente Domino.* The faculty of the University, having considered the matter, sent the thesis to Rome, respectfully asking the Holy See's judgment on the matter. The thesis was sent to Rome on January 30, 1590. On February 2, 1590, Bañez (1528-1604) sent to Sixtus V

[32] " . . . acerca de los dichos votos de los tales estudiantes, fueron por relación de otras personas, a quien probablemente podía creer, y también que muchas de ellas dijo en duda y debajo de condición, y que reguló toda su disputa conforme al parecer de doctores aprobados."—Astrain, *Historia de la Compañia de Jésus,* III, 286; on all this matter confer *ibid.,* pp. 268-287.

a letter and a memorial in which he stated that he did not wish to contravene the decision of the Constitution *Ascendente Domino* or any other mandate of the Holy See, but that he wished to show that the thesis was not in contradiction to that Constitution. In other words, he asked if it was true to say that the definition of religious applied solely to the *professed* of the Institute. If it did, then why was the term to be applied to all the members of the Institute so that all alike could be called religious?

Sixtus V handed the matter over to the Holy Office of the Inquisition, which in January of that same year had given its sentence on Peredo. Since Bañez adhered to the same fundamental error, the same answer was in place. The discussion began on June 13, 1590, and the decision was given on July 14, 1590. The Holy Office of the Inquisition stated that the thesis could be discussed publicly if the word *regulariter* was added to the phrase *quod fit per solam professionem*. In other words, the answer meant that regularly the religious state was constituted by the three solemn vows, but that the Church could, as Gregory had in his Constitution *Ascendente Domino,* establish a religious Institute differently than according to the ordinary law.[83]

In concluding this chapter, one may again be permitted to state that the introduction of simple vows as constituting the religious state was a very notable change in Church legislation. The foregoing examples were chosen as typifying the reaction of the time against this novelty. They show the mind of the time, not only in Spain but throughout the world, since the authors who held the opinion that *solemn* vows were essential for the constituting of the religious state were not confined to one or the other locality or country. The two examples here adduced were "test cases"; they served as an occasion for clarifying and solidifying the Church's doctrine. Special note should be taken of the statement of the Inquisition in the Peredo case, namely, that the matter was very doubtful and that approved authors indeed held contrary opinions. Thus no blame was placed on the men who held the stricter opinion. The case revealed the first appearance of a veering away from the traditional outlook of the past. Simple vows in religion were recognized as truly religious

[83] Astrain, *op. cit.,* III, 291-304.

vows. The simple vows were then distinguished from the solemn vow in regard to perpetuity. The solemn vow signified a perpetual vow in the absolute sense, that is, in relation both to the individual and to the Institute. The simple vow, on the other hand, signified a perpetual vow on the part of the religious but a temporary vow in regard to the Institute since the Institute could dismiss a subject for the reasons stated in law.

CHAPTER III

RELIGIOUS CONGREGATIONS

ARTICLE 1. THE PROHIBITION TO FOUND NEW RELIGIOUS INSTITUTES

THE IV General Lateran Council and the II General Council of Lyons contained two prohibitions. They forbade the erection of any new religious Institute without the approbation of the Holy See, and secondly they forbade anybody to enter such a non-approved Institute. These decrees did not explicitly contain an invalidating clause, but from other texts of the law [1] and from the nature of the religious state the authors commonly held that any foundation of a religious Institute in violation of the prescriptions of these Councils was invalid and did not constitute a true religious Institute.[2] The authors [3] were almost unanimous in stating that the prohibitions of

[1] The reason that such an Institute was regarded as condemned and considered to be not a religious Institute followed from the fact that it was not approved—c. 1, *de religiosis domibus ut episcopo sint subiectae,* III, 11, in Clem.; the only valid profession was one that was made in an approved order—c. un., *de voto et voti redemptione,* III, 15, in VI°; married persons could enter an approved religious Institute—c. un., *de voto et voti redemptione,* VI, in Extravag. Ioann. XXII; the gloss to this last text says: "but not any other Institute because non-approved Institutes are not truly religious Institutes."

[2] Their argument was this: The state of the religious life is a state of perfection; but a papal prohibition renders life in a non-approved Institute a sinful state—Bouix, *Tractatus De Jure Regularium* (2 vols., Parisiis 1857), I, 53-54; 198-201 (henceforth cited as *De Jure Regularium*); Angelus a SS. Corde, *Manuale Juris Communis Regularium* (2 vols. Gandae, 1899), II, 81 (henceforth cited as *Manuale Juris Regularium*); Suarez, *De Statu Perf. et Relig.* tr. VII, Lib. II, c. 15, n. 1; c. 16, n. 9; Schmalzgrueber, *Ius Ecclesiasticum Universum,* lib. III, tit. XXXI, n. 22, q. 5; Benedictus XIV, const. *Quamvis iusto,* § 13, n. 6—*Fontes,* n. 222; Sebastianelli, *Praelectiones Juris Canonici* (2 vols.), Vol. II, *De Personis* (2. ed., Romae, 1905), p. 357.

[3] Suarez, *De statu perfectionis et religionis,* tr. VII, lib. II, c. 16, n. 22 sq.; Pirhing, lib. III, tit. XXXV, n. 27, tit. XXXVI, n. 15 and 33; Craisson,

these Councils extended to the foundation of Institutes whose members take simple vows, even though at that time the terms *religiosus* and *regularis* were considered as synonymous terms.[4] There were only a few dissenters from this opinion.[5] Those, then, who entered any Institute, whether of solemn or simple vows, which was not approved by the Pope took purely *secular* vows and not *religious* vows. They were also *private* vows, since they were not accepted by the Church in the name of God.

Article 2. The Status of Religious Congregations

Before beginning the discussion of the present article one may well define the terms and settle on a set manner of expressions since most of the difficulty in considering the period from the late sixteenth century to the time of the present Code is really one of terminology. Even the Holy See and the Roman Curia, especially in the years just previous to the Code, made use of the word *religio* in at least a twofold sense, and the recurrence of that word in different senses in manuals on *Jus Regulare* has caused a great deal of confusion. The

Manuale Totius Iuris Canonici (3 vols., 5. ed., Pictavii, 1877), II, 430; Pitra, *Commentarium in Constitutiones Apostolicas,* in Const. IX, Gregorii IX, n. 15 sq.; Bouix, *op. cit.*, I, 53, 201; Sebastianelli, *Jus de Personis,* p. 359; Leurenius, *Forum Ecclesiasticum* (5 vols., Venetiis, 1729), lib, III, tit. XXXV, q. 86; Piat, *Praelectiones,* I, 20; *Collectanea in usum Secretariae S. C. Episcoporum et Regularium* (2. ed., Romae: 1885), pp. 423, 798, nota (henceforth cited *Coll. S. C. Ep. et Reg.*); Reiffenstuel, *Jus Canonicum Universum* (4 vols., Romae, 1833), lib. III, tit. XXXI, n. 9; Bastien, *Directoire canonique à l'usage des Congrégations à voeux simples* (3. ed., Bruges: Beyaert, 1923), p. 4 (henceforth cited *Directoire Canonique*); Orth, *Approbation of Religious Institutes,* p. 36.

[4] Reiffenstuel, *op. cit.*, lib. III, tit. XXXI, n. 10: "Religiosus et regularis idem significant nec differunt nisi in hoc quod ly *religiosus* a verbo religio, *regularis* a regula quam quivis regularis profitetur, derivetur"; Antonius a Sancto Spiritu, *Directorium Regularium* (Lugduni, 1675), tr. III, disp. VI, Sect. II, n. 179, p. 161; Molitor, *Religiosi Iuris Capita Selecta,* p. 221; [Konings], *De Jure Regularium* (Wittem, 1851), p. 62, n. 43; Bastien, *op. cit.*, p. 10, note (1).

[5] [Konings], *op. cit.*, p. 37; De Buck—Tinnebroeck, *Examen Historicum Et Canonicum Libri M. Verhoeven* (Bruxellis-Gandavi, 1847), p. 95 (these two authors claim that the Councils condemned only the founding of religious Institutes by *lay persons*); Rodericus, *Quaestiones Regulares* (Lugduni, 1634), Resolutio CXXII, n. 5 (this latter author cites for his opinion Navarrus and Soto).

terminology used by Bouix (which will be treated below) will be employed throughout the rest of the dissertation, and thus will the desired uniformity of expression be achieved.[6]

A *religio* was an Institute which had the essence of the religious state, the approbation of the Holy See, and solemn vows.[7] A religious congregation was an Institute which had the essence of the religious state, the assent of the Holy See, but only simple vows.[8]

This distinction is not an arbitrary one, but is based on pertinent decrees issued by the Holy See. The *Confraternitas Bethlemitarum* was begun in 1653. In 1674 the Holy See approved it as a merely secular Confraternity. Pope Innocent XI in 1687 erected it as a religious congregation[9] in which the rule of St. Augustine was followed and in which simple vows were taken. Over twenty years later Pope Clement XI erected this religious congregation into a *true and formal religious Institute (ordinem religiosum).*[10] In it the members took solemn vows and received the name of religious and of true regulars.[11] The Confraternity of St. Hippolytus for serving the sick

[6] Bouix, *De Jure Regularium,* I, 187-191.

[7] Bouix, *op. cit.,* I, 187. Notice that in these definitions the essentials of the religious state were considered not as essentials which were demanded by the ecclesiastical law but as essentials which were demanded *ex natura rei, i.e.,* the three essential vows, the express profession of these vows, the intention to persevere perpetually—Vermeersch, *De Religiosis,* I, n. 24; Bouix, *op. cit.,* I. 46-48. The ecclesiastical law added the following notes: ecclesiastical approbation, the solemn character of the vows, and the following of an approved rule. Without these there was no *religio stricte dicta.* The essence of the religious state could be realized if there was present all that was required *ex natura rei* plus the approbation of the Church. This was true even apart from solemn vows, for the Church could constitute a new entity, as Gregory XIII had stated in his Constitution *Ascendente Domino.* But whether the lack of solemn vows together with the absence of an approved rule prevented the approved Institute from being a religious Institute formed the real point in dispute.

[8] Bouix, *op. cit.,* I, 187. This author did not explicitly include in his definition the note of the assent or of the approval of the Church, but, in the light of the treatise which follows the definition that note seems contained implicitly, for Bouix held that the prescriptions of the IV General Lateran Council and of II General Council of Lyons were really invalidating laws.

[9] Const. *Ecclesiae Catholicae,* 29 mart. 1687—*Bullarium Romanum,* XIX, 735.

[10] Const. *Ex debito,* 3 apr. 1710—*Bull. Rom.,* XXI, 385-387.

[11] "Nos . . . praefatam congregationem Bethlemitarum in veram religionem

in the hospitals was erected in Mexico City as a secular confraternity. It was raised to the status of a congregation and later in 1700 was made a formal religious Institute.[12] In 1621 Gregory XV erected the Congregation of Priests of the Mother of God, and the Congregation of Clerics Regular of the Pious Schools into religious Institutes with solemn vows.[13] Thus one sees emerging at this period in the Church the clear-cut distinction between religious congregations with simple vows and formal religious Institutes with solemn vows. The word *congregatio* was employed since in those days the word *religio* meant only an institute of solemn vows. The adjective *religious* was used in connection with the word *congregation* in order to distinguish it from a lay or secular congregation. As the years went on, the nature of the congregations approached more and more that of the orders, so that in 1889 the difference was expressed clearly in a decree which distinguished between formal religious Institutes of solemn vows, formal and true religious congregations of simple vows, and pious sodalities in which there was no religious profession and in which the vows were only private in character.[14]

As a result of this decree and of the various decrees of erection in the case of congregations, authors began to make a division among religious Institutes in such a manner as to distinguish between religious properly and truly and in the strict sense (these were the regulars with solemn vows), religious properly and truly in the less

(cum votibus solemnibus, ex integro etiam ab iis qui hactenus vota huiusmodi in eadem congregatione emiserunt, emittendis; . . . ita tamen ut nova vota emittentes, prius de inefficacia praecedentium votorum ad constituendos eos veros religiosos certiorentur) auctoritate Apostolica . . . perpetuo erigimus et instituimus." Bouix, referring to congregations, remarks "praecise et determinate intelligitur institutum in quo adsit essentia status religiosi ita ut ipsum profitentes jam non sint saeculares, sed religiosi, sed cum votis simplicibus."—*De Jure Regularium,* I, 188.

[12] Innocentius XII, const. *Ex debito,* 20 maii 1700: "Praefatam congregationem Sancti Hippolyti in formalem regularem religionem sub regula sancti Augustini, cum votibus solemnibus castitatis, paupertatis, et obedientiae necnon hospitalitatis, auctoritate Apostolica tenore praesentium perpetuo erigimus et instituimus."—*Bull. Rom.,* XX, 931.

[13] Bulla *In Supremo,* 3 nov. 1621 and 18 nov. 1621—*Bull. Rom.,* XII, 608-609; 627-628.

[14] S. C. Ep. et Reg., 11 aug. 1889—*apud* Vermeersch, *De Religiosis,* II, 67.

strict sense (these were the members of religious congregations), and pious congregations which lacked one or the other of the things which were essential *ex natura rei* for the religious state. This lack could result from the absence of all vows, from the absence of all public vows even though private vows had been taken, from the absence of even one or the other for the public vows of religion, or from the absence of papal approbation for the Institute.[15]

As was stated in the first chapter, for the present religious vows are those which are concerned with the evangelical counsels and which are taken in a religious Institute approved by the Church. The word *religio* (or Institute) today according to the Code connotes either solemn or simple vows,[16] so that when one views the pre-Code legislation one must keep in mind that a religious vow even then was acknowledged as including the vow which was taken in a religious congregation of simple vows. Thus there was little difficulty in determining the status of such congregations. Their members were not nor did they ever become religious in the strict sense of regulars. They remained religious in the less strict sense. But the congregation to which they belonged constituted a juridic entity distinct from a pious or a lay congregation and the vows taken by the members were religious vows in the same less strict sense as opposed to secular vows. The Constitution *Sapienti Consilio*[17] and the Code, by including members in simple as well as in solemn vows under the term "religious," changed nothing in the matter of the vows, but merely included members of both these types of religious Institutes under the word which in its strict sense had always been reserved for regulars, and gave congregations of simple vows the rating of religious Institutes in the strict sense.

[15] Vermeersch, *De Religiosis,* I, 64; Wernz, *Ius Decretalium,* III, pars II, n. 610; IV, n. 378; Molitor, *Religiosi Iuris Capita Selecta,* pp. 221, 173.

[16] Canon 488, 1°.

[17] Pius X, const. *Sapienti Consilio,* 29 iun. 1908, § 1, 5°—*Fontes,* n. 682. In repeated decisions the word "religious" was applied to the professed members of Congregations with simple vows: S. C. Ep. et Reg., *Malacitana,* 14 aug. 1891—*Fontes,* n. 2018; instr. 21 iul. 1896—*Fontes,* n. 2031; S. C. S. Off., 5 iul. 1899—*Fontes,* n. 1225. Leo XIII, const, *Conditae a Christo,* 8 dec. 1900—*Fontes,* n. 614; cf. Larraona, "De Religiosis"—*CpR,* I (1920), 209; Goyeneche, "De votis simplicibus in fontibus et in doctrina in ordine ad statum religiosum constituendum"—*Acta Congressus Iuridici Internationalis,* IV, 312-313.

Article 3. Religious Congregations of Men

If one consider the strong opposition which was manifested with reference to the Jesuit simple vows, it will not come as a surprise to find that some held the taking of these vows to be a privilege which could not be shared by others. Theoretically it was proved that the Constitution *Ascendente Domino* was a general doctrinal decision which stated that the Holy See could constitute a religious Institute with simple vows which did not follow one of the four approved rules. But practically it was maintained that as a privilege it could not be shared by others and that if a new Institute was to become truly and properly a religious Institute strictly so-called, then a special indult was needed.[18]

Pope St. Pius V (1566-1572) gave as an answer to the challenge of the reformers the return to and the reform of the old monastic form of life rather than the creation of new forms in the religious life. He had a sharp eye for abuses and corrected them wherever he saw them. If a community failed to heed his words it was suppressed. He strove to render the old general law on religious effective by particular decrees rather than by making new general laws. The Constitution *Lubricum vitae genus* of November 17, 1568, was one of these decrees. Addressed chiefly to the Canons of St. George and the Hermits of St. Jerome, it seemed to include all the congregations of men in which at that time the common life prevailed and in which a distinctive garb was worn as a sign of voluntary obedience. The members of these organizations of simple vows were obliged to embrace a religious Institute, that is, one with solemn vows, and they had to choose one of the approved rules.[19] The extent of the binding

[18] Larraona, "De Religiosis"—*CpR,* I (1920), 45; Angelus a SS. Corde, *Manuale Juris Regularium,* I, 7; *Coll. S. C. Ep. et Reg.* p. 745, note. In a General *Conventus* of the *S. C. super Statu Regularium* of June 15, 1846, one group held that it was not fitting to extend the *particular privilege* of the Jesuits to other Institutes lest a new status of religious Institutes be constituted against the generally reigning discipline of the Church. Pius IX in this instance followed the supporters of this view. Cf. Goyeneche, "De votis simplicibus"—*Acta Congressus Iuridici Internationalis,* IV, 307; Wernz, *Ius Decretalium,* III, n. 599.

[19] *Bull. Rom.,* VII, 725; Orth, *The Approbation of Religious Institutes,* pp. 44-47.

force of this Constitution is not certain. Some held that it was obligatory on all congregations of men.[20] Many were of the opinion that it was not a general decree, for they regarded it as not certainly including those Institutes which had a rule which was approved by the Holy See. It had, they said, no reference to the future, and it did not threaten the invalidity of future professions in congregations which had been approved by the Holy See before the decree.[21]

Shortly after the *Lubricum vitae genus* and upon the death of Pope Pius V many societies of men were approved fully and absolutely at Rome. Yet there is not to be found in these acts of approval any abrogation of the supposed prohibition against the formation of new religious congregations of men. The fact that these congregations had no intention of taking solemn vows did not prevent Rome from approving them without any direct limitation. Besides, in the documents which refer to religious congregations of women the words clearly presuppose that no prohibition existed relative to the formation of congregations of men.[22]

The documents of erection of many of the congregations of Clerics Regular also show that the regulations of the Constitution *Lubricum vitae genus* of Pope St. Pius V were not so strictly enforced at all. To some congregations approbation was given as a preparation for the eventual taking of solemn vows. One such congregation was approved shortly after the death of Pius V. It was a congregation of Clerics Regular the purpose of which was the administering of aid to the sick. It was approved by Pope Sixtus V on March 18, 1586. This act was but a beginning, for many other congregations were likewise approved.[23] It is certain that in the sixteenth and seventeenth cen-

[20] Cf. *Coll. S. C. Ep. et Reg.*, pp. 213, 742, and footnote; Steiger, "De propagatione et diffusione vitae religiosae"—*Periodica*, XIII (1924), (172).

[21] Larraona, "De Religiosis"—*CpR*, I (1920), 48, note (10).

[22] Benedictus XIII, Const. *Pretiosus*, 25 mart. 1727, § 38—*Bull. Rom.*, XXII, 522; Benedictus XIV, *Institutiones Ecclesiasticae*, XXIX, nn. 13, 16; CV, nn. 74, 75, 76; cf. also Pitra, *Commentarium*, in Const. XV Martini V, n. 18 and Matthaeucci, *Officialis Curiae Ecclesiasticae*, C. LII, nn. 3, 6 where this author quotes a decree of the S. C. Ep. et Reg., 20 dec. 1616, § 7.

[23] Larraona, "De Religiosis"—*CpR*, I (1920), 48, note (10); Orth, *Approbation of Religious Institutes*, p. 50; Goyeneche, "De votis simplicibus"—*Acta Congressus Iuridici Internationalis*, IV, 310, notes 9 and 10. Some of the congregations which were founded by way of preparation for the

turies many congregations of men were approved in an *absolute* way by the Holy See. Some were later raised to the status of orders, others kept their first juridical character without change or, having lost it, arose again.[24]

In the eighteenth century these congregations of men received full approbation. The Holy See seemed to favor a stricter discipline, for the pattern of the religious congregations of this century approached more and more closely to that of the strict orders. In consequence of their strict discipline and perpetual simple vows a number of them, particularly the Passionists and the Redemptorists, obtained nearly all the rights and privileges of the orders, notably the privilege of exemption.[25]

Article 4. Religious Congregations of Women

For some years before the Council of Trent a change had come in the religious Institutes of women. Certain communities had risen without Rome's permission and without provision for the observance of the cloister. Besides, many of the older communities which were obliged by the law of the cloister had discontinued its observance. Many of the new Institutes began with a *conservatorium; i. e.*, a home for orphan girls. The women who belonged to such Institutes naturally chose one of their members as the head and began in time

eventual taking of solemn vows were: The Clerics Regular of the Mother of God, October 13, 1595; the Doctrinarians, December 23, 1597; The Poor Clerics of the Mother of God of the Pious Schools, March 6, 1617—*Bull. Rom.*, X, 227-229; 411-413; XII, 382-385. Other congregations were founded perpetually and definitely: The Congregation of the Missions, Sept. 22, 1655; the Congregation of the Most Holy Redeemer, February 25, 1749; the Passionists, December 16, 1769; and the Congregation of the Brothers of the Christian Schools, February 7, 1724—*Bull. Rom.*, XVI, 67-69; *Bullarii Romani Continuatio Summorum Pontificum* (19 vols., Prati, 1835-1858), VII, 73 (henceforth cited as *Bull. Rom. Cont.*); Rules of the Brothers of the Christian Schools (Lembecq-Lez-Hal, 1925); Heimbucher, *Orden und Kongregationen*, II, 347.

[24] *Coll. S. C. Ep. et Reg.*, p. 745; Larraona, "De Religiosis" *CpR*, I (1920), 49; Freriks, *Religious Congregations in their External Relations*, The Catholic University of America Canon Law Studies, n. 1 (Washington, D. C.: Catholic University of America, 1916), p. 23; Wernz, *Ius Decretalium*, III, pars II, 607; Piat, *Praelectiones*, I, 18, 19.

[25] Freriks, *op. cit.*, p. 23.

to feel the need of a rule of life and the need of that stability which could be best furnished through the profession of vows. Their work of charity made the observance of the cloister impossible, so they took simple vows; and some of the old religious Institutes dropped the observance of the cloister in favor of this work. The term *conservatorium* later was extended to embrace those communities of women who lived together as religious under a certain rule but were not obliged to take solemn vows or to observe the cloister; it became synonymous with the term religious congregation.[26] Boniface VIII had commanded all who were professed to live in perpetual cloister and forbade them to leave the cloister for any reason.[27] The Council of Trent demanded a return to the life prescribed by the rule and renewed the law of Boniface VIII, commanding the bishops to restore the cloister where it was not kept, and to preserve it where it was kept.[28] Besides dropping the observance of the cloister, some of the new communities took only simple vows. This was against the general and universal practice from the time of Pope Innocent III (1198-1216) up to the time of the Council of Trent.[29]

The practice which diverged from the general law was reformed by the Constitution *Circa pastoralis* of Pope St. Pius V.[30] The force of this Constitution was to be felt for over two centuries. It set up a policy from which the Holy See receded only because of the necessity caused by the French Revolution. In his Constitution Pius V repeated the law of Boniface VIII and the confirmation of it which was accorded by the Council of Trent. All communities of women, even of Tertiaries living a common life, were obliged to the observance of the cloister even when their vows or constitutions did not demand it. All Institutes of women whose constitutions provided for a life in common without the profession of solemn vows and the observance of the cloister were interdicted and perpetually forbidden

[26] Benedictus XIV, *Institutiones Ecclesiasticae,* XXIX, n. 13; *Coll. S. C. Ep. et Reg.*, p. 743; Larraona, "De Religiosis"—*CpR,* I (1920), 48, n. 9; Bouix, *De Jure Regularium,* I, 187, 329; Orth, *Approbation of Religious Institutes,* pp. 57, 58.

[27] C. un., *de statu regularium,* III, 16, in VI°.

[28] Sess. XXV, *de regularibus,* cc. 1, 5.

[29] Orth, *op. cit.*, pp. 40-43.

[30] Const. *Circa pastoralis,* 29 maii 1566—*Fontes,* n. 112.

for the future. All receptions and professions in such Institutes were in the future invalid. This latter provision condemned them to a slow death, since no new members could be received. The obligation of the cloister began to be connected with the obligation of taking solemn vows, so that both of these began to be regarded as ecclesiastical law essentials for Institutes of women religious. In view of this invalidating clause, congregations of women with simple vows met with much more opposition than the congregations of men. There was a lapse of about two centuries before they were even tolerated. Eventually, they were permitted to exist. They received praise and full approbation much later than the congregations of men.[31]

There were several subsequent laws enforcing this Constitution of Pius V. In 1589 Sixtus V forbade the starting of such foundations.[32] This was not a general prohibition; it was a particular law corroborating the law of Pius V. Urban VIII abolished the Jesuitesses in 1631.[33] A decree of the Sacred Congregation of Bishops and Regulars in 1616 stated that congregations of women tertiaries were bound by the law of the Constitution *Circa Pastoralis* of Pope St. Pius V.[34]

Nevertheless many of the old congregations remained in existence and some new ones sprung up. None of these had papal approbation. They were tolerated, perhaps because of the greater evils feared from their suppression, or because the evils which Pope St. Pius V fought were not present in them or because of the good work they were doing.[35] Clement XI, in deciding some definite questions about certain religious women who lived in simple vows (*e. g.*, the age for admission, the permission to establish a chapel, etc.), clearly revealed that the Pope knew of these Institutes and yet tolerated them.[36] Benedict XIII stated that he did not mean to prohibit the tertiaries who lived a community life with only simple vows (this

[31] *Coll. S. C. Ep. et Reg.*, pp. 412, 742; Larraona, "De Religiosis"—*CpR*, I (1920), 45.

[32] Const. *Cum secuti*, 20 dec. 1589—*Bull. Rom.*, IX, 138.

[33] 13 ian. 1631—*apud Quamvis Iusto*, §§ 2, VI; 5; 8; 13—*Fontes*, n. 398.

[34] Cf. Matthaeucci, c. LII, nn. 3, 6; Pitra, *Commentarium*, in Const. XV, Martini V, n. 19; Benedictus XIV, *Institutiones Ecclesiasticae*, CV, n. 75.

[35] Bouix, *De Jure Regularium*, I, 324-329; Lucidi, *De Visitatione*, II, n. 264; Orth, *Approbation of Religious Institutes*, p. 51.

[36] Const. *Alias propositis*, 10 dec. 1667—*Bull. Rom.*, XVII, 609.

group of tertiaries was under the Dominicans), but that he *desired* that they be persuaded to embrace solemn vows and the observance of the cloisters. He did not bind them to follow out his desire.[37] He also granted a renewal of the privileges of exemption to the tertiaries.

Clement XII revoked any and every implicit approbation which canonists had perhaps connected with these acts of toleration, for he revoked all the privileges mentioned, and in particular the Constitution *Pretiosus* of Benedict XIII, to which he adverted expressly. Thus once again the Constitution *Circa pastoralis* was in full force.[38]

Benedict XIV in his *Institutiones Ecclesiasticae*[39] mentioned that such tertiaries abounded throughout the Church (there were twelve communities of them in Rome), and that they had begun to live as congregations. The Church did not approve them but merely tolerated them and declared them subject to the bishop. Benedict XIV, great canonist that he was, could not let the congregations of women remain in such an anomalous position. Accordingly on April 30, 1749, he issued the Constitution *Quamvis iusto,* which was to be the keystone of the law for congregations of women in simple vows. This Constitution revealed the beginning of a new legal outlook on this type of community, for although it concerned only the *Virgines Anglicanae,* it was this decision which was used for all similar cases in the future. It gives us the foundamentals of this type of religious Institute—the first true, though imperfect, picture of present day Institutes of women with (1) simple vows; (2) no cloister; (3) hierarchical organization, and (4) the exercise of works of charity as their purpose.

In the narrative part of the Constitution *Quamvis iusto*[40] Benedict XIV distinguished the Jesuitesses who had been suppressed by Urban VIII from the *Virgines Anglicanae* who had been approved by Clement XI, for two authors in England had erroneously thought that the approbation of the *Virgines Anglicanae* was a restoration of the Jesuitesses. These *Virgines Anglicanae* were not religious *proprie*

[37] Const. *Pretiosus,* 25 maii 1727, § 28—*Bull. Rom.,* XXII, 522-524.

[38] *Romanus Pontifex,* 31 mart. 1732—*Bull. Rom.,* XXIII, 323, 327.

[39] C. V, pp. 73-78.

[40] §§ 1-8—*Fontes,* n. 398.

dictae, for they had no solemn vows, and the approbation of a rule and way of life together with simple vows was not enough to constitute them religious *proprie dictae.*[41]

They were subject to the ordinary who freely chose the confessors and spiritual directors for them from the secular clergy. The Constitution also sketched the power of the superioress general. In general it was limited to the internal affairs of the house and was always dependent on the authority of the bishop. Her authority was limited to visitation, superintendence over the education of the girls, and the transfer of subjects from house to house, but all in due subjection to the ordinary, for she needed the permission of the ordinary to admit novices to profession, for visitation and for the transfer of her subjects.[42]

In this Constitution Benedict XIV did not approve the *Virgines Anglicanae* as religious,[43] nor did he abrogate the Constitution *Circa pastoralis* of Pius V. Rather he derogated from that law to the extent of giving passive toleration to the Institute. He gave the *Virgines Anglicanae* certain rights and privileges and a standing in law. Just as the Sacred Congregation of Bishops and Regulars [44] stated that these Institutes were subject *omnimode iurisdictioni Episcopi citra tamen approbationem,* so did Pope Benedict XIV add the phrase *caeterum non intendimus per praesentes ipsum conservatorium in aliquo approbare.* Apparently this phrase was added in order that a suppression of these congregations would be easier in case the abuses feared by Pope St. Pius V should appear.[45] This document with the various derogations from it which arose in the course of time became the established guide and norm for all congregations of women until the time of the Constitution *Conditae a Christo,* which was issued by Pope Leo XIII on December 8, 1900.[46]

[41] In his Constitution (§§ 13, 14) Benedict XIV cited the Brief of Clement XI, *Emanavit,* 5 mart. 1796, and the response of the S. C. Ep. et Reg., 21 iul. 1748 (which response is found in *Fontes,* n. 1862)—*Fontes,* n. 398.

[42] §§ 16, 17, 19, 20—*Fontes,* n. 398.

[43] § 13, quinto—*Fontes,* n. 398.

[44] 30 ian. 1723—Benedictus XIV, *Institutiones Ecclesiasticae,* CV, n. 77; XXIX, n. 13.

[45] Const. *Quamvis iusto,* § 5—*Fontes,* n. 398; Cf. Orth, *Approbation of Religious Institutes,* p. 56.

[46] *Fontes,* n. 644.

CHAPTER IV

RELIGIOUS CONGREGATIONS FROM THE FRENCH REVOLUTION TO THE PROMULGATION OF THE CODE

ARTICLE 1. THE RELIGIOUS CONGREGATIONS

IN the consideration of the term *conservatoria* it was seen that many of these were established for the purpose of teaching and education. With the loss of many monasteries and the endowments attached to them as occasioned by the Reformation, the need for new Institutes to care for teaching, to look to the relief of the poor, and to undertake the care of the sick became quite evident. Many congregations both of men and women arose solely for that purpose.

That need was as nothing, however, compared with the crying necessity for works of charity that arose from the public disorders and the total war that ravaged Europe at the end of the eighteenth and the beginning of the nineteenth century. This need was felt most acutely in France, for there the Revolution and the anti-religious laws which followed in its wake left the children of Catholic parents to grow up like pagans without the aids of Catholic education. Orphans were left destitute; the old, the sick, the poor had no help. The orders and monasteries which had cared for them in the past were either despoiled by plunder or suppressed, exiled or denied juridical existence by law. Christ in His mercy raised up men and women who gave their life and fortune to further the spiritual and corporal works of mercy. Experience taught the wisdom of an economy of effort and money which was to be found only in the organization of individuals into bands which were united for furthering the particular works of mercy. Many strove for a more perfect life, by binding themselves through vows to the practice of the evangelical counsels. Their mode of life in common merited and obtained the approval of the Holy See. The conditions in the Americas also gave rise to the need of Institutes which were devoted to the furthering of these spiritual and corporal works of mercy. It was by

Institutes which were fashioned after a more flexible pattern than that of the traditional religious orders within the Church that these needs were to be filled.[1] Centuries had passed since the Jesuits were permitted to profess simple vows as religious. The congregations of women who lived in common with simple vows were still Institutes for which the Church gave nothing more than toleration. But the congregations of men in simple vows had on many sides merited the Church's positive approval. With the appalling spiritual needs of the time the moment had come when the Church desisted from her passive attitude in relation to the congregations of men and hostile attitude in relation to congregations of women and accorded to them not only a cordial welcome, but also positive encouragement and direct approval.

The civil laws in France at the turn of the nineteenth century were quite sweeping in their baneful effect. The laws of the *Directoire* (1795-1799) were renewed on June 22, 1804, dissolving every aggregation or association formed under the pretext of religion and not approved by the State. This law affected France, Belgium, Germany (especially the parts ceded to France in 1801), Spain (where the convents were suppressed during the French occupation from 1808-1814), Holland (by decree of Napoleon, January 3, 1812), and Italy (especially during the French occupation).[2]

The reaction to this situation by the Holy See was immediate. The mere toleration of Institutes of simple vows gave way to decrees of praise and even of approbation. From 1816-1820 five different congregations received decrees of praise or approval from the Holy See; from 1820-1830, thirteen; from 1830-1840, eighteen; from

[1] Lucidi, *De Visitatione,* II, 247-250; Steiger, "De propagatione et diffusione vitae religiosae"—*Periodica,* XIII (1924), (174)-(176); Boudinhon, "Les congregations religieuses à voeux simples"—*Le Canoniste Contemporain,* XXV (1902), 417-423; Larraona, "De Religiosis"—*CpR,* I (1920), 48; Misserey, "La profession religieuse et le voeu solennel"—*Le Canoniste Contemporain,* XLVI (1924), 162, 163.

[2] Tyck, *Notices Historiques sur les Congrégations et Communautés Religieuses . . . du XIXme Siècle* (Louvain, 1892), Appendix I, pp. 293-323 (henceforth referred to as *Notices Historiques*); Keller, *Les Congrégations Religieuses en France* (Paris, 1880), xvii-xxiii; Schuetz, *The Origin of the Teaching Brotherhoods* (Washington, D. C.: Catholic University of America, 1918), *passim.*

1862-1865, seventy-four. In 1865 France alone had one hundred and eighty-five congregations of recent origin with only episcopal approbation, waiting for the approval of the Holy See.[3]

Necessity as well as utility prompted the change. Institutes with solemn vows were in part abolished. Religious with simple vows were needed to take their place. Even when the solemn vows were not revoked, the law often curtailed a number of their effects. The Church, rather than dispense the individual religious from their solemn vows, abrogated solemn profession entirely or at least suspended the juridical effects of solemn profession.[4] The law of the cloister was abrogated during these troublesome times, since the governments recognized the religious communities *only* because of their social worth in education, their care of the sick, etc., which works were incompatible with the cloister. The Holy See left it to the bishops or to the constitutions of the Institute to decide on what kind of cloister the Institute was to observe.[5] According to the law of Pope St. Pius V which was still in force, the only religious women permitted were such as professed solemn vows and observed the papal cloister. With the removal by the Holy See of the necessity of cloister the last barrier to the full approbation of the merely tolerated

[3] Tyck, *op. cit.*, p. 335.

[4] The Sacred Congregation of Bishops and Regulars declared that all future Trappist vows were to be held as simple vows if they were taken within the kingdom of France—decr., 24 mart. 1837, *apud Coll. S. C. Ep. et Reg.*, p. 73; the Redemptoristines because of certain existing laws incompatible with solemn vows had to take simple vows in Belgium and Austria—decr., 3 apr. 1835, *apud Coll. S. C. Ep. et Reg.*, p. 451; the vows of the *moniales* of France ceased to be solemn until the Holy See decided otherwise—decr. *Parisien,* 1 aug. 1839, ad 1, *apud Fontes,* n. 1923; the religious of both sexes who were in solemn vows in the kingdom of Naples were allowed the right to acquire, retain, administer and dispose of their property for honest and pious uses, if that was done with due dependence on legitimate religious superiors—S. Poenit. Ap., 1 dec. 1820, *apud Coll. S. C. Ep. et Reg.*, p. 739; in America a duly appointed religious was allowed to hold and administer the property of his Institute in his own name; but such an arrangement was to be made which allowed the acts to stand as valid solely in the civil law.—15 dec. 1840, *apud Coll. S. C. P. F.*, n. 916, ad 11; *Fontes,* n. 4786.

[5] S. C. Ep. et Reg., *Parisien.*, 1 aug. 1839, ad 2 et 3—*Fontes,* n. 1923; Lucidi, *De Visitatione* II, 325-328; Keller, *Les Congrégations Religieuses en France,* xxvi-xxxvi, etc.

congregations and Institutes of women disappeared.[6] The purpose of the cloister had been to remove the religious from the dangers of the world. The new work and the dangers with which they were faced called for simple and even temporary vows, so that they could leave, if they wished, at the cessation, dispensation, or commutation of these vows. Besides this, another reason for the change to simple vows was that the law of France and of other countries sanctioned what the Church forbade, namely, the state protected the monk or the nun who, in yielding to the temptations and the spirit of the age, had upon leaving the monastery become married. The civil law, to the great harm and scandal of the faithful, made such an act of sacrilege permissible. The effects of the civil law on the rule of the cloister and the vows of poverty and chastity, as well as the needs of the time, contributed the occasion for this change of attitude in regard to religious vows on the part of the Church.[7] So greatly did the Church change its attitude in regard to this that on March 19, 1857, it was prescribed that candidates for all the orders of men in solemn vows were to make simple vows for at least three years before they were admitted to solemn vows.[8] The decree *Perpensis* extended this ruling to all orders of women in solemn vows.[9]

The Holy See, in fact, did not wish to approve any new orders,[10] but rather allowed a great increase in the number of new congregations. So great did these grow in number that Pius IX began to doubt the utility of this growth and asked in a letter of June 6, 1867, which was sent out to the bishops of the world to determine the *agenda* of the Vatican Council, whether this phenomenal growth

[6] Lucidi, *De Visitatione*, II, 268; Schaaf, *The Cloister*, The Catholic University of America Canon Law Studies, n. 13 (Cincinnati: St. Anthony's Messenger, 1921), p. 75.

[7] Lucidi, *De Visitatione*, II, 268, 269.

[8] S. C. super Statu Regularium, litt. encycl. *Neminem latet*, 19 mart. 1857—*Fontes*, n. 4381; S. C. Ep. et Reg., decr. 19 mart. 1857—*Fontes*, n. 1976.

[9] S. C. Ep. et Reg., decr. *Perpensis*, 3 maii 1902—*Fontes*, n. 2039.

[10] The last one approved, it seems, was that of the Order of the Friars of Penance by Pope Pius VI in the Constitution *Ex debito pastoralis*, 27 mart. 1787—*Bull. Rom. Cont.*, Tom. VI, Pars II, 1782; cf. Larraona, "De Religiosis" —*CpR*, I (1920), 133; *Analecta Juris Pontificii*, III (1859), 129, 206; Vermeersch, *De Religiosis*, I, n. 57; Schäfer, *De Religiosis*, pp. 123, 124. Note that canon 492, § 1 has no provision for the founding of a new *order*.

was such a good thing that approbations should continue to be given without limit in number, or whether it would not be better to strengthen and propagate the congregations which already had been founded.[11] The French bishops were the only ones to answer directly (the bishops of Holland and Belgium by their praise answered indirectly) that these Institutes should rather be increased and not decreased.[12]

After the Vatican Council, however, the Sacred Congregation of Bishops and Regulars examined, in 1897, the question of the multiplication of these Institutes and adopted rules to control any inconveniences and abuses which could arise from such a phenomenal growth. A commission was appointed within the Congregation for the approval of the new Institutes; [13] the rules it followed were not promulgated, but they are found incorporated substantially in the Constitution *Conditae a Christo.*[14] The Sacred Congregation of Bishops and Regulars shortly afterwards published its rules for the foundation of new Institutes of simple vows for the guidance of the bishops.[15] Still these provisions were not adequate to curb some of the evils which arose; particularly those of founding Institutes without sufficient funds, of designating them by strange names, or of using an odd form of religious habit for its members. In 1906, Pius X issued a *Motu Proprio* to correct any abuses and irregularities which remained.[16] By this law Pius X demanded that the bishops were to consult the Holy See through the Sacred Congregation of Bishops and Regulars before they founded an Institute, and required explicit information in each case as to the prospective Institute's

[11] *Acta et Decreta Sacrorum Conciliorum Recentiorum, Collectio Lacensis* (7 vols., Friburgi Brisgoviae, 1870-1890), VII, 1028, q. 10 (henceforth cited *Collectio Lacensis*).

[12] *Collectio Lacensis,* VII, 837a, 877a.

[13] Battandier, *Guide Canonique,* n. 16, p. 7.

[14] Leo XIII, const. *Conditae a Christo,* 8 dec. 1900—*Fontes,* n. 644. On this point cf. § 1, III of the Constitution which directed the bishops to choose one of the Institutes already approved rather than to found a new one.

[15] *Normae secundum quas S. Cong. Episcoporum et Regularium procedere solet in approbandis novis institutis votorum simplicium,* 28 iunii 1901 (Romae, 1901), (referred to hereafter as *Normae*).

[16] Pius X, motu propr. *Dei Providentis,* 16 iul. 1906—*Fontes,* n. 675.

name, the name of its founder, reasons for its foundation, its scope, and the form and shape of the religious habit. The underlying purpose of these rules was to check the foundation of new congregations without reason, and to prevent the formation of those which were differentiated only by the use of a new name or by the employment of a new form of religious habit. This law was incorporated in canon 492 of the present Code.

Article 2. The Jurisprudence of This Period

This change in legislation consequent upon the changed attitude bristled with legal difficulties, for there now existed a great number of pious men and women who lived a life which was similar to that of the religious, but for which there existed no common law. The *Jus Regulare* could not be applied to them in very many points such as those regarding the observance of the cloister, the enjoyment of exemption, the solemn character of the vows, etc. Nor could the law on lay confraternities and third orders secular be applied to them. In general it can be said that the *Jus Regulare* was applicable to these new congregations only in such matters which were common to both types of Institutes and in such points wherein the *Jus Regulare* was explicitly applied to them. In all other cases new laws had to be made, or the prescriptions of the *Jus Regulare* had to be changed in order to fit the new conditions.[17]

Several points of uniformity were expressly stated in new decrees. The necessity of testimonial letters for postulants was stated for orders as well as for congregations, societies or Institutes.[18] To both types of Institutes in Italy and the adjacent islands were given the rules for the *exploratio voluntatis* of the novice before profession.[19]

[17] Larraona, "De Religiosis"—*CpR,* I (1920), 135-138; Sanguineti, *Iuris Ecclesiastici Privati Institutiones* (Romae, 1884), p. 294—against Nervegna, *De Institutis Votorum Simplicium Religiosorum et Monialium* (Romae, 1904), p. 22, who maintained that the whole *Jus Regulare* was to be applied to congregations.

[18] S. C. super Statu Regularium, decr. *Romani Pontifices,* 25 ian. 1848—*Fontes,* n. 4375; declar. 1 maii 1851—*Fontes,* n. 4377; 5 nov. 1852—*Fontes,* n. 4380; 29 maii 1857—*Fontes,* n. 4382.

[19] S. C. super Statu Regularium, decr. *Regulari Disciplinae,* 25 ian. 1848—

The Encyclical *Neminem latet* (March 19, 1857) and the Decree *Perpensis* (May 3, 1902) placed simple vows in orders and in congregations on a par as regards the retention of the *dominium radicale* of goods.[20] Several decrees extended the old law to the new congregations. The decrees of the Council of Trent on the ownership of immovable goods, on the election and qualities of superiors, on confession, on communion, on the custody of the Holy Eucharist, on the novitiate and on the age necessary for profession, on the renunciation of goods before profession, on the *exploratio voluntatis* of girls before the taking of solemn vows—all these were applied to religious congregations by the Sacred Congregation of Bishops and Regulars.[21] The law of Pope Benedict XIV on admission of clerics to the Institutes of regulars was applied to the Oblates of Mary.[22] The law of Pope St. Pius V [23] and of Pope Pius IX [24] which forbade the superiors of regular orders to grant dimissorial letters to those who were not yet in solemn vows was applied to congregations regarding those who had not been joined *stabiliter* to the congregation.[25]

Other steps toward uniformity of discipline are manifest in the unifying of discipline for orders and congregations on the canonical process of expulsion, the perpetual suspension of the *eiecti*, their canonical status after dismissal, and the curriculum of studies.[26] The *Normae* extended the ruling of the Encyclical *Neminem latet* (March 19, 1857) to all Institutes of simple vows with pontifical approbation, and achieved uniformity in the following matters: the

Fontes, n. 4376; declar. 1 maii 1851—*Fontes*, n. 4378; declar. 16 ian. 1852, 12 iun. 1855, 24 febr. 1860—*Coll. S. C. Ep. et Reg.*, 850, 851.

[20] *Fontes*, nn. 4381, 2039.

[21] Conc. Trid., Sess. XXV, *de regularibus*, c. 3, 6, 10, 15, 16, 17, 22; *Coll. S. C. Ep. et Reg.*, pp. 120; 432; 710; 778, n. 6; 785, ad 12; 793, ad 5 et 12; Lucidi, *De Visitatione*, II, n. 463, ad 1; 458; Leo XIII, const. *Conditae a Christo*, 8 dec. 1900, § 2, I—*Fontes*, n. 644.

[22] Benedictus XIV, litt. *Ex quo dilectus*, 14 ian. 1747—*Fontes*, n. 374; S. C. Ep. et Reg., *Pinerolien*, 28 iul. 1837, ad 2—*Fontes*, n. 1914; *Aurelianen*, 20 dec. 1859—*Fontes*, n. 1979.

[23] Const. *Romanus Pontifex*, 14 oct. 1568—*Fontes*, n. 129.

[24] S. C. super Statu Regularium, declar. 12 iun. 1858—*Fontes*, n. 4383.

[25] S. C. Ep. et Reg., decr. *Auctis Admodum*, 4 nov. 1892, n. I—*Fontes*, n. 2020.

[26] Decr. *Auctis Admodum*, nn. III, IV, V, VI—*Fontes*, n. 2020.

novitiate, the triennial profession to be made before perpetual profession, the form of government, etc.[27] The decrees of Pope Pius X and of the Sacred Congregation of Religious show openly the trend to constitute a uniform law for orders and congregations with regard to the incurring of debts and obligations by religious Institutes,[28] the exclusion of certain postulants from the religious Institute,[29] the method to be used in passing sentence of dismissal in orders and religious Institutes,[30] and the provisions to be made for the confessions of *moniales* and *sorores*.[31]

On a few points there was an explicit declaration that the *Jus Regulare* was not to be applied to congregations. The latter did not have to observe the laws of the Council of Trent on processions.[32] The law of the papal cloister and the law of attached penal sanctions did not extend to congregations.[33] Simple profession did not induce loss of benefices as did solemn profession.[34] Also the laws of

[27] *Normae,* n. 71-90, 96-109, and pars secunda, nn. 202-320. La Puma, "Evoluzione del diritto dei religiosi de Pio IX a Pio XI"—*Acta Congressus Iuridici Internationalis,* IV, 198.

[28] S. C. de Religiosis, instr. 30 iul. 1909—*Fontes,* n. 4395.

[29] S. C. de Religiosis, decr. 7 sept. 1909—*Fontes,* n. 4396.

[30] S. C. de Religiosis, decr. 16 maii 1911—*Fontes,* n. 4409.

[31] Pope Leo XIII furnished the initial impetus in the legislation which, relative to the confessions to be made by religious, was to become a common law for orders and congregations alike. Cf. S. C. Ep. et Reg., decr. *Quemadmodum,* 17 dec. 1890—*Fontes,* n. 2017. This legislation reached its final form under Pope Pius X. Cf. S. C. de Religiosis, *Cum de sacramentalibus,* 3 febr. 1913—*Acta Apostolicae Sedis,* V (1913), 62-64 (henceforth cited as *AAS*); decr. *In audientia,* 5 aug. 1913—*AAS,* V (1913), 431. The last cited decree guaranteed the same liberty of conscience to all religious whether they belonged to orders or to congregations; the question of the reception of Holy Communion was to be regulated by the confessor; the superior could not deny any religious an extraordinary or a special confessor. This decree was applicable also to all lay religious who were put on an equal basis with other religious in this matter. Cf. La Puma, *art. cit.,* IV, 199.

[32] Conc. Trident., Sess. XXV, *de regularibus,* c. 13; S. C. Ep. et Reg., *Pinerolien.,* 3 maii 1839—*Fontes,* n. 1922.

[33] S. C. Ep. et Reg., *Parisien.,* 1 aug. 1839, ad 2 et 3—*Fontes,* n. 1923; 6 dec. 1839—*Coll. S. C. Ep. et Reg.,* pp. 88, 89.

[34] C. 4, *de regularibus et transeuntibus ad religionem,* III, 14, in VI°; Benedictus XIV, ep. *Ex quo,* 14 ian. 1747—*Fontes,* n. 374; S. C. Ep. et Reg., 25 aug. 1903—*Fontes,* n. 2045.

the novitiate in general were not extended to the congregations because of the difference in purpose, vows, etc.[35]

The biggest knot to untangle was that which involved the question of a bishop's power to found a religious Institute and the extent of his jurisdiction over religious of simple vows. The law of the IV General Lateran Council and of the II General Council of Lyons was rendered inoperative through a contrary custom which existed with the tacit consent of the Pope. By the middle of the eighteenth century authors agreed that bishops had the power to establish and approve religious congregations, and that this power derived from the established contrary custom.[36]

Various examples of the operation of this contrary custom can be given. St. Joan Valois began her society with only the bishop's approbation, but afterwards obtained pontifical approval.[37] The hospital nuns of the diocese of Angers in 1642 founded a monastery and followed the rule of St. Augustine with the permission and approbation of the ordinary, spread into other dioceses with the same permission, and only later obtained the confirmation and approbation of Pope Alexander VII.[38] The Institute of the Sisters of St. Joseph was erected by the Bishop of Le Puy-en-Valay in 1650-1651 without referring to the Holy See for permission.[39] The Brothers of the Christian Schools, organized by St. John Baptist de la Salle, were likewise founded with an initial episcopal approbation.[40]

[35] Bouix, *De Jure Regularium,* I, 577, n. 11.

[36] Piat, *Praelectiones,* I, 21; Bouix, *De Jure Regularium,* I, 326; Wernz, *Ius Decretalium,* III, Pars II, n. 590, footnote 15; Larraona, "De Religiosis"—*CpR,* I (1920), 48; Vermeersch, *De Religiosis,* I, 49; *Acta Sanctae Sedis* (41 vols., Romae, 1865-1908), XXXIX (1906), 345, footnote 2 (hereafter cited *ASS*).

[37] Alexander VI, Bulla *Ea quae,* 14 febr. 1501—Cf. Heimbucher, *Die Orden und Kongregationen,* I, 627, 628.

[38] Const. *Sacrosancti,* 8 ian. 1666—*Bull. Rom.,* XVII, 411; cf. Heimbucher, *op. cit.,* I, 653, 654.

[39] Heimbucher (*Orden und Kongregationen,* II, 492, 493) gives the date of the foundation of the Institute as 1650-1651. Keller (*Les Congrégations Religieuses en France,* pp. 236-239) gives the date as September 23, 1661. Currier (*History of Religious Orders* [New York, 1894], p. 542) gives it as March 10, 1651.

[40] Benedictus XXII, Const. *In apostolicae dignitates*—cf. Rules of the Brothers of the Christian Schools (Lembecq-Lez-Hal, The Mother House, 1925).

There was no dissenting voice against the possession of power on the part of the bishop to approve of religious men. The congregations of religious women, however, could not appeal to the custom which recognized the same power for the bishop relative to such approval, because the continuity of the custom had been broken by the Constitution of Pope Clement XII.[41] Pope Benedict XIV gave them only toleration—which toleration, though, did acknowledge implicitly the practice of the bishops in founding them. The decrees of praise from Rome to the congregations of women still had attached to them the phrase *citra approbationem conservatorii,* but even that was dropped at the beginning of the nineteenth century, and thus there was signified a full approbation of the Holy See.[42]

There was no real uniformity of discipline until the period after the French Revolution. Before that time each case had been handled as a particular matter, but after the Revolution with the rapid growth of the congregations there was a distinct need of norms which could be followed in the founding of these Institutes. These norms were given in a rather sketchy form by the *Methodus* of Archbishop Bizzarri, Secretary of the Congregation of Bishops and Regulars. The *Methodus* appeared in 1884.[43] The *Normae* of 1901 perfected and made more determinate the imperfect and rather general rules of the *Methodus*. These were not laws but rather directive norms for bishops in the founding of new Institutes.[44] However the Constitution *Conditae a Christo* (1900) of Pope Leo XIII gave the bishops the legal right to found new Institutes. Thus was totally abrogated that part of the IV General Lateran Council (1215) and of the

[41] Const. *Romanus Pontifex,* 31 mart. 1732—*Bull. Rom.,* XXIII, 323, 327. Cf. *supra,* p. 36.

[42] Schäfer, *De Religiosis,* pp. 28, 29; *Coll. S. C. Ep. et Reg.,* p. 742, note 1; *Bull. Rom. Cont.,* Tom. VII, Pars II, pp. 1990-1992; Larraona, "De Religiosis" —*CpR,* I (1920), p. 50, note 9; Goyeneche, "De votis simplicibus" *Acta Congressus Iuridici Internationalis,* IV, 308, note 8.

[43] *Methodus quae a S. C. Ep. et Reg. servatur in approbandis novis institutis votorum simplicium—Coll. S. C. Ep. et Reg.,* pp. 772, 773; Lucidi, *De Visitatione,* II, 255-257; Tyck, *Notices Historiques,* pp. 335-337.

[44] Piat, *Praelectiones,* I, 42; Vermeersch, *De Religiosis,* II (130), n. 6. Maroto, "Regulae et particulares constitutiones"—*Acta Congressus Iuridici Internationalis,* IV, p. 297, n. 133; "Studia canonica"—*CpRM,* XVIII (1937), 363.

II General Council of Lyons (1274) which, at least by the common opinion of the authors, had referred to religious congregations. The Holy See determined from the time of this Constitution onward not to approve an Institute unless the bishop had already done so.[45]

The other knotty problem was that of the jurisdiction of the ordinary especially in regard to the congregations of women. The Constitution *Quamvis iusto* (1631) had given him practically full authority over congregations of women, but the prescriptions of that law gradually vanished during this period. Pope Pius IX derogated from the Constitution *Quamvis iusto* when he gave the superioress general wider powers, so that she was subject to the bishop only in regard to local matters.[46] Furthermore the superioress general, as stated in various rules approved during that period, could visit the houses of the Institute, sometimes nominate, always confirm the superioresses of the houses, elect the mistress of novices and the prefect, and transfer subjects from one house to another without the bishop's leave.[47] The power of the superioress general gradually grew, as it had to under the circumstances, when the congregations of women gradually began to enjoy, as the congregations of men long had enjoyed, a separate juridic entity. She began to have full dominative power, separate and independent of the bishop or the Cardinal Protector, though she always remained under the vigilance of these lest she abuse that power.[48]

The spread of many Institutes through several dioceses led to difficulties. The Holy See repeatedly refused to recognize the local ordinary as the superior general of an Institute which had spread through several dioceses, lest he infringe on the jurisdiction of the other local ordinaries where the Institute had spread, and commanded

[45] For the treatment of the Constitution *Conditae a Christo* and the further slight restrictions of the Constitution *Dei Providentis* on the bishop's power, cf. *supra*, article 1 of this chapter.

[46] Pius IX, litt. *Cum maxima*, 13 nov. 1847—apud Lucidi, *De Visitatione*, II, n. 463, p. 327, note 1; Molitor, *Religiosi Iuris Capita Selecta*, p. 54.

[47] *Coll. S. C. Ep. et Reg.*, pp. 775, nn. 1, 2, 3, 5; 501; 709; 710; 775, n. 4; Lucidi, *De Visitatione*, II, n. 305, 306, nn. 16, 17; *S. C. Ep. et Reg.*, *Augustana*, 21 iulii 1748—*Fontes*, n. 1862.

[48] *Coll. S. C. Ep. et Reg.*, pp. 777, n. 13; 667, ad 1 (IV), (V), 780, ad 5; 781, ad 6; 784, ad 1; 785, ad 7; 787, ad 2; 788, ad 1; 789, ad 2; 792, ad 1. Cf. Larraona, "De Religiosis"—*CpR*, I (1920), 138-140.

that any provisions which authorized such powers for the bishop be expunged from the constitutions.[49] The tendency of the Holy See to protect the rights of the local ordinary was shown by the use of the clause which usually was added to the approval of Institutes which had spread through various dioceses: *salva ordinariorum iurisdictione ad praescriptum sacrorum canonum et Apostolicarum constitutionum.*[50] The relations between the superiors and the bishops remained, then, quite vague and obscure until the Constitution *Conditae a Christo,* which distinguished between Institutes of diocesan and pontifical approval, outlined the power of the bishops towards each of these and the nature of their subjection to the bishop. It removed the arbitrary power of the bishop, and gave a strength and juridic stability to these Institutes which obtained right up to the time of the Code.[51]

The law was built up by the collection of this jurisprudence, by the argumentation from these particular cases and by the extension of the particular law to similar cases by way of legal analogy. The law progressed considerably in this way, although somewhat arbitrarily, since many particular resolutions were applied absolutely as general laws or, after the time of the *Normae,* many of the rules of the *Normae* were applied to Institutes erected previous to the *Normae.* In general the *Normae* reflected all the jurisprudence which referred to the internal rule of congregations. It was the *corpus organicum,* and some of its provisions were referred even to regulars. Just before the Code, then, there was achieved a single and a common law for orders and congregations with the sole exception of those provisions which were proper to orders.

[49] *Coll. S. C. Ep. et Reg.,* pp. 780, nn. 5, 6; 784, ad 1; 787; 789, n. 1; 790, n. 2; 792.

[50] *Coll. S. C. Ep. et Reg.,* pp. 778, n. 1; 780, n. 5, etc.

[51] Steiger, "De propagatione et diffusione vitae religiosae". *Periodica,* XIII (1924), (178). For good commentaries on the Constitution *Conditae a Christo* cf. Bastien, *Constitution "Conditae a Christo" de Leon XIII* (Bruges, 1902), esp. pp. 32-91; and the articles "Les Instituts des voeux simples" by Boudinhon in *Le Canoniste Contemporain,* vols. XXV (1902); XXVI (1903); XXVII (1904); XXVIII (1905); esp. Vol. XXV (1902), 520, 521; Vol. XXVI (1903), 5-17; 65-72 (for the relation of the bishop to a diocesan congregation) and Vol. XXVI (1903), 257-270; 321-332; 385-400; 516-537; 624-637 (for the relation of the bishop to a pontifical congregation).

CHAPTER V

TEMPORARY VOWS AND DISMISSAL

Article 1. Temporary Vows

Temporary vows were those which were takeh for a certain specified time, *e. g.*, for one, two, three, or five years, or up to the time when the one professed with vows reached a certain age.[1]

Before the promulgation of the Code the authors were unanimous in their assertion that temporary vows could not furnish the requisite basis for the religious state as understood in its true and proper sense, at most such vows could furnish the basis for the religious state as understood in an improper sense.[2] In fact, the first appearance of temporary vows as a common canonical institute came with the Code.

In a certain sense they did exist before the Code, that is, in the sense that they were temporary from the viewpoint of the religious Institute, though they were perpetual on the part of the one who was professed. This kind of vow had existed ever since the approval of the Jesuit vows which were of this nature,[3] as also were all the simple vows in the religious congregations. When Pope Pius IX ascended the throne political revolt and the spread of irreligion was rampant among almost all nations. This sinister influence was felt also in religious circles. In the religious Institutes with vows it was made manifest in the many defections from these Institutes and in the relaxation of discipline of the vows especially in regard

[1] Lucidi, *De Visitatione*, II, 269.

[2] Goyeneche, "De transitu ad aliam religionem"—*CpR*, I (1920), 110; Larraona, "De Religiosis"—*CpR*, II (1921), 208; Angelus a SS. Corde, *Manuale Juris Regularium*, n. 4; Wernz, *Ius Decretalium*, III, pars II, 590; Piat, *Praelectiones*, I, p. 4, q. 7; Pirhing, *Ius Canonicum*, Lib. III, tit. 31, n. 6; Schmalzgrueber, *Ius Ecclesiasticum Universum*, Lib. III, tit. 34, n. 8; Suarez, *De statu perfectionis et religionis*, Tract. VII, Lib. II, C. 3, n. 2; Vermeersch, *De Religiosis*, II (149)-(150); Battandier, *Guide Canonique*, p. 157, n. 192.

[3] Suarez, *De Statu Perfectionis et Religionis*, Tr. X, Lib. III, C. 10.

to obedience and poverty. Pope Pius IX created the *Congregatio super Statu Regularium,*[4] which issued many important regulations that reflected the Holy Father's mind in regard to the strengthening of discipline in religious congregations.[5] To get to the root of the evil; that is, the admission of unworthy candidates, this Congregation, besides the decree *Regulari disciplinae* on the admission of novices, issued the important encyclical *Neminem latet* of March 19, 1857. In it the Congregation declared that because of the need of the times greater care had to be exercised in the selection of candidates in the orders of solemn vows, lest any be admitted who would be unfit for the religious state. To guard against the admission of such candidates it was decreed that in every order of men with solemn vows each candidate was to take only simple vows at the end of his novitiate (provided that he was sixteen years of age or over), and that only after a period of three years in simple vows was he to be admitted to solemn profession. For a just and reasonable cause the proper superior could defer this profession for even a longer period of time than three years, but the solemn profession was to be made before the candidate had completed his twenty-fifth year. If the candidate at the end of the novitiate was already twenty-five years of age he had to take simple vows for three years, but if his superiors wished to defer his solemn profession, they had in each case to obtain permission from the Congregation in charge of religious affairs.[6] The nature of these vows was explained the following year (1858) in the decree *Sanctissimus.* The vows were perpetual on the part of the one who was professed. They could be

[4] Pius IX, litt. encycl., *Ubi primum arcano,* 17 iun. 1847—*Pii IX Pontificis Maximi Acta,* Pars Prima (7 vols., Romae, 1854-1858), I, 46-54. Cf. Vermeersch, *De Religiosis,* II, 37-41; *Coll. S. C. Ep. et Reg.,* p. 816; Battandier, *Guide Canonique* (5. ed., Paris, 1911), XVI; Schäfer, *De Religiosis,* p. 180.

[5] S. C. super Statu Regularium, decr. *Romani Pontifices,* 25 ian. 1848 (strict rules on testimonial letters)—*Fontes,* n. 4375; decr. *Regulari disciplinae,* 25 ian. 1848 (regulating the admission and formation of novices)—*Fontes,* n. 4376.

[6] S. C. super Statu Regularium, litt. encycl. *Neminem latet,* 19 mart. 1857—*Fontes,* n. 4381; S. C. Ep. et Reg., decr. 19 mart. 1857—*Fontes,* n. 1976; S. C. super Statu Regularium, 20 ian. 1860, ad 3—*Fontes,* n. 4385; *Coll. S. C. Ep. et Reg.,* p. 867, et nota; 869.

dispensed only by the Holy See, but the master general of the order with his general council could dismiss one who was only in simple vows. In such a case of dismissal the religious was freed from all the bonds and obligations of his vows and became a lay person (*i. e.*, if he was not in sacred orders when he entered the Institute).[7] The solemn profession was invalid unless the religious had passed the period of three years in simple vows as required by the Encyclical *Neminem latet*.[8] This law of the Constitution *Ad universalis* referred only to the future; solemn professions which since the Encyclical *Neminem latet* had been made immediately after the novitiate were valid but illicit.[9]

These decrees referred only to orders of men. The orders of women still made solemn profession immediately after the novitiate. There were exceptions and special provisions for some orders. On April 21, 1841, the Sacred Congregation of Bishops and Regulars decreed that, because of the civil laws of the places concerned (the decree is listed as *Incerti loci—Super nonnullis Episcopi postulatis,* etc.), the novices were to take simple vows for three years (the triennial solemn vows demanded by civil law were a contradiction in terms), but these vows were not to be made with the intention of binding oneself to merely temporary vows. These vows could be taken annually or renewed triennially until the time when solemn perpetual vows were to be taken.[10] The *moniales* in France were allowed to take simple vows before they took solemn vows. In the regions under the emperor of Austria the *moniales* could take simple vows until they were twenty-five years of age.[11] In the United States the Nuns of the Visitation at Georgetown, Mobile, Kaskaskia, St. Louis, and Baltimore, were obliged, after their novitiate, to take simple vows for five years. After this period of simple vows they were to be admitted to solemn profession.[12]

[7] S. C. super Statu Regularium, declar. 12 iun. 1858—*Fontes,* n. 4383; 20 ian. 1860, ad 4—*Fontes,* n. 4385.

[8] Pius IX, Const. *Ad universalis* 7 febr. 1862—*Fontes,* n. 532.

[9] S. C. Ep. et Reg., declar. 16 aug. 1866—*Coll. S. C. Ep. et Reg.*, p. 867.

[10] *Coll. S. C. Ep. et Reg.*, pp. 463-464.

[11] *Coll. S. C. Ep. et Reg.*, pp. 736-737.

[12] S. C. Ep. et Reg., litt. 30 sept. 1864—*Fontes,* n. 1995.

In 1902 the Congregation of Bishops and Regulars extended the provisions of the Encyclical *Neminem latet* and of the Constitution *Ad universalis* to all orders of women taking solemn vows. The *moniales* were to take simple vows after the novitiate for a period of three years, and then were to make solemn profession. Any particular indult allowing a longer period of simple vows was not revoked. If the superioress or mistress of novices gave just and reasonable causes in writing, the period of simple vows could be lengthened in particular cases by the local ordinary, or by the superior general or provincial for those monasteries which were exempt. Dispensation from the vows and dismissal from the order were reserved to the Holy See.[13]

As regards congregations, there was no common law expressed about temporary vows. Many of these congregations, in fact the majority of them, stated in their constitutions that temporary vows were to be taken in a variety of ways. Temporary profession could be made annually, biennially, or triennally, with a corresponding renewal of the vows at the end of each such expiration of time, or it could also be made for that period of time which was specified in the constitutions as a preparation for the perpetual vows, the period itself being of varying lengths of one, two, three or five years.[14] The law and the *Normae* in various passages supposed that these Institutes had only temporary vows,[15] both from the viewpoint of the Institute and also on the part of the professed member.[16] This discipline of temporary vows was enjoined on all Congregations in the preparatory schemata of the Code.[17]

[13] S. C. Ep. et Reg., decr. *Perpensis,* 3 maii 1902—*Fontes,* n. 1995.

[14] Tyck, *Notices Historiques,* and Keller, *Les Congrégations Religieuses en France—passim; Coll. S. C. Ep. et Reg.,* pp. 104, 463, 738, 789; Lucidi, *De Visitatione,* II, 252, 270.

[15] S. C. Ep. et Reg., decr. *Auctis Admodum,* 4 nov. 1892, nn. 3 et 4—*Fontes,* n. 2020; *Normae,* nn. 103-106; both of these have explicit reference to temporary vows.

[16] *Coll. S. C. Ep. et Reg.,* pp. 104, 463, 487, 738, 789, 795; Battandier, *Guide Canonique,* p. 151.

[17] Schema of 1912 in can. 447; of 1914 in can. 573. The Schema of 1912, can. 637 reads: "Professus a votis temporaneis, expleto votorum tempore, libere potest religionem deserere: pariter religio ob iustas ac rationa[bi]les causas eundem potest a votorum temporaneorum renovatione vel ab emittenda

Such was the legislation on temporary vows before the Code. The members in the orders of solemn vows took before their final profession triennial simple vows which were temporary from the viewpoint of the Institute. The one who was thus professed with a temporary profession could be dismissed for a reasonable cause.[18] This held for the orders of men from the year 1857 and for the orders of women from the year 1902. For the congregations of simple vows all the legislation was of a particular character and appeared only in the constitutions of each congregation. On the one hand the law assumed the existence of temporary vows; and on the other hand, the *Normae* (which were not properly law) had provisions which presupposed that some constitutions provided for temporary vows. These vows were not truly and properly religious vows. Even up to the time of the preparatory schemata of the Code they were considered as being religious vows in but an improper or analogous sense.[19] It was only in the present Code that they became recognized as furnishing the requisite basis for a true and proper religious status.[20]

professione perpetua excludere, non tamen ratione infirmitatis, nisi certo probetur eam ante professionem fuisse dolose reticitam aut dissimulatam." This was kept in the later Schemata (1914, 1916) and in new Code in can. 637. The Code extended this ruling to the simply professed in religious orders as well as to the simply professed in all Congregations.—Goyeneche, "De egressu a religione"—*CpR,* V (1925), 53-54; cf. also S. C. de Religiosis, declar. 5 apr. 1910, nn. II, IV—*Fontes,* n. 4400.

[18] Schema of 1912-1913, can. 445: "In quolibet ordine, regulari sive virorum sive mulierum, post novitiatum, votis sollemnibus praemittenda est, salvo praescripto C. 506, votorum simplicium professio per se perpetua"; Schema of 1914, can. 571: "In quolibet ordine regulari sive virorum sive mulierum, post novitiatum, votis solemnibus praemittenda est, salvo praescripto Can. 634, votorum simplicium professio rescindibilis ex parte religionis ad normam C. 572"; Schema of 1916 (the draft which immediately preceded the text adopted for the Code) had in can. 571 the provision for simple perpetual profession, perpetual *ex parte voventis,* for orders of solemn vows.—Goyeneche, "De egressu a religione"—*CpR,* V (1924), 53-54; cf. also *S. C. de Religiosis,* declar. 5 apr. 1910, n. II—*Fontes,* n. 4400.

[19] Schema of 1912, can. 369, § 2: "Extensive religionis vocabulum comprehendit quoque societatem, legitima auctoritate ecclesiastica approbatam, in qua tria illa vota nonnisi ad tempus nuncupantur"—Larraona, "Commentarium Codicis"—*CpR,* II (1921), 208.

[20] Canon 488, 1°, compared with can. 488, 7°.

Article II. Dismissal of Religious in Temporary Vows

Dismissal in the pre-Code law was the act by which a religious in simple vows was sent away from the congregation by the competent superior without the judicial form prescribed for an expulsion (*eiectio*), that is, in view solely of an examination of the truth in the case which revealed just and grave causes, even though these causes did not necessarily involve guilt or incorrigibility on the part of the dismissed member of the Institute.[21] Dismissal was thus distinct from expulsion (*eiectio*).[22] The latter term was used with reference to religious in solemn vows. It presupposed the use of the juridical form and connoted incorrigibility as the cause which justified the expulsion.[23]

The chief sources for this law as current before the Code were the Encyclical *Neminem latet* (1857), the decree *Auctis Admodum* (1892), and the Constitution *Conditae a Christo* (1900), together with the directive *Normae* (1901). The decree *Auctis Admodum* held for religious in temporary vows only if they were in sacred orders. This kind of religious was classed with those who were in perpetual simple vows. This legislation covered a case which soon ceased to appear, namely, a religious of temporary vows in sacred orders, since n. III of the decree *Auctis Admodum* forbade such a one to be ordained until he had perpetual vows. This ruling was carried over into the Code.[24] For these it was stated that the laws of Pope Urban VIII and of Pope Innocent XII were to be observed.[25]

[21] Wernz, *Ius Decretalium*, III, pars II, 377-378; Palombo, *De Dismissione Religiosorum* (Taurini-Romae: Marietti, 1931), p. 2.

[22] S. C. Ep. et Reg., 22 maii 1896, ad 34—apud Battandier, *Guide Canonique*, pp. 269-270; Palombo, *loc. cit.*

[23] S. C. C., decr. 21 sept. 1624—*Fontes*, n. 2454; 24 iul. 1694—*Fontes*, n. 2942. Cf. Benedictus XIV, *De Synodo Dioecesana*, Lib. XIII., Cap. XI, n. 15, *ad finem*: Palombo, *op. cit.*, p. 8; Sebastianelli, *Jus De Personis*, p. 432; Battandier, *Guide Canonique*, p. 270; Wernz, *Ius Decretalium*, III, pars II, n. 676; and Piat, *Praelectiones*, I, 218. These authors stated, however, that occasionally the word *eiectio* was used with reference to the dismissal of religious in simple vows.

[24] S. C. Ep. et Reg., decr. *Auctis Admodum*, 4 nov. 1892—*Fontes*, n. 2020; Canon 964, 3°, 4°.

[25] S. C. C., decr. 21 sept. 1624—*Fontes*, n. 2454; 24 iul. 1694—*Fontes*, n. 2942.

According to these earlier provisions the sole reason for dismissal was true incorrigibility. To contract such a cause all the conditions stated in common law were essential: (1) that a grave and public fault was committed before the members of the community or before the laity, so that the delinquent could not be kept in the order without grave infamy; [26] (2) that the delinquent was previously corrected, admonished, and punished three times; and (3) that if after this he was still unrepentant he was to be dismissed after a judicial trial. The delinquent could defend himself or select another member of the same Institute to defend him. If he did neither, the suprior or the tribunal was to appoint a defender for him.

After all these preliminaries had been observed the Superior and his council could pass the sentence of dismissal on a religious of temporary vows in sacred orders. If there were grave reasons which prevented the observance of these preliminaries, the superior was to have recourse to the Sacred Congregation of Bishops and Regulars for a dispensation from the observance of these solemnities and for permission to use the summary process permitted by this Congregation.[27]

Upon his dismissal the religious was not dispensed from his vows, nor was it considered expedient that the Superior be given power to dispense from the vows in the act of dismissal. The religious was to have recourse to the Sacred Congregation of Bishops and Regulars for this dispensation when he was dismissed.[28] When one in sacred orders was dismissed, he was perpetually suspended from exercising his office until he found an *episcopus benevolus*. This suspension was not properly a censure for it was of its nature perpetual. It was

[26] The culpa could be constituted by a series of misdemeanors which were not grave in themselves, but nevertheless constituted a grave disturbance of discipline. A grave fault in general was one which offended seriously against the substance of the vows or the common good of the Institute—Piat, *Praelectiones* I, 220; *Analecta Ecclesiastica,* I (1893), 94.

[27] Decr. *Auctis Admodum,* n. VIII—*Fontes,* n. 2020.

[28] S. C. Ep. et Reg., 10 iun. 1896—Vermeersch, *De Religiosis,* II, 281. Though this rescript was issued with relation to an Institute which had only perpetual simple vows, it seems that in its import it comprehended also the case of one in sacred orders who had only temporary vows. Cf. *Normae,* n. 201, which put the perpetually professed and the temporarily professed who were in sacred orders on the same plane. Cf. also Vermeersch, *De Religiosis,* I, 217.

not even removed by any grant of the Holy See until such a bishop had been found. The most that was ever permitted was to grant to a bishop the faculty to permit such a former religious to exercise his orders *ad tempus* in a given diocese. The obligation of trying to find an *episcopus benevolus* still remained on the former religious.[29] Furthermore, he could not validly enter the novitiate nor could he validly be professed in another religious Institute,[30] but if he had been equivalently dismissed, *i. e.*, if he had been exhorted to leave the novitiate by his superiors, the profession was illicit but not invalid.[31]

As has been stated, these cases of a religious in temporary vows who were in sacred orders were comparatively few. By far the greater number of religious in temporary vows were those religious who had professed the quasi-temporary vows mentioned in the Encyclical *Neminem latet,* as well as those who were not formally recognized in law as religious (*i. e.,* those in temporary vows in congregations). Into the constitutions of these congregations with temporary vows were introduced shortly afterwards the provisions of the Encyclical *Neminem latet,* and for the same reasons the discipline regarding dismissal which had been enacted with reference to a religious of simple vows in an order was made applicable to religious in congregations with simple vows.[32] It is appropriate, therefore, to treat here the discipline of the Encyclical *Neminem latet* as to the form of dismissal, the superior authorized for effecting the dismissal, the causes necessary to justify a dismissal and the effects deriving from the dismissal. The law applied *expressly* to those who were professed with simple vows which were taken in orders before the profession of solemn vows. These simple vows were considered as per-

[29] S. C. Ep. et Reg., *Abulen.*, 20 nov. 1895—*Fontes,* n. 2026; S. C. de Religiosis, decr. *Quum singulae,* 16 maii 1911, n. 20—*Fontes,* n. 4409; *Appendix ad Concilium Plenarium Americae Latinae Romae Celebratum Anno Domini MDCCCXCIX* (Romae: 1910), n. 571. Cf. Battandier, *Guide Canonique,* p. 333; Vermeersch, *De Religiosis,* II, 279-280; Angelus a SS. Corde, *Manuale Juris Regularium,* p. 476.

[30] S. C. de Religiosis, decr. *Ecclesia Catholica,* 7 sept. 1909—*Fontes,* n. 4396.

[31] S. C. de Religiosis, declar. 5 apr. 1910, ad III—*Fontes,* n. 4400.

[32] *Coll. S. C. Ep. et Reg.*, p. 777; *Animadversiones ad Constitutiones Congregationum Religiosarum:* 22 maii, 1896, ad 34; 15 nov. 1898, ad 10, pp. 791, 796, 804. Cf. Battandier, *Guide Canonique,* p. 271; *Normae,* nn. 193, 201; Tabera, "De dimissione religiosorum"—*CpR,* XII (1931), 140.

petual on the part of the one who professed them, but as temporary from the viewpoint of the order. Equivalently the law applied also to the religious of those congregations in which only simple vows were taken.

For the dismissal no judicial form was needed, but solely the certain knowledge of the truth. The power to dismiss resided in the master general and his general chapter. In the cases of religious whose houses were established throughout the world this faculty could be delegated to a tribunal of at least three prudent and upright men. They were to proceed with the greatest charity and prudence.[33] The superior properly authorized to dismiss members who took temporary vows in congregations of diocesan right was the local ordinary. He however was to inform the superior, for the superior was not to have been unaware of or seriously opposed to the dismissal.[34] The superior who was empowered to dismiss members in congregations of pontifical approval was the superior general (*Praeses*) of that Institute. He had to follow the rules of the Institute and the pontifical decrees.[35] The only pontifical decree in question here was the *Auctis Admodum,* which has already been treated above.[36] The *Normae* repeated this provision for all such Institutes which sought to obtain pontifical approbation. They prescribed that the council of the moderator general had a decisive vote in the dismissal of those who were temporarily professed, and that the members of the council were to reside in the general's house.[37] The preparatory schemata of the Code held to this ruling. The authorized superior in the matter of dismissal was the supreme moderator or, if it was a congregation of diocesan right, the local ordinary.[38]

[33] S. C. super Statu Regularium, decr. *Sanctissimus,* 12 iun. 1858, nn. III, IV—*Fontes,* n. 4383; Micheletti, *Jus Pianum* (Augustae Taurinorum, 1914), pp. 589, 590.

[34] Leo XIII, const. *Conditae a Christo,* 8 dec. 1900, § 1, VIII—*Fontes,* n. 644; Bastien, *Constitution "Conditae a Christo,"* pp. 47, 48.

[35] Const. *Conditae a Christo,* § 2, I—*Fontes,* n. 644.

[36] Bastien, *Directoire Canonique,* pp. 60-62.

[37] Normae, nn. 192; 193; 201; 271, 5; 276.

[38] Schema of 1912: cans. 446; 447; of 1914: cans. 572, § 3; 573; of 1916: cans. 572, § 3; 573; 667—Tabera, "De dimissione religiosorum"—*CpR,* XII (1931), 141.

As regards the causes for dismissal from the Institute while in temporary vows, only a few causes were definitely indicated. On the part of the religious there was the lack of a religious spirit, or his ineptitude to fulfill either the common duties of a religious or the special duties required by the constitutions of his Institute. On the part of the religious Institute there was the inability to provide for all the members, or some like cause. However varied in species these causes were, they had one thing in common: they had to be grave and just. This was always held to be so even when the vows were such as were temporary only on the part of the religious.[39] Many dependable authors held that dismissal without a just and reasonable cause was invalid, though there have been no cases in which any such dismissal was declared invalid.[40]

But what is a just and reasonable cause? The Holy See was asked that question; and it was asked, besides, to decide whether certain causes were just and reasonable, viz., a cause which would be sufficient to keep a novice from profession: (1) lack of aptitude for fulfilling the duties of the Institute, even though these were the lesser and ordinary duties; (2) ineptitude to fulfill the duties of the religious state, whether from levity of character or from lack of judgment. The Holy See answered that it should not be asked (*interloquendum*) such a question, since the matter was one which was left to the judgment and conscience of the superiors.[41]

[39] S. C. super Statu Regularium, decr. *Sanctissimus,* 12 iun. 1858, n. VII—*Fontes,* n. 4383; declar. 7 febr. 1862—*Fontes,* n. 4387; S. C. Ep et Reg., decr. *Perpensis,* 3 maii 1902—*Fontes,* n. 2039; *Normae,* nn. 193, 201; Preparatory Schema of 1912: can. 446, § 1—Tabera, "De dimissione religiosorum"—*CpR,* XII (1931), 141; *Coll. S. C. Ep. et Reg.,* p. 789; Suarez, *De Statu Perfectionis et Religionis,* Tr. X, Lib. III, C. 9, n. 7 sq.; Bouix, *De Jure Regularium,* II, 468-486; Battandier, *Guide Canonique,* p. 271; Angelus a SS. Corde, *Manuale Juris Regularium,* I, p. 175, q. 219; p. 219, qq. 199, 200; the preparatory schemata of 1914 and 1916 contained substantially the same law as the present Code in canon 647, § 2: " . . . graviter eorum onerata conscientia, . . . 1° Causae dimissionis debent esse graves. . . ."

[40] Suarez, *De Statu Perfectionis Et Religionis,* Tr. X, Lib. III, C. 9, n. 7 sq.; Piat, *Praelectiones Iuris Regularis,* I, 142; Bouix, *De Jure Regularium,* II, 486, q. II; Craisson, *Manuale Totius Juris Canonici,* n. 3093.

[41] S. C. Ep. et Reg., resp. 15 sept. 1873. This answer is found in another answer of the same congregation: 13 maii 1904—*Fontes,* n. 2048. A decree almost identical in its wording is found in Vermeersch (*De Religiosis,* II, 278);

Prümmer remarked on this decision that the causes mentioned in the petition were not repudiated as insufficient, otherwise the Sacred Congregation would have said so. He offered as a general rule the teaching of Benedict XIV: Whenever it can be judged with moral certainty that the professed in simple vows will not be able to finish his studies or to live the kind of life demanded by the constitutions, dismissal is allowed.[42] A grave cause in general was present: (1) if the superior judged that the bad example of the professed would cause grave harm; (2) if the religious gave grave offense to others by his words or deeds; (3) if the religious could not adapt himself to a life of obedience according to his rule; (4) if the faults and unworthy affections of the religious which offended the Divine Majesty could not be corrected, even if they were not of a public character.[43]

Quite a dispute arose on the justness of the cause concerned with insufficient talent, especially in regard to clerical Institutes (and, for similar reasons, in the case of lay religious devoted to education). As is evident from the teaching of Pope Benedict XIV and of Suarez, and also from the whole purpose of the Jesuit vows,[44] inability to fit oneself for the work of teaching, the special duty of the Institute, was a cause for dismissal. After the decisions of 1873 and 1893, Ferrari[45] stated that he had been told by the Secretary of the Sacred Congregation of Bishops and Regulars that great (*nimia*) ignorance or ineptitude for studies in clerics professed in simple vows was not a sufficient cause for dismissal. In general, he said, nobody can be dismissed after taking simple vows except for a grave cause or for grave defects in the moral order. Piat and Appeltern

the decree, however, is of the S. C. super Statu Regularium, dated 15 dec. 1893, and it is this latter decree which is quoted by Schäfer (*De Religiosis*, p. 994) and Prümmer (*Manuale Iuris Canonici*, p. 341, q. 258).

[42] Prümmer, *Jus Regularium Speciale* (Friburgi-Brisgoviae, 1907), p. 137; Benedictus XIV, *De Synodo Dioecesana*, Lib. XIII, C. XI, n. 17.

[43] *Institutum S. J., Constitutio*, pars II, c. III, nn. 1-5; pars I, c. III, n. 16; Suarez, *op. cit.*, Tr. X, Lib. III, C. 9, n. 7 sq.; Bouix, *De Jure Regularium*, II, 468; Angelus a SS. Corde, *Manuale Juris Regularium*, pp. 175, 2; 160.

[44] Cf. *supra*, Chapter II, article 1, p. 18.

[45] *De Statu Religioso Commentarium* (Romae, 1899), pp. 104, note 1; 127.

agreed with him.[46] All the other authors abstained from mentioning this as a cause, and many contradicted his statement by insisting that one cannot use a private opinion as the equivalent of a common law.[47]

After this decision of the Sacred Congregation the authors generally held that ineptitude for the duties of the Institute flowing from any cause (except sickness) was a sufficient cause for the dismissal of one who was only temporarily professed.[48] This, of course, did not hold if the ineptitude was fully known before the temporary profession. Nor is it cause enough if the inability to study was caused by sickness.[49]

Sickness which came on after temporary profession or which was present at the time of temporary profession was not a just cause for the dismissal of a religious. While it is true that good health was a requisite for profession in the religious state,[50] still it was held to be unjust to dismiss a religious for ill health which arose after his profession. This has always been the discipline of the Church, as is evident from the doctrine of Pope Benedict XIV,[51] and the decrees of the Sacred Congregation of Bishops and Regulars.[52]

The loss of the religious spirit was surely a just cause for dismissal. But solely the often and tenaciously repeated assertion that

[46] Piat, *Praelectiones,* I, 142, q. 154, n. 6; Appeltern, *Compendium Praelectionum Juris Regularis* (Tornaci, 1903), p. 88, note.

[47] Wernz, *Ius Decretalium,* III, pars II, n. 676; Bouix, *De Jure Regularium,* II, 486 sq.; Vermeersch, *De Religiosis,* I, 215; Angelus a SS. Corde, *Manuale Juris Regularium,* I, 160; Bachofen, *Compendium Juris Regularium* (New York, 1903), p. 339.

[48] Goyeneche, "Consultationes"—*CpR,* I (1920), 232, 233; Langogne, "Le Decret *Auctis Admodum*"—*Analecta Ecclesiastica,* I (1893), 93. The latter says that in the light of strict law ineptitude for the religious life is cause enough for the dismissal of the religious.

[49] Goyeneche, "Consultationes"—*CpR,* III (1922), 82.

[50] Nervegna, *De Jure Practico Regularium* (Romae, 1900), p. 155.

[51] *De Synodo Dioecesana,* Lib. III, c. XI, n. 1 sq.

[52] 10 mart. 1650—*Fontes,* n. 1790; *Animadversiones ad Constitutiones Congregationum Religiosarum,* 1860, ad 10—*Coll. S. C. Ep. et Reg.,* p. 777; 22 maii 1895, ad 21—Battandier, *Guide Canonique,* pp. 281, 282; S. C. super Statu Regularium, decr. *Sanctissimus,* 12 iun. 1858, n. V—*Fontes,* n. 4383; *Normae,* n. 199; S. C. Ep. et Reg., 13 maii 1904—*Fontes,* n. 2048; Suarez, *De Statu Perfectionis Et Religionis,* Tr. X, Lib. III, C. 10, n. 11 sq.

a religious had lost this spirit was not cause enough to dismiss a religious from vows which were temporary from the viewpoint of the order but perpetual on the part of the professed.[53] The secret vote of the majority or even the unanimous vote of the general's council was not a just and reasonable cause to dismiss one who was in simple vows prior to solemn profession. The vote alone without further inquiry or investigation of the matter did not suffice.[54] It was considered to be a very dangerous policy to regard talkativeness alone as a sufficient cause for the dismissal of a sister in the absence of other contributing causes, such as the violation of fraternal charity.[55]

When a religious was dismissed while he was professed with the simple vows which were to precede his solemn vows, he was *ipso facto* freed from his vows.[56] In regard to congregations with temporary vows, it depended on the constitutions of that Institute whether or not the dismissed religious was freed from his vows by the dismissal.[57] The preparatory schemata of the Code contained the provision for a release from the vows effective *ipso facto* at dismissal.[58] The pious vows which the religious had taken before he entered and which had remained suspended during his life in religion, revived and bound him again when he was dismissed.[59]

[53] S. C. Ep. et Reg., resp. 19 nov. 1886—Vermeersch, *De Religiosis,* II, 275; Piat, *Praelectiones,* I, p. 142, 2. q. 154 ad II, 5°.

[54] S. C. super Statu Regularium, 7 febr. 1862, n. 2—*Fontes,* n. 4387.

[55] S. C. Ep. et Reg., 12 aug. 1891, ad 8—Battandier, *Guide Canonique,* p. 271; Angelus a SS. Corde, *Manuale Juris Regularium,* I, p. 221, q. 200.

[56] S. C. super Statu Regularium, 12 iun. 1858, art. 3—*Fontes,* n. 4383; Lucidi, *De Visitatione,* II, pp. 39, 107-109; Angelus a SS. Corde, *Manuale Juris Regularium,* p. 221, q. 201; p. 176, q. 181; Vermeersch, *De Religiosis,* I, 216; Piat, *Praelectiones,* I, 146. This provision had existed in the particular laws of some religious, *e. g.,* the Jesuits: *Institutum S. J.: Examen,* C. VII, n. 1, 2; *Constitutio,* Pars Secunda, C. IV, n. 1; Pars Quinta, C. IV; Suarez, *op. cit.,* Tr. X, Lib. III, C. 1.

[57] S. C. Ep. et Reg., *Bergomen.,* 14 mart. 1861, ad 16; and 23 sept. 1836—*apud* Lucidi, *De Visitatione,* II, 284. Cf. Angelus a SS. Corde, *Manuale Juris Regularium,* I, p. 219, q. 199.

[58] Schema of 1912, can. 486, § 4; of 1914-1916; same as canon 648 of the present Code.

[59] Ballay, "De votis simplicibus quae votis solemnibus praemittuntur"—*AKKR,* XVII (1867), 29.

The last noteworthy effect of dismissal was the ineligibility of the religious if he desired to enter another religious Institute. He could not validly enter the novitiate, nor could he be validly professed in another Institute. But if he was but equivalently dismissed, *i. e.,* in view of the exhortation of his superiors to leave the novitiate, then the novitiate and the profession in the new Institute were undertaken illicitly, but not invalidly.[60]

[60] S. C. de Religiosis, decr. *Ecclesia Catholica,* 7 sept. 1909; declar. 5 apr. 1910, ad III—*Fontes,* n. 4396, 4400.

PART TWO

CANONICAL COMMENTARY

CHAPTER I

TEMPORARY VOWS AND DISMISSAL

ARTICLE 1. TEMPORARY VOWS

A. Definition and Division

Temporary vows are vows which are taken for a certain specified time, *e. g.*, for one, two, three or five years, or until the time the religious reaches a certain specified age.[1] The New Code of Canon Law envisions two kinds of temporary vows: those taken as a preparation for perpetual vows and those taken as absolutely temporary with no view to perpetual vows but to be renewed at stated intervals.[2]

Those taken as a preparation for perpetual profession are obligatory, according to the Code, in every Order, both of men and of women, and in every Congregation of perpetual vows. In these Institutes the perpetual vows must be preceded by a profession of simple vows which the novice, on the completion of his novitiate, is required to make in the novitiate house itself. This profession is to last for three years, or more if a period of more than three years is required for the subject to attain the age prescribed for perpetual profession.[3] In this latter case he must take his vows to bind until he is twenty-one years old (*i. e.*, to the day after his twenty-first

[1] Lucidi, *De Visitatione,* II, 269; Schäfer, *De Religiosis,* p. 567.

[2] Cervia, *De Professione Religiosa* (Dissertatio ad Lauream in Iuris Canonici facultate Pontificiae Universitatis Gregorianae: Bologna, 1938), p. 103.

[3] Canons 574, § 1; 572, § 2. The wording of the text is taken from *Canonical Legislation Concerning Religious* (Authorized English Translation, Vatican Printing Office: Rome, 1919). As stated in the Foreword of this translation, it has not the official character of the Latin text, although it has been specially authorized by the Holy See. When necessary, the official Latin text will

birthday anniversary). The duration of the vows may be expressed in years, months, and days, *e. g.*, "for four years, three months, and fifteen days," or generically, *e. g.*, "until I have completed my twenty-first year."[4]

There are exceptions to this rule requiring the preparatory profession of triennial vows before perpetual vows. Thus, for instance, the Code itself leaves room for the existence of Institutes the constitutions of which prescribe annual profession instead of triennial profession before the perpetual profession. In such Institutes the annual profession will be made three times or more before the making of perpetual profession, depending upon the age of the novice.[5] As is stated in canon 574, § 1, it may be necessary that these vows shall be taken for a period longer than three years. Thus, if a religious is only sixteen years of age at the time of his first profession, he will take vows until he is twenty-one years of age (the age required for a valid perpetual profession). A religious may, therefore, be in temporary vows as long as five years before his perpetual profession.[6] The second paragraph of canon 574 states that the legitimate superior can prolong this period, but not beyond a second term of three years, the religious meanwhile renewing the temporary profession.[7]

be given when reference is made to the Code in this dissertation; when the English is used this authorized translation will be employed.

[4] Coronata, "Professione temporanea dei novizi"—*Perfice Munus*, IX (1934), 98; Orth, *Religious Profession*, p. 109; Beste, *Introductio In Codicem* (Collegeville, Minnesota: St. John's Abbey Press, 1938), p. 385.

[5] Canon 574, § 1. Cervia (*De Professione Religiosa*, p. 108) thinks that if the novice is not yet eighteen at the time of his first annual profession, then at the time of the last annual profession before he becomes twenty-one, he may make profession to bind not for one year but only until he reaches the age of twenty-one. In this he agrees with Schäfer (*De Religiosis*, p. 596). The validity of another opinion of Cervia which relies upon the analogy to canon 577 seems doubtful. He states that if the last annual profession of a religious (who was not eighteen years of age when he made his first profession) will reach a month beyond his twenty-first year, then he can take the last annual vows for a full year and anticipate the perpetual vows by one month. Cf. Woywod, "Answers to Questions"—*HPR*, XXXVII (1936-1937), 856.

[6] Canons 555, § 1, 1° and 2°; 572, § 1, 1° and 3°; 573.

[7] "Hoc tempus legitimus superior potest, renovata a religioso temporaria professione, prorogare, non tamen ultra aliud triennium."

It is a very disputed point whether the words *hoc tempus* refer to the period of three years alone or also to the period in general; *i. e.*, to the three years for one who was eighteen years of age at the time of the temporary profession as well as to the four or five years for the religious who was only seventeen or sixteen years of age at the end of his novitiate. In other words, in the Institutes of perpetual vows mentioned in canon 574 is it possible for the superior, by using paragraph two of that canon, to prolong the period of temporary vows to seven or eight years, or did the legislator wish to limit this time of temporary vows to six years? Many authors hold that the phase *hoc tempus* refers to the period prior to perpetual profession, no matter whether it be of three, four, or five years' duration, so that the period of temporary vows may conceivably be prolonged to last for eight years.[8] The view held by a greater number of authors is that the phrase *hoc tempus* refers only to the three-year period, so that in no case can the period of temporary vows in these Institutes total more than six years.[9]

Space does not permit a thorough review of all the arguments of both sides. It seems that the opinion allowing the prorogation

[8] Fanfani, *De Iure Religiosorum Ad Normam Codicis Iuris Canonici* (ed. altera, Taurini—Romae: Marietti, 1925), p. 302; Augustine, *Commentary,* III, 260; Schäfer, *De Religiosis,* p. 588; Mothon, *Traité Sur L'État Religieux* (Paris: Desclée, De Brouwer & Cie., 1922), p. 368; Frey, *Religious Profession,* pp. 111, 112; "Annotatio"—*Il Monitore Ecclesiastico,* VI (1924), 51 (henceforth cited as *Il Monitore*); Blat, *Commentarium Textus Codicis Iuris Canonici,* Liber II, Partes II et III (3. ed. Romae: apud "Angelicum," 1938), p. 383 (henceforth cited as *De Religiosis*); Coronata, *Institutiones Iuris Canonici,* I, (2. ed., Taurini: Marietti, 1939) n. 757 (henceforth cited as *Institutiones*); A. Ledwolorz in reviewing the third volume of Mayer's *Ordensrecht* says (*Apollinaris,* X [1937], 478) of the other opinion: "non est certa. . . . Concedo tamen S. C. de Religiosis non favere prorogationi ultra sexennium." Schönsteiner, *Grundriss Des Ordensrechtes* (Wien: L. Auer, 1930), pp. 365, 366. Geser, *The Canon Law Governing Communities of Sisters* (Herder, St. Louis, 1938), pp. 256, 257. Geser, however, quotes Pejska (*Ius Canonicum Religiosorum,* 3. ed. Friburgi Brisgoviae, 1927, p. 108) in support of his opinion. In the place cited, however, it does not seem certain that Pejska holds this opinion.

[9] Vermeersch-Creusen, *Epitome Iuris Canonici* (3 vols., Vols. I and II: 5. ed., 1933 and 1934; Vol. III: 4. ed., 1931, Brugis: Beyaert), I, 523; Creusen, *Religieux et Religieuses D'apres Le Droit Canonique Ecclesiastique* (2. ed., Bruxelles,

of vows for an absolute three-year period, no matter what the length of time of the first period of temporary vows, has the more solid foundation in consideration of the text and context of the Code. Both sides present valid arguments derived from the purpose of the law and the mind of the legislator. The opinion allowing temporary vows in these Institutes to last for six years at most has by far the greater weight of external authority and is strengthened by Goyeneche's statement as to the constant practice of the Sacred Congregation of Religious in not allowing religious in such Institutes to be in temporary vows for a period longer than six years.[10] The *praxis Curiae* is not, however, a norm of interpretation, but simply a help to fill in *lacunae* of the Code.[11] A prorogation which would cause the period of temporary vows to go beyond six years would not, even if forbidden, render the profession invalid.[12] It

1921), n. 187; Bastien, *Directoire Canonique,* n. 144; Palombo, *De Dimissione Religiosorum,* p. 200, note 1; Cocchi, *Commentarium In Codicem Iuris Canonici Ad Usum Scholarum,* II, pars II (2 ed., Taurinorum Augustae: Marietti, 1926), n. 78, p. 160 (henceforth cited as *Commentarium*); De Meester, *Iuris Canonici Et Iuris Canonico-Civilis Compendium* (3 tomes in 4, Brugis: Desclée, De Brouwer & Cie: 1921-1928), II, 447 (henceforth cited as *Compendium*); Bouuaert-Simenon, *Manuale Iuris Canonici Ad Usum Seminariorum,* I (3. ed., Gandae et Leodii: Dessain, 1930-1931), 382 (henceforth cited as *Manuale*); Wernz-Vidal, *Ius Canonicum,* III, p. 274, note 4; Sipos, *Enchiridion Iuris Canonici* (3. ed., Pécs: Haladás, R. T., 1936), p. 259 (henceforth cited as *Enchiridion*); Prümmer, *Manuale Iuris Canonici* (ed. altera, Friburgi Brisgoviae, 1920), q. 214; Jansen, *Ordensrecht* (2. ed., Paderborn, 1920), p. 126; Cervia, *De Professione Religiosa,* pp. 117-125; Mayer, *Benediktinisches Ordensrecht in der Beuroner Kongregation* (3. ed., 4 vols., Beuron: Beuroner Kunstverlag, 1929-1936), III, 393 (henceforth cited *Benediktinisches Ordensrecht*); Caviglioli, G., *Manuale di Diritto Canonico* (Società Editrice Internazionale, Torino, 1934), p. 406; Vermeersch, "De accidentali causa cur vota temporaria nunquam in perpetua convertantur"—*Periodica,* XVII (1928), 222*, 223*; cf. also *Periodica,* XVI (1927), 160*; Creusen, "Prolongations des voeux temporaires"—*Revue des Communatés Religieuses,* V (1929), 116 (henceforth cited *RCR*); Goyeneche, "Consultatio"—*CpR,* XIV (1933), 49-53; La Puma, "Acta et Documenta"—*CpR,* XIV (1933), 164, note 46.

[10] Goyeneche, "Consultatio"—*CpR,* XIV (1933), 50.

[11] Compare canons 18 and 20.

[12] Goyeneche, "Consultationes"—*CpR,* XIV (1933), 357, 358; Creusen, *Religieux et Religieuses,* n. 187; Coronata, *Institutiones,* I, 138. Against this

seems theoretically that the superior can validly and licitly prolong the period of temporary vows, no matter what its length, by three years so that a subject could be under temporary vows as long as eight years. In practice, however, it will generally be safer and more prudent to follow the side which restricts the time of temporary vows in these Institutes to six years at the most. The reason is that this is the practice of the Sacred Congregation of Religious. Although this practice does not constitute law nor even an authentic interpretation of the law, still it seems to give us the mind of the legislator. In a particular case a superior can prolong the period of temporary vows so that the total time in temporary vows will be longer than six years (just so long as the time of the prolongation itself does not extend beyond three years). Such would be the case particularly when a superior has not been able to make up his mind as to a candidate whose vocation, after a trial of six years, is still doubtful. This view has enough intrinsic and extrinsic authority to permit its application to practice at least in a particular case.[13]

A second exception to the provision requiring this period of triennial vows is made for the religious who transfers from one Institute to another, provided that, already perpetually or solemnly professed in one Institute, he transfers to another Institute whose members make either solemn or perpetual simple profession. In this case, after a year of novitiate, he is immediately admitted either to solemn or perpetual simple vows, as the case may be, without a previous three-year period of temporary vows.[14] By an analogy with canons 633 and 634, those who transfer from one class to another in the

opinion and holding that such prolongations are invalid if the total time of temporary vows is more than six years: Vermeersch-Creusen, *Epitome,* I, 524; Creusen, "De prorogatione professionis temporariae"—*Periodica,* XII (1924), (57)-(58); De Meester, *Compendium,* II, p. 449, note 4; Schäfer, *De Religiosis,* p. 587; Bastien, *Directoire Canonique,* p. 144.

[13] Beste, *Introductio,* p. 386.

[14] Canon 634. Note, however, that if he had not taken perpetual vows in the Institute, then when he transfers to another Institute he must after having completed his novitiate in the second Institute make temporary profession to last for a period of three years. Woywod, "Novitiate and profession of religious who have permission to leave their community and join another"—*Homiletic and Pastoral Review,* XXIV (1923-1924), 75, 76 (cited henceforth as *HPR*).

same Institute, if they have already finished three years' temporary vows and are twenty-one years of age, may take perpetual vows immediately after the year of novitiate made according to canon 558.[15]

Another exception is the case of those religious who take vows with the formula "as long as I live in the congregation," or with some like condition. These vows need not be preceded by the period of temporary vows prescribed in canon 574.[16]

There is in the Code provision for Institutes in which temporary vows are so taken that they are renewed at stated intervals, and in which perpetual vows are never taken. It is apparent that there is no prescription of a three-year period of temporary vows in Institutes of this kind.[17]

Finally, there are some Institutes in which, because of approved constitutions, the religious are not bound to this law at all. In such Institutes perpetual vows are taken immediately after the novitiate. Two such religious Institutes are the Society of Jesus and the Sisters of the Most Sacred Heart.[18]

[15] Ellis, "De transitu ad alium ejusdem religionis classem"—*Periodica*, XXV (1936), 103*-104*.

[16] *Pontificia Commissio Interpretationis* (*PCI*), 1 mart. 1921—*AAS*, XIII (1921), 177.

[17] Canon 574. Included under this category are religious of the type described by Vermeersch. He states that he knows of a case in which a sister, afflicted with nervousness, found the bond of perpetual profession unbearable although she could easily live under temporary vows. Since the Institute to which she belonged had provision only for a preparatory period of temporary vows, she was faced with the alternative either of taking perpetual vows, the burden of which affected her abnormally, or of returning to the world. In this case, the Holy See granted permission that she be allowed to take temporary vows (even annual) to be renewed indefinitely. The only provisions demanded were that the superiors agree to this arrangement and that a competent physician give testimony as to her condition of mind regarding the bond of perpetual profession. Cf. Vermeersch, "De accidentali causa cur vota temporaria nunquam in perpetua convertantur"—*Periodica*, XVII (1928), 222*-223*.

[18] Schäfer, *De Religiosis*, p. 585; Vermeersch-Creusen, *Epitome*, I, 522; Biederlack-Führich, *De Religiosis* (Oeniponte, 1919), n. 94, note 4. Coronata (*Institutiones*, I, p. 756, note 8) in quoting Maroto (*CpR*, II [1921], 132, IV) states that Maroto holds that some orders retain the privilege of taking perpetual simple vows before solemn profession against the prescriptions of canon 574, § 1. Maroto, in the place cited, is speaking only of the law before the Code.

B. Temporary Vows and the Religious State

The present Code defines the religious state as "the firmly established manner of living in community, by which the faithful undertake to observe, not only the ordinary precepts, but also the evangelical counsels, by means of the vows of obedience, chastity, and poverty." [19] An Institute is defined as "every society, approved by legitimate ecclesiastical authority, the members of which tend to evangelical perfection according to the laws proper to their Society, by the profession of public vows, whether perpetual or temporary, the latter renewable after the lapse of a fixed time." [20] As was seen in the historical part of this dissertation, this is the first instance in which the Church has recognized religious of temporary vows as religious in the full and true sense of the word.[21]

In ecclesiastical law the religious *state* is called a state precisely because it connotes the firmness and stability necessary for the observance of the counsels of poverty, chastity and obedience. As is apparent from the very word, counsels are not in themselves of obligation; therefore, in order that this manner of life may be styled a *state,* there must be something to make these counsels obligatory.[22] But how can temporary vows effect this necessary stability? The very concept or nature of temporary vows as defined in papal documents, in the rules and constitutions of religious Institutes, and in the authors seems to militate against stability. The whole tenor of the Encyclical *Neminem latet* is that the three-year period of simple vows prior to solemn vows is a time of trial and probation.[23] Various

[19] Canon 487.

[20] Canon 488, 1°.

[21] Canons 574; 575, § 1; Schäfer, *De Religiosis,* p. 61, *supra,* p. 54.

[22] Jombart, "L'essence de l'etat religieux"—*RCR,* I (1925), 175; Vermeersch, "De status religiosi essentia et interpretatione can. 487 et 488, 1°"—*Periodica,* XV (1927), (1)-(13); Schäfer, *De Religiosis,* p. 57 sq.; Larraona, "Commentarium Codicis"—*CpR,* II (1921), 209; Goyeneche, "De transitu ad aliam religionem"—*CpR,* I (1920), 22-30; 73-77; 107-112.

[23] S. C. super Statu Regularium, litt. encycl. *Neminem latet,* 19 mart. 1857 —*Fontes,* n. 4381; S. C. Ep. et Reg., *Ordinis S. Benedicti,* 13 maii 1904, Colliges n. 2—*ASS,* XXXVII (1904-1905), 450.

rules and constitutions state this very clearly,[24] and the authors also call it a period of probation.[25]

In the Code, it has been noted, the only temporary vows admitted are those which precede perpetual vows and those which are taken as absolutely temporary to be renewed at stated intervals throughout the religious life. Any society which would have vows which were so absolutely temporary that they could not be renewed would not be an Institute as defined in canon 488, 1°, and surely would not have the stability necessary for the religious state.[26] The Code requires that the novice have the intention, at least indefinitely, of renewing the temporary vows or of taking perpetual vows. It is enough if he takes them with this in mind: "as the constitutions prescribe" or "as the Code prescribes." This intention should not be taken absolutely but with the provision "if no impediment intervenes." These provisions are usually made mentally.[27] By this means the Code has given to these temporary vows the necessary stability or firmness which temporary vows in themselves do not possess, enough stability to constitute a person in the religious state, even though juridically he is free at the end of a definite period to return to the world if he so wishes.[28]

Though he has at the time of his temporary profession the ex-

[24] "Cum vota temporaria quodammodo sint probatio prorogata . . . "—*Declarationes et Statuta Sive Constitutiones Congregationis Ottiliensis O. S. B. Pro Missionibus Exteris* (Ottilae, 1925), p. 70; "Cum toto professionis votorum annualium tempore religiosi adhuc in statu probationis permaneant"—*Regulae et Praescriptiones* . . . (pro Congregatione Sacerdotum a Sacro Corde Jesu), (Romae, 1934), p. 115; "The minor Religious (those in temporary vows) are in a sort of probation . . . "—*Manual of the Clerics of Saint Viator* (Jette-Saint-Pierre, Belgium, 1926), p. 72.

[25] Battandier, *Guide Canonique*, pp. 157 and 162; Bastien, *Directoire Canonique*, p. 131; Schäfer, *De Religiosis*, p. 995; Prümmer, *Manuale Iuris Canonici*, p. 348, q. 258; Palombo, *De Dimissione Religiosorum*, pp. 181, 182; Maroto, "Annotatio"—*CpR*, II (1921), 132, V; Goyeneche, "De transitu ad aliam religionem"—*CpR*, I (1920), 110; "Consultatio"—*CpR*, XI (1930), 441.

[26] Fanfani, *De Iure Religiosorum*, pp. 4 sq.; Wernz-Vidal, *Ius Canonicum*, III, 273, 274; Schäfer, *De Religiosis*, pp. 59-62; Misserey, "La profession religieuse et le voeu solennel"—*Le Canoniste Contemporain*, XLVI (1924), 164.

[27] Biederlack-Führich, *De Religiosis*, p. 14, note 2; Schäfer, *De Religiosis*, p. 62; Cervia, *De Professione Religiosa*, p. 104.

[28] Canon 637.

press intention either of not renewing his vows or of not making perpetual profession at the end of his temporary vows, he makes a valid profession, but he is not in the religious state.[29] Such a profession is always illicit and the religious cannot make it willingly without sin nor can the superior without sin admit one whom he knows to have such an intention.[30] However, if the constitutions of the Institute expressly declare that it does not intend to admit a novice unless he has the intention of proceeding to perpetual profession, then the temporary profession made with the intention of not proceeding to perpetual profession is invalid in view of the defect of lawful admission to profession.[31]

C. Temporary Vows and the Contract

It is almost the unanimous opinion of post-Code authors that religious profession is a contract.[32] This contract is a bilateral contract in a proper but less strict sense.[33] It is a contract contained

[29] Nevin, "Novice who takes temporary vows intending to leave institute on their expiry"—*Australasian Catholic Record,* XV (1938), 64 (henceforth cited as *ACR*); "Casus de intentione eius qui vota temporanea emissurus est"—*Periodica,* XXI (1932), 192*; 226*-227*. The case is not listed under the defects which render a profession invalid (canon 572).

[30] Cervia, *De Professione Religiosa,* p. 104; Schäfer, *De Religiosis,* p. 59; Wernz-Vidal, *Ius Canonicum,* III, 13; Vermeersch, "Quaesita de religiosis"—*Periodica,* XXI (1932), 122*-123*; Goyeneche, "Consultatio"—*CpRM,* XVI (1935), 315-318.

[31] Canon 572, § 1, 2°; Goyeneche, *loc. cit.;* Nevin, *loc. cit.*

[32] Schäfer, *op. cit.,* p. 565; Cervia, *op. cit.,* p. 68; Coronata, *Institutiones,* I, n. 589; Bastien, *Directoire Canonique,* n. 147; Pejska, *Ius Canonicum Religiosorum* (3. ed., Friburgi-Brisgoviae: Herder, 1927), p. 103; Fanfani, *De Iure Religiosorum,* p. 269; Chelodi, *Ius De Personis* (Tridenti, 1922), p. 420; De Meester, *Compendium,* II, 447; Wernz-Vidal, *Ius Canonicum,* III, 262; Vermeersch-Creusen, *Epitome,* I, 519; Tabera, "De dimissione religiosorum"—*CpR,* XII (1931), 277; Orth, *Religious Profession,* p. 4; Sipos, *Enchiridion,* p. 314; Papi, *Religious in Church Law* (New York: Kenedy, 1924), p. 268.

[33] Cervia, *De Professione Religiosa,* pp. 54, 65. Most moderns consider a contract to be a bilateral contract only when it is such in the strict sense; *i.e.,* when it is binding both parties in commutative justice, each of whom is equal in right, about something not due by another title. Cf. Cavagnis, *Institutiones Iuris Publici Ecclesiastici* (4. ed., 3 vols., Romae, 1906), I, p. 419, n. 662. In the less strict sense the bilateral contract obliges both parties and is to the advantage of both. It prescinds from the questions whether the parties are equal in right concerning the matter of the contract and whether the parties

in the act of incorporation into the Institute much like the contract which is entered into every time one joins a free society. It is clear that such a contract cannot give rise to an obligation of strict or commutative justice (the very prime requisite, that it be between equals, is lacking), but rather of legal or distributive justice.[34]

The religious binds himself to obey by vow, oath, or promise the rules and constitutions of the Institute. He gives the Institute the right to the legitimate use of the faculties of his body and soul; he deprives himself of the free use of himself, of his own action, of his liberty, of all the faculties of his body and of all his effects. He intends to obey and live, according to obedience, in poverty and chastity, and he binds himself to the observance of all the laws of the Institute and to its spiritual and temporal demands. The Institute on its part is obliged to direct the religious in spiritual affairs, and is bound to provide him with food, clothing, and dwelling; to admit him to the communion of all the goods of the Institute and to community life with the other religious; to keep him perpetually or temporarily (if he is in temporary vows), unless he prove a harmful member; and, finally, to treat him as a son. All these obligations are measured by the vows, the rules and constitutions as well as by the will of the superior, which in turn is limited and ruled by these same vows, rules and constitutions. The rights of the Institute correspond to the duties of the religious and *vice versa*.[35] Temporary profession is such a contract.[36] This seems the better explanation of the nature of religious temporary profession; that it is a bilateral contract between a society and its members and that it gives rise to obligations of distributive or legal justice.[37]

give what is their own, or only promise what is already due under another title. Cf. Cervia, *op. cit.*, pp. 54-56; 65. For a review of the various opinions confer also Bergh, "Elements et nature de la profession religieuse"—*Ephemerides Theologicae Lovanienses,* XIV (1934), 5-32 (henceforth cited as *ETL*).

34 Cervia, *op. cit.*, pp. 68, 69.

35 Cervia, *op. cit.*, p. 65.

36 Vermeersch-Creusen (*Epitome,* I, 519) however state that only "ratione minus universali" can temporary profession be considered a contract.

37 Cf. Cervia, *op. cit.*, pp. 51-65, for a full explanation of this matter. Not all authors after the Code agree that profession is a contract. Confer on this: Tabera, "De dimissione religiosorum"—*CpR,* XII (1931), 277, note 9; Vermeersch-Creusen, *supra,* note 36.

Article 2. Dismissal

Dismissal is the forced or unwilled egress of a religious from an Institute while his vows are still in force.[38] Dismissal is thus distinct from: (1) the voluntary egress which can take place even during vows: licitly, by means of an indult of permanent or temporary dissociation from the Institute (*indultum saecularizationis seu exclaustrationis*); [39] illicitly, by means of apostasy; [40] (2) the exclusion of the religious from the making of perpetual vows or from the renewal of temporary vows; [41] (3) the transferring to another Institute or monastery of the same Institute; [42] (4) the provisory sending of the religious away from the religious house.[43]

There are four species of dismissal: (1) the dismissal which takes effect *ipso facto;* [44] (2) the authoritative dismissal of clerical exempt religious in perpetual vows; [45] (3) the authoritative dismissal of clerical non-exempt and lay religious in perpetual vows; [46] (4) the authoritative dismissal of religious in temporary vows.[47] This dissertation deals with the last species of dismissal. The law on the dismissal of religious in temporary vows applies to all those of whom mention was made in Section A of Article 1. Besides these there are other groups included either by laws or by authentic interpetation.

The members of societies which are not properly religious Institutes but the members of which imitate the manner of life of reli-

[38] Tabera, *art. cit.*, p. 277. Tabera notes that the Code uses the word *dimissio* throughout Title XVI of Liber II with the exceptions of canons 653 and 668, in which the phrase *ad saeculum remitti* is used (however, in canon 668 there immediately follows the phrase: *religioso autem dimisso*). He gathers from this that the word *dimissio* is the word officially adopted by the Code and that the *ad saeculum remitti* of canons 653 and 668 is used because of the provisory nature of this dismissal. Note, too, in canons 649, 651, and in canons 654-668 the abandonment of term used in the old law, *eiectio*.

[39] Canons 638, 639, 640.

[40] Canon 644.

[41] Canon 637.

[42] Canons 632-636.

[43] Canons 653 and 668.

[44] Canon 646.

[45] Canons 654-668.

[46] Canons 649-653.

[47] Canons 647, 648.

gious by living in community under the government of superiors according to approved constitutions, but without being bound by the usual three vows, cannot properly be designated by the name of religious.[48] However, in regard to dismissal, the members of such societies are ruled by canons 647 and 648 if the bond by which they are bound to the Institute is of a temporary character.[49] As Maroto [50] and Vermeersch [51] note, there must be a bond of some sort, *e. g.*, an oath, a promise, a pledge, etc., which binds them to the Institute. Otherwise there is no firm bond between the Institute and the members, and no solemnities or prescriptions of law are needed in dismissal. They seem to be on a par rather with novices than with professed members, and just causes are enough for their dismissal.[52]

By an authentic interpretation, conditional vows, *e. g.*, those taken to last "as long as I live in the Congregation" or some such words, are to be considered in regard to dismissal, as temporary vows.[53] As Vermeersch correctly notes, such vows are improperly called "conditional." The profession is not conditioned, but is made for a period of time the duration of which is uncertain.[54]

This dissertation, then, concerns all religious in temporary vows as well as those who, by law or authentic interpretation of the law,

[48] Canon 673.

[49] *PCI*, 1 mart. 1921—*AAS*, XIII (1921), 177.

[50] "Annotationes"—*CpR*, II (1921), 129-133.

[51] "Annotationes"—*Periodica*, X (1922), 326, 327.

[52] Canon 571.

[53] *PCI*, 1 mart. 1921—*AAS*, XIII (1921), 177; Maroto, "Annotatio"—*CpR*, II (1921), 129; Schäfer, *De Religiosis*, pp. 585, 990. Bastien (*Directoire Canonique*, I, 132, note 3) states that this answer meant that canon 647 was to be followed in regard to the dismissal of those who *had* taken vows with this condition. In this he agrees with other authors. He differs with them when he says and with no apparent justification that the answer means that in regard to the dismissal of those who will take these vows in the future the prescriptions of canons 649 sq. (for the dismissal of those who have taken perpetual vows) are to be followed.

[54] Vermeersch, "Annotatio"—*Periodica*, X (1922), 325. If it were a resolutive condition then it would, as soon as the condition is actualized, annul and revoke the juridical consequences which had been effected throughout the period of the vows. Nobody holds this.

have been included under the phrase "religious in temporary vows" at least as far as there is question of their dismissal. Included then are:

(1) Religious men in orders who take simple temporary vows prior to their solemn profession, whether they be *in sacris* or in minor orders (canon 574).

(2) *Moniales, i. e.,* religious women in orders who take simple temporary vows prior to their solemn profession; also those *moniales* whose final vows are normally solemn but which by disposition of the Holy See are simple in certain regions (canons 574 and 488, 7°).

(3) Religious men and women in Congregations of perpetual vows, no matter whether these are of pontifical or of diocesan approval, when they have entered upon a preparatory period of temporary vows. In regard to men, all are included whether *in sacris* or in minor orders (canon 574).

(4) Religious men and women in Institutes the constitutions of which prescribe only temporary vows which are to be renewed at certain specified times (canon 488, 1°).

(5) Religious men and women bound to their Institutes not by temporary vows but by some other temporary bond, *e. g.,* an oath, a promise, etc., whether the Institute is of pontifical or of diocesan approval.

(6) Religious men and women who take so-called conditional vows, whether the Institute is of pontifical or of diocesan approval.

CHAPTER II

THE SUPERIOR AUTHORIZED TO DISMISS

THE Church enacts general rules for moral collegiate persons and their acts; [1] and in Book II, Part II of the Code, entitled *De Religiosis,* it gives special rules for the actions of the moral persons designated as religious Institutes. One of the acts of a religious society is the expulsion of one of its members. This could be accomplished in a variety of ways, but the law is very specific concerning expulsion or dismissal, with a different set of rules for the different types of Institutes. In the case of dismissal of a member from a religious Institute when the member is still in temporary vows, the authority to perform this task is vested very particularly in certain definitely designated superiors. These superiors are designated in canon 647, § 1, and since a number of different Institutes are there considered with a corresponding number of different superiors, it will be best to divide this chapter into various sections for a clearer treatment of the matter. The sections treated successively are: A. Orders and congregations of pontifical approval; B. Orders with independent monasteries; C. The consent of the council; D. Orders of women (*Moniales*); E. Congregations of diocesan approval; F. The power of major and local superiors; G. In mission lands; and H. The delegation of this power.

A. Orders and Congregations Approved by the Holy See

"Professum a votis temporariis sive in Ordinibus sive in Congregationibus iuris pontificii dimittere potest supremus religionis Moderator. . . ." [2]

The dismissal of a religious in temporary vows in these Institutes is effected by the superior general. In the present section, the word

[1] Canons 101; 105; 161-178.

[2] "In Orders and in Congregations approved by the Holy See, the dismissal of a religious with temporary vows can be effected by the Superior-General . . ." —Canon 647, § 1.

order will be taken to comprise every Institute the members of which make profession of solemn vows, *with the exception of those orders which have independent monasteries (monasteria sui iuris) and of orders of women (moniales).* These exceptions will be treated under the following sections. The term *Institute approved by the Holy See* includes every Institute which has obtained from the Holy See either approbation or at least a decree of commendation (*decretum laudis*). Included in the present section are: (1) Orders in the sense just explained; (2) Congregations of men both clerical and lay (whether exempt or non-exempt) and congregations of women, provided they are of pontifical approval; (3) Societies of men (clerical and lay, whether exempt or non-exempt) and of women living in common without vows, as long as these have at least the decree of commendation.[3]

In these Institutes the superior named by law for effecting the dismissal of a subject in temporary vows is the superior general. He is designated in the Code or constitutions by various names: *Praepositus Generalis, Superior Generalis, Director Generalis, Magister Generalis, Minister Generalis, Rector Maior, Praeses, Moderator Supremus,* etc.[4] Included in the term *Superior General* is the *Moderatrix Suprema* of congregations of women of pontifical approval, for in this matter she is not dependent on the bishop.[5] The Code does not give an essential definition of the term *Superior General,* as it does, for example, of the terms: *church,*[6] *sacramentals,*[7] etc. However it has described his juridic character and capacity. By the term *Superior General* is not meant the Roman Pontiff who is the Supreme Superior of all Institutes,[8] but rather the superior general of each single Institute. The superior general must have spent at least ten years in the Institute (to be reckoned from the date of his first profession), he must have been born of a legitimate marriage,

[3] Canon 681; *PCI,* 1 mart. 1921—*AAS,* XIII (1921), 177.

[4] Larraona, "Commentarium Codicis—Canon 488"—*CpR,* II (1923), 44.

[5] Canon 490; Biederlack-Führich, *De Religiosis,* p. 298; Fanfani, *De Iure Religiosorum,* p. 500; Schäfer, *De Religiosis,* p. 990; Coronata, *Institutiones,* I, p. 868, note 4; Bastien, *Directoire Canonique,* p. 129.

[6] Canon 1161.

[7] Canon 1144.

[8] Canon 499, §1 .

and he must have completed his fortieth year.[9] He is surely a major superior and to him is to be attributed all the prescriptions of law which are attributed to major superiors. He is distinguished from the other major superiors by the greater extent of his powers, *i. e.*, he has authority over *all* the provinces, houses, and members of the Institute.[10] It is true that the Code is rather vague in describing so generally his juridic character and powers. But this rather vague characterization can apply only to one member of an Institute, for no other person has power over the whole Institute. Much of the determination of his qualities and powers is left to the constitutions. These constitutions cannot take away any of his power, but they can limit its exercise especially in the manner of its use. He must follow the restrictions of his constitutions and *a fortiori* the restrictions which are placed on him by common law, especially the law requiring the consent or advice of his council.[11] This consent of his council is needed for the dismissal of religious in temporary vows, and will be treated in full below.

B. Orders with Independent Monasteries

"Professum a votis temporariis sive in Ordinibus sive in Congregationibus iuris pontificii dimittere potest . . . Abbas monasterii sui iuris. . . ." [12]

One cannot so easily make a general statement as to who is the proper superior to dismiss religious who are attached to independent houses. Before being able to single out the superior authorized to dismiss, several questions must first be decided; *i. e.*, what is an independent monastery, and whether or not independent monasteries of women religious of solemn vows and independent houses of congregations of simple vows are included under the phrase *independent*

[9] Canon 504.

[10] Canon 502.

[11] Larroana, "Commentarium Codicis—Canones 502-504"—*CpR*, VII (1926), 239-241.

[12] In Orders and in Congregations approved by the Holy See, the dismissal of a religious with temporary vows can be effected by . . . the Abbot of an independent monastery . . ."—Canon 647, § 1.

monastery in canon 647. One must first define and settle on the essential condition of an independent house and apply the definition to the various types of houses and monasteries before a decision can be reached.

An independent monastery or house is one which is self-ruling in its internal government.[13]

This self-rule or autonomy must not be confused with exemption. Exemption frees the Institute, according to the norms of law, from the jurisdiction of the local ordinary. All orders are exempt by law and some Institutes of simple vows are exempt by privilege,[14] but only certain houses of certain orders and of certain congregations of simple vows are independent.[15]

In order to clarify the problem of interpretation of the phrase *independent house* of canon 647, it will be helpful first to state which monasteries surely come under the phrase; secondly, to list those monasteries which in some way approach the definition of the independent monasteries but are surely not included under the term; and finally, to consider those houses which, even though they come under the term *independent house,* are probably not included under the term as it is taken in canon 647.

Many orders have monasteries of this juridic character of full independence; *e. g.*, the Benedictines, the Cistercians (except the Italian Congregation of the Primitive Observance), the Premonstratensians, etc.[16] These independent monasteries have as their head

[13] Larraona, "Commentarium Codicis—Canon 488"—*CpR,* III (1922), 133.

[14] Canons 615, 618.

[15] It is not true, then, to say that every independent monastery or house is exempt. When Mayer (*Benediktinisches Ordensrecht,* I, p. 140) and Schäfer (*De Religiosis,* p. 80) say that every independent house is exempt they are speaking of independent houses of the Benedictines or, at least, of orders in general. In this sense the statement is true, since every house of an order is exempt.

[16] Schäfer, *De Religiosis,* pp. 80, 81; Larraona, *loc. cit.,* Vermeersch, "De monasteriis seu domibus sui iuris"—*Periodica,* X (1922), (7)-(9). These independent monasteries have various names: Abbey, Conventual Priorate, *Coenobium,* and even *Ecclesia.* An Abbey is a monastery which has, besides the Abbot, at least twelve monks in solemn vows. A Conventual Priorate is smaller but still independent. For its erection there are required, besides the Prior, at least eight monks in solemn vows. Such a Priorate is distinct from a

a superior elected by the members of that house. He is called an Abbot if the house is an Abbey or a Prior if the house is a Priorate. Other names or titles may also be used in accordance with the constitutions or rules.

There are in the orders also the following: the *Abbas Primas,* the *Abbas Praeses,* the *Abbas Praesidens,* the *Abbas Generalis,* the *Archiabbas.* The *Abbas Primas* (Abbot Primate) is the head of the confederation of all the houses of the Black Benedictines.[17] The Benedictines and other non-centralized orders are formed into confederations of houses called monastic congregations. The head of such a confederation is designated by various names. In the Benedictine Congregation of Beuron, and in the Brazilian and Cassinese Congregation, he is called the *Archabbot.* In the American-Cassinese Congregation, the Abbot of Latrobe, Pa., is called *Archabbot, honoris causa,* but the real head of that congregation is elected periodically and has the name of *Abbas Praeses.* In the Congregation of Bavaria and Switzerland, etc., the superior is called the *Abbas Praeses.* In the Cassinese Congregation of the Primitive Observance he is called the *Abbas Generalis* and, in the Congregation of Solesmes, *Superior Generalis.*[18]

These monasteries of men which are independent in the strict sense described above are the only type of monastery contained under this heading. One may then ask which superior in the Institute

simple Priorate which depends in all spiritual and temporal matters on the founding Abbey. A simple Priorate is usually founded in mission lands; it needs only four monks in solemn vows besides the Prior. This Prior is not elected by members of the house (as in an Abbey or Priorate *proprie dictum*) but is appointed *ad nutum* by the Abbot of the founding Abbey. *Coenobium* is a word often used in the rules for an Abbey. *Ecclesia* is a word used in the Beuron Congregation of the Benedictine Order for an Abbey. No matter whether the independent monastery is called an Abbey, a Conventual Priorate, a *Coenobium,* or an *Ecclesia,* the juridical character of autonomy or independence is the essential constitutive note. Confer Mayer, *Benediktinisches Ordensrecht,* I, 151-154; II, 7-26; 26-29; 30-32, etc.; Molitor, *Religiosi Iuris Capita Selecta,* p. 230; Vermeersch, *art. cit.,* p. (9).

[17] Leo XIII, litt. ap. *Summum Semper,* 12 iul. 1893, nn. I, II—*Fontes,* n. 619. He is mentioned in canons 223, § 1, 4°; 501, § 3; 510, etc.

[18] Larraona, "Commentarium Codicis—Canon 488"—*CpR,* IV (1923), 40; Molitor, *Religiosi Iuris Capita Selecta,* 396, 397.

is authorized to dismiss a religious during his temporary vows. Can the Abbot Primate or the Superior of a monastic congregation dismiss a religious who is in temporary vows? The Abbot Primate or the Superior of a monastic congregation can dismiss only a subject of the house over which he is the abbot; neither of them can dismiss a subject of any other house. Any other opinion is untenable.[19] The Abbot Primate and the Superior of the monastic congregation have not even all the powers which are conceded to major superiors much less those which are conceded to superiors general. Their power is limited by the constitutions of their Institute and the decrees of the Holy See.[20] Thus in common law the Abbot Primate or the superior of a monastic congregation has not the power to effect the dismissal of a religious in temporary vows in an abbey other than that over which he is the superior. Nor can this power to dismiss such a religious be given him except in extraordinary circumstances. The only superior, then, who can dismiss a religious in temporary vows in a fully and completely independent house of an order of men is the Abbot of an Abbacy or the Prior of a Conventual Priory; and these can proceed in the act of dismissal only with the consent of their council.

Many houses of different types of Institutes approach the requirements of the term *independent house* but lack one or more of its essential notes. These types of monasteries, as shall be seen, are expressly provided for in the Code with but one exception. The treatment of the rest of the section, therefore, will follow this order: an analysis of the independent houses which are included in other sections of canon 647 (and are thus provided for in the Code), and the investigation of one type of independent house for which there is no express provision in the Code.

Some *moniales* have such independent monasteries with the full independence described above; *e. g.*, the Carmelites, the Colettines, and the Visitation nuns. Although it is the better opinion that the

[19] Schäfer, *De Religiosis*, p. 991; Larraona, "Commentarium Codicis—Canon 488"—*CpR*, III (1922), 133; 137, notes 207-209; IV (1923), 44, note 302; Tabera, "De dimissione religiosorum"—*CpR*, XII (1931), 142.

[20] Canon 501, § 3.

superior of an independent monastery of nuns is a major superior,[21] in no other way does she possess equal juridical status with the abbot of an independent monastery. Canon 490 states that the dispositions of the Code, even when expressed in the masculine gender, apply equally to religious women, unless the text or context of the Code state otherwise. This canon does not apply in this case because the text of the canon 647 does, in fact, state otherwise when it gives a separate and distinct ruling in regard to the superior authorized to dismiss nuns who are still in temporary vows. This ruling will be considered below.[22]

There are degrees of independence, depending on the greater or less power granted by the rule and constitutions to the Abbot Primate and on the consequent approach of his power to that of the superior general in congregations of simple vows.[23] Many orders have a superior general in the true and proper sense of canon 502 explained above. In these orders the independence and autonomy of each house excludes only an intermediary major superior who would exercise power in his own name over the independent monastery, but it does not exclude the power of the superior general over them. Such are, for instance, the Olivetans, the Camaldolese, the Reformed Cistercians of La Trappe, the Carthusians, the Vallumbrosians and many others.[24] In this type of Institute, the head of the Institute is a superior general not in the limited sense of the Abbot Primate in the Benedictines but in the full and complete sense of the word, and hence he alone can dismiss as was stated in Section A above.

21 Larraona, "Commentarium Codicis—Canon 488"—*CpR,* IV (1923), 40-44; Tabera, "De dimissione religiosorum"—*CpR,* XII (1931), 142.

22 Tabera, *art. cit.;* Larraona, *art. cit.*—*CpR,* IV (1923), 11-14; 40; Schäfer, *De Religiosis,* pp. 991 and 218 (n. 103, 5) against Fanfani, *Il Diritto delle Religiose* (Torino-Roma: Marietti, 1922), p. 242.

23 Canon 501, § 3. For a discussion on the development of these different degrees of independence and the approach of many of these monastic congregations to centralization, confer Jombart, "Autonomie et centralization"—*RCR,* X (1934), 124; 132-139; 148, 149.

24 Larraona, "Commentarium Codicis—Canon 488"—*CpR,* III (1922), 137; Schäfer, *De Religiosis,* pp. 226, 227. As opposed to this concept of degrees of independence, confer Gomez, "De Abbatum potestate tonsuram minoresque ordines conferendi"—*CpR,* IX (1928), 445, 446 note (18), and Larraona's remark in *CpR,* IX (1928), 434 note (*).

There are also independent monasteries or houses in religious congregations of simple vows. Tabera denies that there are such houses and, admitting them only as hypothetical cases, says that they are to be considered as *moniales*.[25] It is well to note that every discussion on this matter which was available to the writer refers to independent houses in congregations of religious *women* in simple vow Institutes. No mention is made of such houses of religious men. The consideration will be limited to those Institutes of religious women of simple vows whose houses are independent, and only a note added concerning Institutes of religious men of simple vows with independent houses.

There can be no doubt that there are such congregations, *e. g.*, the Sisters of Mercy and the Sisters of St. Joseph who have not been amalgamated into the union of houses which took place in comparatively recent times. An investigation of the constitutions will show that they have simple vows and that each house is independent.[26] These congregations are quite old and widespread, hence Vermeersch's statement is not fully accurate when he says that such a situation (*i. e.*, independent houses in congregations whose members take simple vows) usually is accidental because the congregation has not yet expanded.[27]

These independent monasteries in religious congregations of simple vows are not included under the term *independent monastery* in canon 647 because it seems that in regard to dismissal they are subject to the local ordinary who alone can dismiss. In the last analysis it is for the rules and constitutions of these congregations to decide who is the superior authorized to dismiss. If the congregation is of pontifical approval (as is the case of the Sisters of Mercy not in the

[25] Tabera, "De dimissione religiosorum"—*CpR*, XII (1931), 144.

[26] *The Rule and Constitutions of the Religious Called the Sisters of Mercy*, for the use of the Sisters in the diocese of Philadelphia (Philadelphia: The Catholic Standard and Times, 1928), *passim*; *Rule and Constitutions of the Religious Sisters of Mercy in the Archdiocese of Baltimore, Maryland*, pp. 49, 50, 85 ff.; *The Rule and Constitutions of the Religious Called the Sisters of Mercy* (Dublin: Browne & Nolan, 1926), *passim*, especially pp. 31-34, 68 ff.

[27] Vermeersch, "De monasteriis seu domibus sui iuris"—*Periodica*. X (1922), (9).

union) [28] the Code has no provision for them. There are three analogies of law possible in this case. The analogy might be made to other congregations of pontifical approval whose houses are dependent; it might be made, as Tabera suggests, to Institutes of *moniales*; or, finally, it might be made to independent houses of men in solemn vows. In the first case, the superioress of the independent house would be considered as the superior general and be empowered to dismiss; in the second case, the local ordinary would be the superior authorized to dismiss; [29] and in the last case, the superioress of the house would be considered on a par with the Abbot of an independent monastery, and would be authorized to dismiss the religious.

The analogy to the Institutes of *moniales* seems the best of the three. First of all, an investigation of the rules available to the writer (those of the Sisters of Mercy not in the Union) designate the local ordinary as the superior empowered to dismiss.[30] Secondly, a complete view of the provisions of canon 647 seem to point to the analogy to Institutes of *moniales* as the more correct one. In regard to the dismissal of religious during temporary vows, the Code distinguishes between centralized and non-centralized Institutes. Each of these divisions is subdivided further into Institutes of pontifical and of diocesan approval. The question under consideration concerns solely Institutes of pontifical approval. Of these Institutes of pontifical approval the Code places all centralized Institutes on a par and rules that in these Institutes the superior general dismisses. In regard to non-centralized Institutes the Code distinguishes between those of men and of women religious. In both cases, however, the ruling of the Code is for Institutes of solemn vows. In non-centralized Institutes of men the Abbot of the independent monastery is authorized by the Code to dismiss and in Institutes of

[28] S. C. de Religiosis, declàr., 24 nov. 1925—*AAS*, XVIII (1926), 14; Maroto, "Annotationes"—*CpR*, VII (1926), 84-92; cf. *Periodica*, XV (1927), 52, 53.

[29] Tabera, "De dimissione religiosorum"—*CpR*, XII (1931), 144.

[30] *The Rule and Constitutions of the Religious Called the Sisters of Mercy* (Philadelphia), n. 101, p. 67; *The Rule and Constitutions of the Religious Called the Sisters of Mercy* (Dublin), n. 101, p. 61; *Rule and Constitutions of the Religious Sisters of Mercy in the Archdiocese of Baltimore, Maryland*, pp. 49, 50; 85 sq.

women (*i. e.*, of *moniales*) the local ordinary or regular superior dismisses. There is no provision in the Code for non-centralized Institutes of simple vows, so recourse must be had to an analogy of law. It seems that the analogy is closer to *independent* monasteries of *moniales* than to *dependent* houses in centralized simple vow Institutes of pontifical approval. The difference between an independent house of a simple vow Institute of pontifical approval and an independent house of *moniales* is solely in the solemnity of the vows. This difference is often only one of law and not of fact, for example, the Ursulines of the Paris Congregation whose vows are solemn by their constitutions but simple because of a special provision of the Holy See. The difference between an independent and a dependent house in simple vow Institutes of pontifical approval is one of centralization. The independent house is in an Institute which is non-centralized, whereas the dependent house is in a centralized Institute. The Code seems to distinguish between centralized and non-centralized Institutes in determining the superior authorized to dismiss a religious during the time of temporary vows. Therefore it seems to the writer that the analogy should be made to independent houses of *moniales* because they as well as independent houses of simple vow Institutes of pontifical approval are parts of non-centralized Institutes. These reasons coupled with the prescriptions of the three rules and constitutions examined above lead the writer to believe that it is the better opinion to say that the local ordinary is the superior to dismiss in this case.

One could object that the third analogy (*i. e.*, between independent houses in simple vow Institutes of religious women to independent monasteries of men of solemn vows) could just as easily and logically be made because in this case, too, the difference is only one of the solemnity of vows and not of centralization. The Code, however, does not in its law on dismissal of religious provide for a house of women so independent that they are under no superior other than the local superior. Thus houses of religious women are always under either the local ordinary, the regular superior, or the superioress general even when the house is totally independent in other matters. By analogy it would seem that any independent house of religious women of simple vows would not be completely independent in regard to dismissal as is the independent house of religious men with solemn vows. It would seem rather that they would have a superior other than the superior of the house to dismiss the religious. Therefore the analogy should be made to independent houses of *moniales* rather than to independent houses of religious men of solemn vows.

In regard to independent houses in simple vow Institutes of religious men there seems to be no reason why the analogy should not be made to independent monasteries of solemn vow Institutes of men. In this case, the superior of the house is equaled to the Abbot of the monastery and is empowered to dismiss.

C. *The Consent of the Council*

". . . cum consensu sui cuiusque Consilii per secreta suffragia manifestato. . . ." [31]

The Code demands the consent of the Council in relation only to the two superiors here mentioned: the Superior General in Orders and in congregations of pontifical approval and the abbot of an independent monastery. But of whom does their Council consist? And when must it be called to furnish its secret vote in the act of dismissal?

A Council is a group designated by the common law or the constitutions to help the superior in some designated and especially grave cases. Canon 516 demands that

> "Supremus religionis aut monasticae Congregationis Moderator, Superior provincialis et localis saltem formatae domus habeant suos consiliarios, quorum consensum aut consilium exquirant ad normam constitutionum et sacrorum canonum." [32]

The Code states in this canon only the necessity of these superiors' having a Council; it leaves the designation of the number of its mem-

[31] ". . . each with the consent of his respective Council, manifested by secret voting. . . ."—Canon 647, § 1.

[32] "The Superior-General of every Institute or monastic Congregation, also every Provincial Superior and local Superior at least of every formal house, shall have their Councillors whose consent or counsel they must seek according to the terms of the constitutions and the sacred canons."—Canon 516.

bers, the method used in selecting them, the time of their election and many details concerning their juridical capacity to the constitutions. As to whether their advice or consent is to be asked the Code sometimes specifies; if it does not, then the specification is left to the constitutions.[33]

Since the Code often uses the terms *Council* and *Chapter* in the same canon, it will be best to see the distinction between the two. The Code uses the word *Capitulum* in two senses. In the first it is used to designate a collegiate moral person which is usually elective.[34] In the second sense it is used to designate a board of consultors; in this sense it is not a collegiate moral person. When used in this latter sense the Code usually places *Capitulum* in apposition to *Consilium* and places a *seu* or *vel* between them.[35] This distinction follows the one made very clearly in the *Normae*.[36]

The Council is very clearly distinct from the Chapter both externally and internally. Externally, the Council usually has few members (the Superior and from two to six councillors) who are fixed and determined by law, or are personally elected or designated; the Chapter usually has (and should have) more members than a Council. Internally, or in juridic character, they are also distinct. The Chapter, as stated, is a real law-making body and its power to make laws is limited only by the Code or the constitutions. It helps the superior in the use of his executive power and watches over his exercise of legislative power. The Council is an advisory or consultative board with no law-making power. It is constituted rather a part of the superior's executive power, because in some cases so stated in law, he cannot act without it. The Chapter is a moral person in the sense that it forms a legitimate representation of the house, of the province, or of the whole Institute. It implies the joining of its members into one moral unity and juridic personality. The Council does not necessarily form a moral person, nor does it

[33] Canon 516, § 1; Schäfer, *op. cit.*, pp. 235, 324, 325. The Council is mentioned in the Code in canons 510, 516, § 1, 549, 647, § 1, 650, § 1, 653, 668, 896, etc.

[34] It is used in this sense in canons 494, § 2; 501, 506, 507, 587, § 1, 597, § 3.

[35] Cf. canon 534, § 1; 543; 575, § 2, 646, § 2, 655, § 1, 667.

[36] *De Capitulo—Normae*, nn. 202, 251; *De Consilio—Normae*, nn. 271-280.

necessarily constitute a true *collegium,* even though it sometimes, in the cases determined by the law or the constitutions, acts as such. But only in the cases so determined does the Council act as a collegiate moral person, for in all other cases its acts are not collegiate acts but the personal acts of the individual councillors. The acts of the Chapter cannot be ascribed to the Superior, for that body is a co-elector or co-legislator with the superior; the Council, however, never acts on a par with the superior and the superior's action, taken with their counsel or consent, is always his and not theirs. The Council is less *sui iuris* than the Chapter.[37]

If the Code, in treating of the act of a superior who rules a moral person, requires that he receive the consent or the counsel of several persons at once who form a moral person or are constituted according to the manner of a moral person, then the rules of canons 101, 162-172 are followed.[38] When there is demanded, by the law or by the constitutions, the counsel or consent of the councillors they then act in the manner of a moral person. The superior must convoke them and indicate to them the time and place (if it is not already known to them), in order that they may engage in common deliberation, give their opinions, and vote freely. No special convocation is needed if the meetings take place regularly on days stated by the constitutions, by custom, or by the prescription of the superior. Since common deliberation is needed it is not enough to send in one's opinion by letter unless the constitutions allow it.[39]

In neglecting to make this summons or convocation, does the superior act invalidly or illicitly? The neglect of convocation does not render the proceeding invalid if the required consent is obtained or the required counsel sought.[40] If he neglects to summon one of

[37] Schäfer, *De Religiosis,* p. 235; pp. 324-327; Larraona, "Commentarium Codicis"—*CpR,* VI (1925), 428, 429; Vermeersch-Creusen, *Epitome,* I, 198; Maroto, *Institutiones Iuris Canonici* (3. ed., Romae: Apud Commentarium pro Religiosis, 1922), I, 550.

[38] Maroto, *Institutiones,* pp. 546, 547, note 1; 555; Chelodi, *Ius De Personis,* n. 102, p. 167; n. 99, pp. 162, 163; Vromant, "De actibus personae moralis collegialis et superioris"—*ETL,* VII (1930), 677-680.

[39] Canons 105, 2°, 162, § 4; Schäfer, *op. cit.,* pp. 326, 327; Goyeneche, "Consultatio"—*CpR,* III (1922), 215, 329 sq.; XV (1934), 211.

[40] Canon 105, 2°; 162, § 4; Vromant, "De actibus personae moralis col-

the councillors (unless there are only two in the Council) he does not act invalidly; the councillor who was not summoned may, however, within three days after receiving notice of the transacted meeting invalidate the proceedings through a competent superior by proving to him that he was not summoned and in consequence was absent from the meeting. But if a major portion (more than one-third of the Council) is not summoned then the proceeding is invalid. But if, notwithstanding the neglect of the superior to convoke more than one-third of the members of the Council, at least two-thirds of the Council are present anyhow, the proceeding is valid, but rescindable by any one of those not present because they were not convoked.[41]

Must those who are not able to be present be nevertheless convoked under pain of invalidating the proceedings? Goyeneche cites a case when two members of a Council of five were absent from the country when there arose a case of the dismissal of a religious in temporary vows. Must the two absentees be convoked even though it is known that they are too far away to be present on the day specified? If so, then the lack of their convocation makes the proceeding invalid. Practically the case is always covered, for either the constitutions or the announcements or prescriptions of the superior fixes certain days for the meeting of the Council. But if the time of the meeting were not fixed, must these two be sent a summons under pain of nullity for the ensuing proceedings? The pre-Code law demanded that only those be summoned *"Qui debent et volunt et possunt interesse"*; therefore there was no need to summon those who had lost the right to vote, who had renounced it, or who were so far away from the place of election that it could be foreseen that they would not be able to arrive in time for the voting. Is this interpretation still in force? Many say it is.[42] Others say that there

legialis ac superioris"—*ETL*, VII (1930), 677; Toso, *Ad Codicem Juris Canonici Commentaria Minora*, Liber II, *De Personis*, Tome I (Taurini-Romae: Marietti, 1922), p. 54 (henceforth cited as *Commentaria Minora*).

[41] Canon 162; Schäfer, *op. cit.*, pp. 327, 328; Parsons, *Canonical Elections*, The Catholic University of America Canon Law Studies, n. 118 (Washington, D. C.: Catholic University of America Press, 1939), pp. 98-108.

[42] Maroto, *Institutiones* I, p. 734; Goyeneche, *Iuris Canonici Summa Principia* (Romae, Tip. Pol. "Cuore Di Maria," 1938), I, 193; Coronata, *Institutiones*, I, 172; Sipos, *Enchiridion*, p. 136; Wernz-Vidal, *Ius Canonicum*, II,

is a definite change in the law.[43] It seems, then, that there is a doubt as to whether the pre-Code law has been changed, and therefore, according to canon 6, 2°, 4°, the approved interpretation of the pre-Code law is to be followed; namely, that those do not have to be summoned who have lost the right to vote, who have renounced it, or who are so far away from the place of voting that it can be foreseen that they will not be able to arrive in time for the voting. The rules given in the older authors concerning the impossibility of reaching the place of meeting can no longer be followed, because of the great change in methods of transportation. Circumstances of place and person, and the ease or difficulty of the journey are all to be considered. Either custom or particular law is the best judge of these circumstances.[44]

If, after the summons of convocation, one or several or even all of the Council do not come or refuse to come, what is the effect on the validity of the proceedings? If one neglects to come the gathering can proceed to the business at hand.[45] If all are convoked and several fail to appear, indeed if only one appears at the meeting with the superior, the right devolves on these two. The full right to proceed belongs to those who are actually present, regardless of how small this number may be.[46] But, as is so often true in following the letter of the law, *summum ius,, summa iniuria,* and the superior who in a matter of such great importance as dismissal would use this manner of seeking consent would commit a great injustice. Thus the constitutions of various Institutes commonly determine

267, note 23; Vromant, "De actibus personae moralis collegialis et superioris" —*ETL,* VII (1930), 677, 678. Larraona ("Consultatio"—*CpR,* IX [1928], 337, note 106) agrees with this opinion but says that it can be maintained only with difficulty.

[43] Ayrinhac, *General Legislation in the New Code of Canon Law* (New York: Longmans, 1930), p. 331; Augustine, *Commentary,* II, 125; Toso, *Commentaria Minora,* Lib. II, Tome I, p. 131; Parsons, *Canonical Elections,* p. 101.

[44] Maroto, *Institutiones* I, pp. 734, 735, 744, C.

[45] Canon 163; Goyeneche, "Consultatio"—*CpR,* III (1922), 215, 333; XI (1930), 357; *CpRM,* XVIII (1937), 158-160; Pejska, *Ius Canonicum Religiosorum,* p. 233; Maroto, *op. cit.,* I, 555, 556.

[46] Goyeneche, "Consultatio"—*CpRM,* XVIII (1937), 159; Maroto, *op. cit.,* I, 747; Parsons, *Canonical Elections,* pp. 109-111; Vromant, *art. cit.*—*ETL,* VII (1930), 678, 679.

the number of Councillors who must necessarily be present for the validity of the acts transacted at these meetings.[47] If all are convoked and none appear, the superior cannot proceed because the seeking either of consent or, probably, of counsel, is a *sine qua non* condition for valid action according to canon 105.[48] The rights of the Council do not revert to the superior, for it is of the very nature and purpose of the Council to restrict his will and to circumscribe his power. Thus he must consult or ask for and receive the consent of at least one of them when the Code or constitutions so demand. He can, and should command them to come and to appear when they are convoked. He should, if necessary, threaten them with penalties for their refusal to do their duty.

As to supplying members who are not councillors, to make up for the lack of the necessary number of councillors, the Code mentions the question only once, viz., in canon 655, § 1, for the dismissal of religious in perpetual vows in a clerical exempt religious Institute. The constitutions can prescribe that the superior fill in the vacancies in order to constitute a quorum, since this is not against the Code.[49] If the constitutions demand a full Council for action and there are vacancies caused by absentees, the superior is not bound to, nor can he, so it seems, fill the vacancies. The right of proceeding with the

[47] *Constitutions of the Catholic Foreign Mission Society of America* (2. ed., Maryknoll, N. Y., 1938), p. 14, n. 78: there are five in the general Council; a majority must be present for the validity of the acts of the meeting; *The Rule and General Constitutions of the Friars Minor* (Paterson, N. J.: St. Anthony's Guild Press, 1936), p. 103, n. 475: at least five voters are needed; *Constitutiones Ordinis Fratrum Beatissimae Virginis Mariae de Monte Carmelo* (Romae: Typis Polyglottis Vaticanis, 1930), pp. 182, 183, art. 529: "*Praesentibus tribus saltem gremialibus*" (there are five members in the Supreme Council), etc., etc.

[48] As to the necessity of seeking the required advice, this is a statement of opinion. There is no need to go into the vexing question of whether or not the phrase *satis ad valide agendum* of canon 105 demands the seeking of the counsel for validity or licitness only. The general principles of conciliar action are treated here only in so far as they concern canon 647, which demands the *consent* of the Council.

[49] *The Rule and General Constitutions of the Friars Minor*, p. 103, n. 475, allow for substitution or for supplying for the absent members of the *Definitorium*, and likewise *Reglè De Saint Augustine et Constitutions des "Augustin de L'Assomption"* (Paris: Typographie Augustinienne, 1935), p. 90, n. 221.

matter in hand pertains only to those who are present. The absent cannot send in their vote by mail or proxy, and the admission of an outsider to the voting would render the proceeding invalid. It seems that an *outsider* in this regard is anyone who is not a member of the voting body.[50]

When the constitutions demand a full Council for action and further do not provide for substitution for absent members, the superior should legitimately convoke all of his Council and, if need be, constrain them by threat of penalties to assist. If, after enough time has been allowed to enable them to come, there are still some vacancies, the proceeding will be valid even if there is not a full Council, for juridically, although not actually, a full Council is present.[51]

In regard to the dismissal of religious in temporary vows, the Superior General and the Abbot of an independent monastery (as described above) must have the consent of his Council indicated upon a secret ballot. He must convoke the members of his Council. If he does not convoke at least two-thirds of the Council, the subsequent proceeding is rendered invalid. If one or even more were not convoked (but less than one-third of the Council), any one of them may, within three days of obtaining knowledge of the transacted meeting, invalidate the proceeding through a competent superior by proving to him that he was not convoked and in consequence was not present at the meeting. For if he is present despite the lack of his being convoked, then the proceeding is valid. No convocation is necessary if the meeting is held on the day specified

[50] Canons 163, 165; Goyeneche, "Consultatio"—*CpRM,* XVIII (1937), 160; Pejska, *Ius Canonicum Religiosorum,* p. 233; Schäfer, *De Religiosis,* pp. 328, 329. Cf. Parsons, *Canonical Elections,* p. 118.

[51] Goyeneche, "Consultatio"—*CpR,* III (1922), 335, note 15; XI (1930), 357; *CpRM,* XVIII (1937), 160. This seems to hold unless the constitutions demand a full Council for validity. They should then also make provision for the filling of vacancies, otherwise many grave inconveniences may arise inasmuch as important matters cannot be expedited because of the absence of even one consultor. Goyeneche states that if the constitutiones which demand a full Council are based on the *Normae* (which command the superior to fill in vacancies in the Council), then they demand a full Council in the sense of the *Normae,* and the places of the absent Councillors should be supplied, even though the constitutions do not state this expressly.

by law, by the constitutions, or by the standing decision of the superior. The superior should not act in a matter so serious as that of dismissal if only one member of the Council is present, but should urge the others to be present and threaten them with penalties for their failure to be present. Nevertheless it seems that the action of dismissal in the case would not be invalid. Unless the constitutions allow him to do so, he shall not supply the vacancies in the Council caused by the failure of some of the members to appear after the summons of convocation. After mature discussion and deliberation the matter of dismissal shall be voted upon secretly. This secrecy of the ballot is required only for the licitness of the procedure and not for its validity.[52]

It may be disputed whether or not the neglect to consult the councillors *collegialiter* (*i. e.*, by having them in assembly express their opinion and vote on the matter) is necessary for validity. It is the more common opinion that collegiate action is necessary under pain of invalidity.[53] This opinion, not without its opponents,[54] is surely the preferable one and follows more logically the doctrine treated above on the necessity of convocation. The convocation would be more or less useless if the vote was not to be taken *collegialiter.*[55]

In the computation of the votes, canon 101, § 1, 1° is to be followed. First, all invalid votes are discarded. On the first two ballotings an absolute majority is required, *i. e.*, more than half of the total of the valid votes which were cast. On the third balloting a relative majority suffices, *i. e.*, a number of votes greater than the number cast for any other single candidate. In the case of the dis-

[52] Blat, *De Religiosis,* pp. 570, 571; Coronata, *Institutiones,* I, 868, note 5.

[53] Michiels, *Principia Generalia De Personis In Ecclesia* (Lublin: Universitas Catholica, 1932), pp. 427-430; Chelodi, *Jus De Personis,* n. 102; Coronata, *Institutiones,* I, n. 154, b; Brandys, *Kirchliches Rechtsbuch für die religiösen Laiengenossenschaften der Brüder und Schwestern* (2. ed., Paderborn: Schöningh, 1920), n. 186; Goyeneche, "Consultatio"—*CpR,* III (1922), 215-216.

[54] Toso, *Commentaria Minora,* Liber II, *De Personis,* Tome I, p. 54; Vromant, "De actibus personae moralis collegialis ac superioris"—*ETL,* VII (1930), 677; Fallon, "Consequence of failure to consult diocesan consultors collegialiter" —*IER,* LIII (1939), 299.

[55] Confer Michiels, *loc. cit.*, for a full exposition of this matter.

missal of a religious in temporary vows, since the vote is either positive or negative there is no chance for a third or fourth category of votes as in an election for office. Because of this fact the relative majority will always be the absolute majority. If the ballotings result each time in an equal voting for and against dismissal, the superior on the third balloting shall break the tie by his vote. If the majority vote is against the dismissal he cannot, under pain of invalidity, dismiss the subject.[56]

D. Institutes of Moniales

> ". . . vel, si agatur de monialibus, Ordinarius loci, et si monasterium sit regularibus obnoxium, Superior regularis, postquam monasterii Antistita cum suo Consilio fidem de causis scripto fecerit; . . .[57]

This portion of canon 647 includes *all* nuns, even those whose vows are normally solemn but which, by a disposition of the Holy See, are simple in certain regions.[58] Even though the monastery of the nuns be independent, and even though generally what is applied to the word *Abbot* can, by force of canon 490, be applied also to the word *Abbess,* still as touching the question of dismissal as enacted in canon 647 nuns are all placed under one category, the one considered here. It is clear from the text and context that the Abbess of an independent monastery cannot dismiss a subject in temporary vows.[59]

There is no difficulty when the monastery is subject to the local ordinary. It is he alone who can effect the dismissal after hearing

[56] Canons 647, §§ 1 and 105, 1°; Schäfer, *De Religiosis,* n. 155, 5, c, p. 327; n. 578, p. 990. For a complete treatment of the power and working of the Council together with data on the Rules and Constitutions of various orders and congregations, confer Hofmeister, *Der Ordensrat* (Bonn: L. Röhrscheid, 1937).

[57] ". . . or, in the case of nuns, by the local Ordinary and, if the monastery be subject to Regulars, by the Regular Superior, after the Superioress of the monastery with her Council will have given a written attestation of the motives for the dismissal"—Canon 647, § 1.

[58] Canon 488, 7°; Larraona, "Commentarium Codicis"—*CpR,* IV (1923), 11-14.

[59] Tabera, "De dimissione religiosorum"—*CpR,* XII (1931), 142; Schäfer, *op. cit.,* p. 991.

the written testimony of the Superioress and of her councillors. But when the monastery is subject to a regular superior, it is not so clear which superior is qualified to effect the dismissal. The wording of canon 647, § 1, is:

> *"Vel, si agatur de monialibus, Ordinarius loci et, si monasterium sit regularibus obnoxium, Superior regularis postquam monasterii Antistita cum suo Consilio fidem de causis scripto fecerit."*

One opinion on this dispute is that of Augustine, who is alone in holding that each separate superior has this power, and that the first one who touches the matter is the one who has the power to effect the dismissal.[60] Another opinion is that which contends that both the local Ordinary and the regular superior must concur in the dismissal.[61] This opinion has for its principal arguments: (1) the actual wording of the clause, for *et* is employed, not *vel*; (2) the discipline preceding the Code in which a religious was dismissed by the superioress, but the just and grave causes were to be approved by the local Ordinary and, if the monastery was subject to Regulars,

[60] Augustine, *Commentary*, III, 388.

[61] Chelodi, *Ius De Personis*, p. 451, note 6; Schäfer, *De Religiosis* (ed. altera, Münster: Aschendorff, 1931), p. 591; Coronata, *Institutiones*, I, 868, note 6; Creusen, *Religieux et Religieuses*, p. 122, n. 235; Biederlack-Führich, *De Religiosis*, p. 298; Blat, *De Religiosis*, p. 571; Claeys Bouuaert-Simenon, *Manuale*, p. 387; Sipos, *Enchiridion*, p. 391; De Meester, *Compendium*, II, 484, note 7; Vermeersch-Creusen, *Epitome*, I, 598; Fanfani, *De Iure Religiosorum* (2. ed.), p. 500; Palombo, *De Dimissione Religiosorum*, p. 174; Wernz-Vidal, *Ius Canonicum*, III, 476; Berutti, *Institutiones Iuris Canonici* (3 vols., Taurini-Romae: Marietti, 1936-1938), Vol. III (1936), *De Religiosis*, p. 341 (henceforth cited as *De Religiosis*); Schönsteiner, *Grundriss des Ordensrechtes*, pp. 628, 629; Oesterle, *Praelectiones Iuris Canonici*, Vol. I (Romae: Collegio S. Anselmi, 1931), p. 371; Jardi, *El Derecho De Las Religiosas* (2. ed., Vich: Editorial Seráfica, 1927), 413; Thévenot, *Le Noveau Droit Canonique Des Religieuses* (2. ed. Paris: Téqui, 1922), pp. 151-152; Eichner, *Lehrbuch des Kirchensrechts auf Grund des Codex Iuris Canonici* (2. ed. Paderborn, Schöningh, 1926), p. 258; Geser, *The Canon Law Governing Communities of Sisters*, p. 363; Sabino, Alonso, "Situación canónica de las monjas sujetas a los regulares"—*La Ciencia Tomistica*, XXX (1924), p. 120; Jombart, "Le renvoi au cours des voeux temporaires"—*RCR*, V (1929), 196.

also by the Regular Superior;[62] (3) the analogy of the law with canon 652, § 2, in which for the dismissal of nuns in perpetual vows the local Ordinary is required to transmit to the Sacred Congregation of Religious all the acts and documents with a statement of his own judgment in the case *and* that of the Regular Superior if the monastery is subject to Regulars; (4) the constant rule of the Code in subjecting these monasteries to both superiors, as it does, for instance, in canons 525, 535, § 1, 1°, 549, 603, 652, § 2.

A third opinion considered by the present writer as the most acceptable of the three, states that, when the monastery is subject to Regulars, only the Regular Superior can effect the dismissal.[63] This opinion has for its chief arguments: (1) The grammatical structure of the sentence. The canon employs the singular *potest* and not the plural *possunt,* which would be required if both were to concur in the dismissal; (2) the fact that in all the preparatory schemata of the Code the word *vel* was used, and not *et*; (3) the fact that any other interpretation would appear to presuppose an inelegance of structure in the canon; and (4) the fact that grave perplexities could readily be occasioned if joint action were demanded from two co-

[62] S. C. de Religiosis, Decr. *Quum singulae,* 16 maii, 1911, n. 21—*Fontes,* n. 4409.

[63] Prümmer, *Manuale Iuris Canonici,* p. 347, note 2; Pejska, *Ius Canonicum Religiosorum,* p. 190; Schäfer, *De Religiosis* (3. ed., Romae: Typis polyglottis vaticanis, 1940), p. 992; Battandier, *Guide Canonique,* p. 272; Stadtmüller, *Das neue Ordensrecht* (Dülmen i. w., 1919), p. 77; Tabera, "De dimissione religiosorum"—*CpR,* XII (1931), 143-147; Goyeneche, *De Religiosis,* p. 212; "Consultatio"—*CpRM,* XVII (1936), 347-349; Leitner, *Handbuch des katholischen Kirchenrechts auf Grund des neuen Kodex,* 5 vols., Vol. III, *Das Ordensrecht* (2. ed., Regensberg, Pustet, 1922), p. 496; Bouuaert, *Selecta Capita Codicis Iuris Canonici* (Gandae, 1919), p. 63; Arndt, *Die Kirchlichen und Weltlichen Rechtsbestimmung für Orden und Kongregationen* (2. ed., Paderborn, 1919), p. 82; Haring, *Grundzüge des Katholischen Kirchenrecht* (3. ed., 2 vols., Graz: Meyerhoff, 1924), p. 823; Jansen, *Ordensrecht,* p. 288; Tabera quotes Jansen's *Ordensrecht,* p. 219, for the opinion that both the local ordinary and the regular superior must concur in dismissal. But in both the second (1922) and the third (1931) edition Jansen holds that the regular superior alone dismisses. Note also that Bouuaert when he collaborated with Simenon in writing the *Manuale* changed from this opinion. cf. note (61). Note also that in his latest edition, Schäfer has changed from the opinion he held formerly. Cf. *supra,* note (61).

responsible persons. Would each of these two have to hear the other? Would their decision have to be mutually conformed? Would the dismissal when effected by the one remain invalid in the face of the disagreement of the other, or even apart from his agreement? The Code quite generally obviates the possible conflict of authority when the powers of two superiors are involved either by subjecting the power of one to the other [64] or by defining clearly the relative measure of each one's power and authority.[65]

These arguments are strengthened by a refutation of the reasons employed in defense of the second opinion. (1) the word *et* is a simple connective which points to the possibility of yet another case. It is not a connective which implies action from two superiors. The word *vel* could not feasibly be used when it already appeared at the beginning of the clause in which the two superiors are to be differentiated. (2) The decree *Quum singulae* gave the superioress of nuns the power to dismiss a subject in temporary vows, but, in the case of nuns who were subject to regulars, only after the ordinary and the regular superior had examined and approved the causes for the dismissal. This is not the same case as that contemplated in canon 647, according to which not the superioress, but either the regular superior alone or in conjunction with the local ordinary, effects the dismissal. (3) Canon 652, § 2 is not strictly analogous to canon 647 for the very same reason, since neither the local ordinary nor the regular superior effects the dismissal of a nun in final vows, but only sends his opinion on the validity of the causes set forth by the superioress. (4) It is falsely asserted that the Code follows the constant rule of subjecting such monasteries to both the local ordinary and the regular superior by empowering them to act with joint power. This can be seen for example, from canons 512, § 2, 1°; 529; 535, § 1, 2°, which clearly define the respective power of each with regard to the monasteries of nuns which are subject to regulars.

It is a matter much in doubt. Because of the general principle stated in canon 500, § 2, namely, that nuns who are placed by their constitutions under the jurisdiction of regular superiors are subject to the local ordinary only in the cases provided for in the law, it

[64] Cf., for example, canons 456; 506, § 2; 525; 527; etc.
[65] Cf., for example, canons 534, § 1; 535, § 1, 1°, 2°; 1338-1340.

seems that, until it can be proved conclusively that the monasteries of nuns which are subject to regulars are, by canon 647, subjected also to the authority of the local ordinary, there is no obligation of consulting the local ordinary in this matter. However, since both of the opinions here discussed have intrinsic probability, and since the opinion which gives the local ordinary power together with the regular superior in the matter of dismissal has greater extrinsic authority, one cannot say that the opinion which demands that both concur in the act of effecting the dismissal is improbable. Indeed, even though one opinion he selected as preferable to the other, one will readily join with Vermeersch and Tabera in the desire for an authentic interpretation of this knotty problem.[66]

Who is the regular superior? The Code does not specify, but leaves it to the constitutions to decide which of the regular superiors is authorized to dismiss. If the constitutions do not make it clear, the major superior of the order of men can dismiss, because the word regular superior is placed on a par with local ordinary. Further, in no other place in the Code is a local superior given permission to dismiss. Since the major superior is not specified either the provincial or the superior general may dismiss.[67] If the *moniales* are subject to an independent house of men it seems that only the Abbot and not the superior of the monastic congregation nor the Abbot Primate can dismiss the *moniales*.

As to the rôle of the superioress of nuns in the dismissal of religious in temporary vows, she and her Council must first give a written attestation of the motives for the dismissal. A formal balloting is not necessary for this, but the *votum* of the majority of the Council must be manifested by means of a definite vote. Therefore all that was said about the consent of the Council in the section above applies equally here. This attestation is signed by the superioress and her Council.[68]

[66] Vermeersch-Creusen, *Epitome*, I, p. 598, n. 808; Tabera, "De dimissione religiosorum"—*CpR*, XII (1931), 147.

[67] Goyeneche, "Consultatio"—*CpRM*, XVII (1936), 349, 350.

[68] Schäfer, *De Religiosis*, p. 991, note 2; Tabera, "Consultatio"—*CpR*, XII (1931), 372; Larraona, "Consultatio"—*CpR*, II (1921), 365, note 7; Chelodi, *Ius De Personis*, p. 452, note 1. Confer, however, Coronata (*Institutiones*, I, 868, note 7), who says that the Code by this phrase does not demand a delibera-

Although the testimony given in writing has great weight of authority the local ordinary or the regular superior is not freed from the obligation of prudently investigating the matter and the causes of the dismissal. Even though the sufficiency of the cause is generally proved by sworn testimony, still on account of the gravity of the matter it is the duty of the local ordinary or of the regular superior to examine the attestation. Canon 647, § 2, 3°, demands that the causes or motives of dismissal be really known to the superior who effects the dismissal. But to know them he must examine them. Further, from the general principle, *cuius est pronuntiare, eius est iudicare,* since the pronouncement in the present case turns about the existence and the gravity of the cause it is for the local ordinary to judge the existence and gravity of the causes. Although the testimony has great force, and the presumption is that the superioress and her Council acted prudently and without prejudice, the ordinary or the regular superior is not by this fact dispensed from examining the case himself, especially, if on having been told the causes of dismissal, the subject uses his right to reply to the charges.[69]

E. Congregations of Diocesan Approval

". . . in Congregationibus vero iuris dioecesani, Ordinarius loci in quo religiosa domus sita est, qui tamen iure suo ne utatur Moderatoribus insciis vel iuste dissentientibus. . . ." [70]

tive vote. The *Antistita* sends the vote of her Council whether positive or negative to the local ordinary who then decides. Palombo (*De Dimissione Religiosorum,* pp. 187-188) says that no certain argument can be found in Canon 647, § 1. He suggests an analogy to Canon 646, § 2, which leaves the type of vote to the constitutions. Since the Code says simply *"cum suo consilio"* it leaves the decision as to the type of vote to the constitutions. If they are silent she must hear the Council but she need not follow its counsel under pain of invalidity. Oesterle (*Praelectiones Iuris Canonici,* I, 371) states that since the superioress and her Council are giving merely an attestation, a vote in the strict sense is not required. If one of the Councillors does not wish to attest, the fact should be noted in writing.

[69] Vermeersch, "De dimissione monialis votis temporariis adstrictae"—*Periodica,* XII (1924), (63), sq.

[70] ". . . finally, in diocesan Congregations, this dismissal is to be effected by the Ordinary of the place in which the religious house is situated, but the Ordinary must not exercise this right without the knowledge or against the just opposition of the Superiors."—Canon 647, § 1.

This section of the canon is quite clear and needs little explanation. It concerns diocesan congregations; *i. e.,* Institutes erected by a local ordinary which have not yet obtained the decree of commendation of the Holy See. The canon comprises also those diocesan Institutes the members of which live in common without vows (canons 673, 681). The superior authorized for effecting the dismissal is the ordinary of the place in which the religious house is situated; *i. e.,* the house to which the religious who is to be dismissed is attached. The local ordinary, then, is not the ordinary of the place in which the mother house is situated. In exercising his power, the local ordinary must not act without the knowledge or against the just opposition of the superior; but if he does so the dismissal is valid. The superior of the Institute cannot dismiss but can only ask for the dismissal from the ordinary of the place in which is situated the house to which the subject is attached.[71] If the Institute thinks that it has been harmed by the manner of acting of the ordinary, or if he dismisses a subject without the knowledge or against the just will of the superior, the superior of the Institute can appeal to the Holy See.[72]

F. The Major Superior. The Local Superior.

There is an urgent and extraordinary dismissal committed to the care of the major and local superiors in canons 653 and 668. Canon 653 states:

> *"In casu gravis scandali exterioris vel gravissimi nocumenti communitati imminentis, religiosus statim potest a Superiore maiore cum consensu sui Consilii vel etiam, si periculum sit in mora et tempus non adsit adeundi Superiorem maiorem, a Superiore locali cum consensu sui Consilii et Ordinarii loci, ad saeculum remitti, habitu religioso illico deposito, ita tamen ut res per ipsum Ordinarium aut per Superiorem maiorem, si adsit, Sanctae Sedis iudicio sine mora subiiciatur."* [73]

[71] Schäfer, *De Religiosis,* p. 992; Bastien, *Directoire Canonique,* p. 130; Jombart, "Congregations de droit pontifical"—*RCR,* III (1927), 81; "Le renvoi au cours des voeux temporaires"—*RCR,* V (1929), 196, 197.

[72] Bastien, *Directoire Canonique,* p. 130.

[73] "In the case of grave external scandal or of very serious imminent injury to the community, the religious can be dismissed immediately by the higher Superior with the consent of his Council or even, if there be danger in delay

Canon 668 has the same wording as canon 653 with these exceptions: it does not demand that the major superior have the consent of the local ordinary, nor does it demand that the local superior have the consent of the local ordinary; further, it does not demand that the matter be placed before the Holy See, but simply that the process against the religious be started immediately. Canon 653 applies to religious of perpetual vows in a clerical non-exempt or in a lay Institute; canon 668 applies to a religious in perpetual vows in a clerical exempt Institute. By analogy of law it seems, however, that the prescriptions of these canons apply *mutatis mutandis* to religious in temporary vows. By reason of canon 681 and a similar analogy of law it seems that the same prescriptions apply to religious who are bound by a temporary bond to those Institutes in which the members live in community without vows.[74]

It is to be noted first of all that there is no question here of a true and juridic dismissal; it is only the fact of the temporary and provisory sending of the religious out of the Institute into the world which is better expressed by the original text of the Code *ad saeculum remitti* than by the wording of the authorized translation, *i. e., dismissal.* This sending of the religious into the world is done in order to avoid harm which would otherwise befall the Institute. It is accomplished by means of a definite decree by the proper superior.[75]

Although the rulings of canons 653 and 668 can by analogy of law be applied to religious in temporary vows, they must be applied *mutatis mutandis*. There is no process for the dismissal of religious in temporary vows as there is for the dismissal of religious in perpetual vows. The extraordinary and provisory "dismissal" of which mention is made in canon 653 has for its purpose the removal of the religious from the Institute provisionally until the matter is decided

and time does not admit of recourse to the higher Superior, by the local Superior with the consent of his Council and of the local Ordinary; the religious must immediately put off the religious habit; the Ordinary, however, or the higher Superior, if he be present, must without delay submit the matter to the judgment of the Holy See."—Canon 653.

[74] Coronata, *Institutiones*, I, 877, 5°; Fanfani, *De Iure Religiosorum*, p. 479, Tabera, "De dimissione religiosorum"—*CpR*, XII (1931), 372; Berutti, *De Religiosis*, p. 350.

[75] Chelodi, *Ius De Personis*, p. 456; Coronata, *op. cit.*, I, 887.

by trial. Since no trial is needed for the dismissal of religious in temporary vows, this extraordinary form of dismissal or ejection will have to be used far less often for them; in fact, it will be used only in those cases in which the superior authorized to dismiss as outlined in canon 647, § 1 cannot be reached and in which there is grave danger in any delay of effective action. There is no need previously to obtain the consent of the ordinary or subsequently to refer the matter to the Holy See. The procedure to dismiss juridically is begun at once.[76]

When a fault of the type mentioned in canons 653 or 668 has been committed by a religious in temporary vows, it is grave enough to justify his dismissal. If the superior mentioned in canon 647, §1 can be reached there is verified the ordinary case of dismissal. It is not such a case that is contemplated here, for here there is question of the extraordinary case. In this latter instance the local superior shall refer the matter, if there is time, to the major superior. Thus, in an Institute of pontifical approval (whether of men or of women), the matter shall be sent to the Provincial who shall investigate the case and send the religious into the world (if he sees fit to do so after obtaining the consent of his Council). He shall then send the matter to the Supreme Moderator who will issue the decree of dismissal according to canon 647, if he be convinced of the gravity of the offence. In monasteries of *moniales* the Abbess shall send the matter to the local ordinary or, if the monastery be subject to regulars, to the regular superior whose duty it will be to issue the decree of dismissal whenever it seems to be the proper measure.

In case the Provincial cannot be reached, the local superior or superioress with the consent of the Council can send the religious into the world. In Institutes of pontifical approval the local superior shall then send the whole matter to the Provincial who, with his Councillors shall send the matter to the Superior General for the decree of dismissal. If, in the case of Institutes of nuns (*moniales*), the local ordinary or the regular superior (when they are subject to regulars) cannot be reached and there is danger in any delay of definite action, the superioress of a dependent house with the consent of her Council can send the offender into the world and thereupon

[76] Palombo, *De Dimissione Religiosorum*, pp. 227-229.

remit the matter to the local ordinary or to the regular superior for the decree of dismissal. If, in the case of religious Institutes of diocesan approval, the local ordinary cannot be reached and at the same time there is danger in any delay of definite action, the local superior or the superioress with the consent of her Council can send the offender into the world and thereupon remit the matter to the local ordinary for the decree of dismissal.

G. In Mission Lands

To avoid any difficulty with regard to the respective limits of the power of the religious superior and that of the ecclesiastical superior in mission lands, the Sacred Congregation for the Propagation of the Faith issued an instruction on the matter. The ecclesiastical superior in mission lands cannot act in regard to those things which pertain to the life of the religious within the Institute even though they be under his jurisdiction. The dismissal of a religious is one of the things which pertain to the life of the religious within the Institute. However, with regard to the dismissal which is effected according to the requirements of canon 653, *i. e.*, in the case of grave external scandal, the ecclesiastical superior can act if the religious superior does not, since canon 307, § 2 gives the former the power to remove such a religious from the mission, though it does not give him power to send him out of the Institute into the world in the sense of canon 653. In other words, he has the power, when a fault such as the one in canon 653 or 668 has been committed by a religious, of insisting that the religious be transferred from the territory over which he has jurisdiction.[77]

H. Delegation of This Power

Is the power to effect a dismissal committed to the superiors enumerated above as a *munus* or duty in such a way that it cannot

[77] S. Cong. de Prop. Fide, instr. 8 dec. 1929—*AAS*, XXIII (1930), 111; Larraona, "Annotatio"—*CpR*, XI (1930), 151 and "Animadversio"—*Apollinaris*, III (1930), 217; Vermeersch, "Annotatio"—*Periodica*, XIX (1930), 260-265; Creusen, "Gouvernement des religieuses en mission"—*RCR*, XIV (1938), 28-29; 33-37; "Relations entre les Vicaires ou Préfets Apostoliques et les supérieurs religieuses"—*RCR*, VI (1930), 118-119.

be delegated to others? Or is it a power which they may delegate to others? One opinion, sponsored at first by Goyeneche, maintained that some matters pertain to the superior general so exclusively that they cannot be committed to others. Such are the powers which imply real duties and not mere authority. Such powers are enumerated in canons 646, § 2, 647, § 1, 545, § 1, etc. Goyeneche maintained that the general principle of canon 199, § 1 concerns the power or faculties of a superior and does not touch the case of a *munus* or duty which is specific and entrusted to a certain superior.[78]

A far greater weight of authority supports the other opinion. The duty of dismissing a religious constitutes a part of the proper superior's ecclesiastical *officium*. Canon 197, § 1 states that ordinary power of jurisdiction is that which is annexed by law to an office. The canonical act of dismissal is a power which is annexed in this way to an office. Therefore its exercise implies the use of an ordinary power.

All the rights accorded to major superiors in the Code reflect an ordinary power because they are attached by law to the office.[79] Now, inasfar as all ordinary power of jurisdiction (and, as we have seen, all ordinary dominative power) can be delegated to others in accordance with the expressed principle of canon 199, § 1, as long

[78] Goyeneche, "Consultatio"—*CpR*, XII (1931), 131-133.

[79] Pejska, *Ius Canonicum Religiosorum*, pp. 230-231. There is no difficulty in the application of this principle of ordinary power to the superioress general in Institutes of pontifical approval. The fifth title of the first part of the second book in the Code is inscribed *De potestate ordinaria et delegata*. It does not specify that it treats solely of jurisdictional power and, as is apparent from canon 210 and from the application of canons 209 and 199 to marriage delegation, it has a wider ambit than mere jurisdiction. Kearney (*Principles of Delegation*, Catholic University of America Canon Law Studies, No. 55 [Washington, D. C.: Catholic University of America, 1929], pp. 49, 50), Vermeersch-Creusen (*Epitome*, I, 275) and Maroto (*Institutiones*, I, 824) all agree that this title of the Code is to be extended to dominative power. From the context and arguments of these authors it is seen that *officium* in the case of dismissal is taken in the wide sense, since at least in regard to a woman religious there can be no power of orders or jurisdiction connected with her *officium*. Consequently her *officium* is taken in the wide sense as expressed in canon 145, that is, as a *munus* exercised for a spiritual purpose. The principles of delegation are applied to that *officium* of dominative power.

as provision to the contrary is not made by the law, and inasfar as no such contrary provision is enacted relative to the matter of effecting the dismissal of a religious, this latter power can be delegated even when it simultaneously connotes the performance of a duty. This doctrine is supported by several authors, even by Goyeneche, who in more recent years relinquished the opinion he formerly held.[80] So it seems that the more acceptable doctrine is the one which acknowledges the possibility of delegating the power of dismissing a religious on the part of those superiors to whom the Code has accorded this power.

[80] Goyeneche, *De Religiosis,* p. 212; Tabera, "De dimissione religiosorum" —*CpR,* XII (1931), 148; Coronata, *Institutiones,* I, 869. Hanssen ("De sanctione nullitatis in processu canonico"—*Apollinaris,* XI [1938], 220) says *"neque superior religiosus tenetur per se cognoscere causam."* Though this statement of Hanssen's treats of judicial cases for the dismissal of a perpetually professed religious in a clerical exempt Institute, it seems *a fortiori* that it can be applied to canon 647 which treats of a case less strict in process. Cf. also Augustine, *Commentary,* III, 388 and Battandier, *Guide Canonique,* p. 367. At least one Rule allows this delegation: *Constitutiones Piae Societatis Missionum* (Ratisbonae: Pustet), p. 86.

CHAPTER III

CAUSES SUFFICIENT FOR DISMISSAL

The determination of what constitutes a sufficient cause for the dismissal of religious in temporary vows is no easier after the Code than before. In 1893 the Holy See answered that it should not be asked what is a just and reasonable cause in this matter, since this was a question left to the judgment and conscience of the superiors.[1] Just as before the Code the Holy See did not wish to determine the causes for dismissal, so even now it refuses to determine them further than this: namely, that they be grave, certain, external, and existing either in relation to the Institute or on the part of the religious. On the part of the religious only one cause is specified, namely the lack of religious spirit which constitutes an occasion of scandal to others. Negatively the Code provides that ill health which was not deceitfully hidden or dissimulated at the time of profession cannot be accepted as a cause for dismissal.[2] Beyond this the Code does not go. An attempt will be made through an inspection of the opinions of authors and of the prescriptions of constitutions approved by the Holy See to elaborate on the causes for dismissal. The plan to be followed will be:

I. Causes on the part of the Religious:
  - A. Causes in General.
  - B. Causes in Particular.
    1. Negative Causes (which are surely not sufficient for the act of dismissal).
       - a. Ill Health: mental or physical.
       - b. Other Negative Causes:
         - (1) Cases Reserved to the Holy Office.
         - (2) Causes Which Effect a Dismissal by Their Very Existence.

[1] S. C. Ep. et Reg., resp. 15, Sept. 1873. The response is found embodied in another response of the same Congregation May 13, 1904—*Fontes,* n. 2048.

[2] Goyeneche, "Consultatio"—*CpR,* XIV (1933) 183, 184.

(3) Mutual consent—Consent of Superior and His Council Only.
(4) Failure to Receive Holy Communion Daily.
(5) Other Causes.

2. Positive Causes:
   a. In the Moral Order:
      (1) Absence of the Religious Spirit—Scandal—Warning.
      (2) Delicts and Graver Causes:
         (a) Delicts.
         (b) Fugitives and Quasi-Apostates.
         (c) Causes Sufficient to Dismiss a Religious in Perpetual Vows.
         (d) Extraordinary Causes of Canons 653 and 668.
   b. In the Physical Order.
   c. In the Intellectual Order.
   d. Causes Sufficient for Dismissal from a Seminary.

II. Causes in Relation to the Institute.

I. Causes on the part of the Religious.

A. Causes in General

In the matter of dismissal the Superior is faced with a very difficult duty. On the one hand he is charged with the welfare of the Institute. He must see that no unworthy member is admitted, whether this unworthiness be the result of the inculpable lack of the qualities required by the Institute, or the result of the lack of the required standards in the moral order. The welfare of the Institute often rests on his decision, for, as St. Paul says, "Expel the wicked man from your midst." [3] The reason is clear: one diseased and infected sheep may imperil and compromise the welfare of the entire flock.[4] The individual good of the religious cannot be neglected, still

[3] I Cor., V, 13.

[4] I Cor., VII, 15; Butler, *Sancti Benedicti Regula Monasteriorum*, Caput XXVIII, pp. 62-64.

the common good of the Institute or of the community must prevail. The superior, then, must avoid false pity, counterfeit charity and excessive kindness, since pity, charity and kindness of that misdirected sort can occasion the ruin of the spirit of the Institute, and can eventually place the other religious in spiritual danger. Experience has manifested this truth day by day.[5] The prosperity of the Institute depends less upon the number of its members than upon their fervor and regularity. The retention of unworthy subjects damages the interior peace of the Institute. It often discredits and even nullifies the work and good name of the Institute. Further, the toleration of such unworthy members in the Institute can become a source of troublesome disgust for the other members, or, what is even worse, induce them to the same laxity and unworthiness. Finally, the bad example of the unworthy members discourages and estranges those who would enter the Institute.[6] It is false pity, too, to the individual delinquent. Since he is not suited for the religious life in this particular Institute, he can never really be happy there. It is counterfeit charity and dissimulated cruelty to keep him there because of false and misdirected kindness.

On the other hand, the superior has very grave obligations in relation to his subject. By profession the subject has entered into a contract with the Institute, so that the superior who acts for the Institute cannot dismiss him without a grave reason. He must have moral certainty regarding the existence of this reason; that is, an assurance which is sufficient to exclude all prudent fear that he is unjustly expelling the subject from a state which he possesses legitimately. The superior must in this case of dismissal, more than in any other, avoid extreme rigor on the one hand and false pity and kindness on the other. He is often aided by his Rule or Constitutions which frequently list faults according to their gravity and indicate the corresponding penalties for such faults.[7] The superior should use

[5] Bastien, *Directoire Canonique*, p. 131, note (1).

[6] *Manual of the Clerics of St. Viator* (Jette-Saint-Pierre, Belgium, 1926), p. 147.

[7] It is to be noted that in several rules the list of penalties includes such severe penances as the loss of vote, removal from and disability for office, and even excommunication, suspension or interdict by means of special precept as the punishments to be imposed prior to the ultimate penalty of dismissal from

every means of correction and every kindness possible to bring the delinquent back to his duty and to the observance of the obligations he has taken on himself by his vows. But if his good intentions and efforts should fail to produce an emendation, it would still be more prudent to settle the matter amicably and have the religious ask for a dispensation. This will avoid great inconveniences to the Institute and the subject. If the religious refuses to ask for a dispensation, then the superior must act prudently, sincerely and very kindly in the dismissal, so that the subject will recognize that he was at fault. For if the superior's conduct is not blameless, the religious will more easily be inclined to have recourse against his dismissal to the Holy See.[8]

The Code says that the cause for dismissal must be grave. Note that it places the phrase *causae graves* in the plural number. That does not mean that for each dismissal there must be several causes. One cause, grave enough, may suffice. The cumulation of several causes, *e. g.*, lack of religious spirit and ineptitude for studies, may constitute a sufficient motive for dismissal, although each one of them standing alone without the other would not be a sufficient cause. In general, then, it can be said that the cause must be grave, *i. e.*, that the Institute will suffer a notable harm or grave inconvenience in the keeping of this religious. The grave cause includes, besides the causes resulting from delinquences, the lack of the qualities or aptitude necessary to fulfill the duties common to all religious or special to the members of this Institute since the Institute has a right to expect these from its subjects.[9] When canon 647, § 2, 1° states that the causes for the dismissal of a religious in temporary vows must be

the order according to the norms of the law. Note, however, that the Rules here consulted are for orders, and that these penalties refer to all the members including those in solemn perpetual, as well as those who are in simple temporary vows, so that it cannot be said that for religious of temporary vows dismissal cannot precede such severe penalties. It does, however, show the correct estimate of the gravity of dismissal. Cf. *The Rules and General Constitutions of the Friars Minor*, nn. 356-358, pp. 76, 77; *Constitutiones Ordinis Fratrum Beatissimae Virginis de Monte Carmelo*, art. 279, 280, pp. 102, 103.

[8] Palombo, *De Dimissione Religiosorum*, p. 5; Michelletti, *Jus Pianum* (Augustae Taurnorum, 1914), p. 587.

[9] Canon 538.

grave, what does it mean and in what manner are these causes different from those which in canon 637 are called *just* and *reasonable?* In selecting words to describe the causes which are necessary for the giving of dispensations the Code uses a wide variety of words: *just, reasonable, special, equitable, public, canonical, just and reasonable, just and grave, just and canonical, just and necessary, grave, grave and reasonable, grave and urgent, most grave, most grave and reasonable,* etc. Such a variety of phraseology cannot but indicate that the legislator, keeping in mind both the quality of the cause and the gravity of the law which is dispensed, has devised a scale of graduated causes.[10] Each time these words are found in the Code, therefore, attention must first be paid to their intrinsic meaning and secondly to their relation to the law under consideration.

According to some authors, under the case considered in canon 637, there no longer exists any contract between the Institute and the religious; at the end of three years the contract has expired and the religious is free to leave. He has not bound himself to stay longer nor has the Institute contracted to accept him at the end of this period. The Institute fails solely against charity and obedience to ecclesiastical law, but not against justice because there is no contract.[11]

It seems however that if the whole period of temporary profession is considered there are really two contracts involved, one with a resolutive and one with a suspensive condition. Dismissal of a religious without the cause required by canon 647 would be effected in contravention to a contract with a resolutive condition. Dismissal without the cause required by canon 637 would violate a contract with a suspensive condition.

10 Michiels, *Normae Generales Juris Canonici* (2 vols., Lublin, Universitas Catholica, 1929), II, 506; *L'Ami du Clergé,* XLV (1928), 121; O'Mara, *Canonical Causes for Matrimonial Dispensations,* The Catholic University of America Canon Law Studies, n. 96 (Washington D. C.: Catholic University of America, 1935), pp. 46-53.

11 Blat, *De Religiosis,* pp. 545, 546; Beste, *op. cit.,* p. 430; Passerini, *De Hominum Statibus* (Lucae, 1739), q. CLXXXIX, Inspectio VII, nn. 231-236, q. 16; Suarez, *Operis De Religione,* Pars II, *De Statu Perfectionis et Religionis,* Tr. VII, Lib. V, Cap. 11, nn. 4-5; Goyeneche, *De Religiosis,* p. 193; "Consultatio"—*CpR,* V (1924), 212-214. In the last mentioned article, Goyeneche calls this opinion "common."

The contract with a resolutive condition expires when it has run its full term. But during the time it endures the Institute fails in justice if it dismisses a subject without sufficient reason. All the authors agree on this because the contract was entered upon with the resolutive condition: "I take my vows to last . . . years, unless some grave cause intervenes."

One should keep in mind the doctrine on the condition by which temporary vows place one in the religious *state;* namely, that the novice shall have the intention, at least tacit and indefinite, of renewing his temporary vows or of taking perpetual vows at their expiration. The intention should not be made absolutely but rather with the condition: "if no grave cause intervenes." The Institute must be of the same mind; namely, it must intend to admit the religious to a renewal of temporary profession or to perpetual profession "if no grace cause intervenes." A profession made knowingly and willingly with the intention of not renewing the vows or of not making perpetual profession, although it be valid, always remains illicit. The religious cannot make it without sin, nor can the superior without sin admit one who has not the intention of renewing his vows or of proceeding to perpetual profession.[12] This is an intention totally different on the part of both the religious and the Institute from the intention on the part of the religious not to ask for a dispensation *during* the period of temporary vows, and on the part of the Institute not to dismiss the religious *during* the period of temporary vows. The whole doctrine on the stability of the religious state demands that the intention to renew temporary vows or to take perpetual vows be made at least tacitly. This intention in turn gives rise to a contract with a suspensive condition just as the former intention gave rise to a contract with a resolutive condition. The contract with the suspensive condition, although it be entered upon at the time of first profession, begins to bind only at the end of the period of vows. It would be worded as stated above: "I intend to take perpetual profession (or renew my temporary vows) unless some grave cause intervenes," and on the part of the Institute: "he will be admitted to perpetual profession (or to a renewal of the temporary profession) unless some grave cause intervenes." The refusal to admit one to

[12] Cf. *supra,* pp. 70-72.

renewal of temporary vows or to perpetual profession without a sufficient cause is a violation of a contract and an injustice.[13]

There is, it is true, a gradation in the gravity of the causes which justify a dismissal in these two cases. But this difference is not due, as has been said, to the existence of a contract in one case and its absence in another. The difference lies in this that the dismissal before the expiration of the vows includes an implicit dispensation from the vows, while exclusion of the religious from profession at the end of his period of temporary profession does not. A graver cause is needed when a dispensation from the vows is involved.

In both the cases considered, the gravity of the cause must be apparent and based on the common good of the Institute. It must be of such weight as to counterbalance the right of the subject to remain in the Institute.

The causes must be *external; i. e.,* in some way public, so that they can be known by witnesses. There are several reasons for this. As was seen, canon 647 in some cases demands the consent of the Councillors. They cannot consent unless they have knowledge of the professed religious and of the causes for dismissal which can be known only by external means; *i. e.,* by personal observation or by the report of witnesses. Moreover, one of these causes, namely, the defect of the religious spirit, is qualified by the phrase "which is a cause of scandal to others." It cannot become a cause of scandal except through knowledge which is derived from the external action of the delinquent. The remedy of recourse which by law is made available for the subject also shows the necessity of external causes; otherwise proof of the lack of the gravity of the causes is not possible.[14] Further, the causes must be certain; *i. e.,* the superior who dismisses the religious must have moral certainty as to the existence and gravity of the causes. No formal trial is necessary. It is enough

[13] A writer in *Il Monitore Ecclesiastico* states that a religious in temporary vows has an acquired right to remain in the Institute saving, of course, the prescriptions of canons 637 and 647—"Questioni"—*Il Monitore Ecclesiastico,* Series IV, V (1923), 57-58.

[14] Tabera, "De dimissione religiosorum"—*CpR,* XII (1931), 371; Jombart, "De dimissione ex mutuo consensu"—*Periodica,* XII (1924), (58)-(60); "Le renvoi au cours des voeux temporaires"—*RCR,* V (1929), 197; Schäfer, *De Religiosis,* pp. 993, 997.

that the superior attain certainty in the ordinary way; *i. e.,* from his own knowledge or from the credible attestation of others.[15]

B. Causes in Particular

In the treatment of the causes in particular those which are mentioned in the Code will first be considered, then those assigned by the authors, and finally those listed in the various Rules and Constitutions which were available to the writer. Even though the causes listed in the Rules and Constitutions have received the approval of the Holy See in their nature as reasons for dismissal, still it is true that they are particular law which is binding only upon the members of the respective Institutes. They have, however, the approval of the Holy See in this that they have been authoritatively deemed sufficient as reasons which will enable the superior to proceed with a clear conscience when he dismisses any religious for the causes listed in the Constitutions. The approval of the Rule is not a general law but it is an approval of an individual application or interpretation of the general law. It should not be feared that a cause for dismissal as approved for an Institute in which vows are not taken would not be grave enough for the dismissal of a member of an Institute who is bound by vows. The contract between the individual and the Institute is just as strong in both cases, and the gravity of the cause must be the same.

1. Negative Causes (which are surely not sufficient for the act of dismissal)

a. Ill Health: mental or physical

> ". . . non vero infirma valetudo, nisi certo constet eam ante professionem fuisse dolose reticitam aut dissumulatam;" [16]

Ill health may be either mental or physical, but in either case there can be no cause for dismissal in consequence of it, unless it can be proved with certainty that the condition of ill health was

[15] Schäfer, *op. cit.,* p. 993; Tabera, *art. cit.,* p. 373.

[16] ". . . ill-health is not a sufficient motive for dismissal unless it is proved with certainty that it has been fraudently hidden or dissimulated before profession;"—Canon 647, § 2, 2°.

fraudulently hidden or dissimulated before profession. In the case of complete mental illness; *i. e.*, of perpetual insanity, there was need of an authoritative decision. If a subject became perpetually insane during the period of temporary vows, he could not make perpetual profession or renew his temporary vows at the end of that period, since he was incapable of a human act. Canon 575 states that at the end of that period he must either make perpetual profession, whether solemn or simple, or renew his temporary vows, or return to the world. Thus, according to the strict sense of the law, the subject who became insane had to return to the world because he was incapable of making a profession of vows. This manner of acting did not violate the rule of canon 637, since the Institute was not excluding him. But the strict following of the letter of the law would have worked great harm to the religious in this case. Even though the Sacred Congregation had never allowed dismissal for such a reason,[17] an interpretation of the law was necessary in order to cover such a case. Strictly taken, this problem concerns only canon 637. But it was equally applicable to canon 647, for if the religious could not be sent away for this cause when his vows expired, then *a fortiori* he could not be sent away while the vows still bound him.

This difficulty was solved by an answer to a doubt sent to the Sacred Congregation of Religious:

> Since it sometimes happens that a religious man or woman, during the three years of vows which, according to c. 574, must precede every perpetual or solemn profession, becomes insane, so that at the end of the three years, being still out of his mind, he cannot be admitted to the profession since he is incapable of such an act, the question has been raised what is to be done in such a case.
>
> As the matter is of some practical importance, the Sacred Congregation, after taking the counsel of several consultors, presented the following question for decision to the Eminent Fathers:
>
> Questions. I. Whether one who is professed of the simple vows in an Order or Congregation, and who during the three years loses his mind, even incurably according to the judgment of physicians, can at the end of three years be sent back to his relatives or into the world, or whether he must be kept in the religious institute. And if he must be kept:

[17] Nervegna, *De Jure Practico Regularium,* pp. 155-157.

II. What is the juridical condition of such a religious, and what are the obligations of a religious institute in the matter?

The S. C. Rel. in full session, on the 28 Nov., 1924, after mature consideration, replied:

Reply. I. In the negative to the first part; in the affirmative to the second.

II. The religious in question belongs to the religious institute in the state in which he was when he lost his mind, and the institute has the same obligation toward him that it had at that time.

Approved by His Holiness, Pius XI, in the audience of 30 Nov., 1924.[18]

First of all, it is to be noted that the *dubium* refers to a sickness of the mind which in the opinion of the physician takes away the use of reason totally, whether this be permanent (incurable) or temporary (curable). All other aberrations and similar diseases are indeed sicknesses, but they are not included in the case in question. It is also to be noted that this insanity must have come on after temporary profession. If it can be proved that the person was afflicted before profession, then the profession was invalid, for then the person was not *sui compos* or capable of a human act. The Institute is not bound in justice by any obligation to this person, nor need it recognize him as a member of the Institute. A further necessary postulate is that this cause was not deliberately hidden or concealed either by the person himself or by his parents or guardians. This ill health is of a special kind. In all other cases the sick person can renounce his right and return to the world but not so in the case of the insane who must be presumed not to consent in any way to being sent into the world. In other words, insanity is a destruction within the subject of his moral capacity to act juridically. However, when he sustains this loss of capacity his juridic condition should not change; it should remain what it was when he lost his capacity to act juridically. This is the basis underlying the answer to the doubt: the religious lives physically and bears inherently in himself that juridic status which he had at the moment he lost his capacity to act juridically.[19]

[18] Bouscaren, *The Canon Law Digest* (2 vols. and Supplement, 1941, Milwaukee: Bruce Publishing Co., 1934-1941), I, 309-310, canon 574. The Latin text: S. C. de Relig., dubium 5 febr. 1925—*AAS*, XVII (1925), 107.

[19] Maroto, "Annotationes"—*CpR*, VI (1925), 170-179; "Annotazioni"—

He remains, then, in the same juridic status in which he was when he became insane. Does this mean that his vows are suspended at that moment and begin to run again at the moment when he regains sanity? Or does the time of his vows keep running, so that even after the time they would ordinarily have elapsed, he still retains the status of a religious in temporary vows? It seems that in the interim his vows are suspended, especially from the reading of the wording of the answer to the second *dubium*: "the religious belongs to the institute in the state in which he was when he lost his mind." From this it seems that the vows are suspended; being unable to act juridically he remains in the state in which he was. If he recovers and becomes juridically capable to act again, his vows continue from the point at which their operativeness was suspended. However, when the whole response is considered, and especially the first *dubium, i. e., whether at the end of three years* he may be sent into the world, etc., it seems that the negative answer rather presupposed that the vows were not suspended. It is not absurd to say that one can be a member of an Institute and still not be bound by his vows. There is a parallel case, *e. g.*, those bound to military service take their vows "until I am called etc." At the moment of their call to service the vows cease but in consequence of their profession they are still members of the Institute. The solution of this question is not clear, and practically it is not of much moment, for even if the vows are suspended, who can assign definitely the first moment of insanity at which the vows are suspended, or the first moment of cure at which they begin to bind? The Sacred Congregation seemed not to be concerned about this as much as the practical solution. The religious, even after the three years in which his vows would normally have expired, was to be kept in the Institute as a member of it and the Institute was obligated to him by the same duties which it had when he was *sui compos* and in vows. It seems to the writer that the better opinion is the one which holds that the vows do run and do expire even though the religious cannot act juridically.[20]

Il Monitore Ecclesiastico, 4th series, VII (1925), 73-75 (hereafter cited *Il Monitore*).

[20] Creusen, "Profés des voeux temporaires atteinte d'alienation mental"—

It may happen that a religious becomes violently insane, or that in the judgment of the physician proper care cannot be given him in the religious house. The Institute is not bound to keep him in the house in this case, but can send him to a home or to an asylum. He can even be sent to his own home if his family freely asks or accepts the care of him. Even then he still remains a member of the Institute and the expenses are to be borne by the Institute unless his family freely takes this financial burden on itself. If it is foreseen that he will be out of his religious house for more than six months, permission must be had from the Holy See unless the home or asylum is a part of a house of his own Institute.[21]

If the religious recovers his sanity he is to be admitted to a renewal of his temporary vows or to perpetual profession, unless there is some obstacle in the way. He has no obligation of making his novitiate again for such an obligation presupposes a dismissal or voluntary egress from the religious Institute. Canon 577, § 1, which demands the taking of perpetual vows or the renewal of temporary vows when the period of temporary vows has expired, has indeed been violated, but only materially so because circumstances rendered the renewal of the vows impossible. There should be no delay in the renewal of his vows when the religious is cured. Though there is no obligation in law to force the superior to use the power given him by canon 574, § 2 for prolonging the period of temporary vows, still it would be better if he did so. The law has been materially fulfilled because three years have been spent in temporary vows, but its purpose, a probation for three years, has not been fulfilled. The superior can prolong the period by making the subject renew his temporary vows for as long a period as seems necessary for a trial, but not longer than three years.[22]

Nouvelle Revue Théologique, LII (1925), 332 (henceforth cited *NRT*); Maroto, *art. cit.* 178, 179; Coronata, *Institutiones,* I, 854; Nevin, "How to deal with a temporarily professed sister who recovers from insanity"—*ACR,* XI (1934), 340-343. Goyeneche ("Consultatio"—*CpR,* XI [1930], 440, 441) seems to presuppose the vows were not suspended after the religious becomes insane.

[21] Canon 606, § 2; Berutti, *De Religiosis,* p. 271; Bastien, *Directoire Canonique,* p. 172; Vermeersch-Creusen, *Epitome,* I, 589.

[22] Maroto, *art. cit.*—*CpR,* VI (1925), 176; Goyeneche, "Consultatio"—*CpR,* XI (1930), 440, 441; Nevin, "How to deal with a temporarily professed sister who recovers from insanity"—*ACR,* XI (1934), 340-343.

Often, because of the insanity from which he has recovered, the religious has been rendered unfit or unequal to the task of sustaining the burdens of religious life, or his condition may even be such that, in the opinion of the physicians, he will be in great danger of relapsing into insanity in consequence of the strict mode of life led in the Institute. Since this danger will be more easily avoided if he should lead the life of a lay person in the midst of his family (especially if his cure was due greatly to the influence of the less strenuous and more nerve-relaxing life in his own home), he should generally be advised, for his own good, to leave the Institute willingly. Such advice depends much on the mental and physical condition of the individual as well as on the conditions he will encounter in the world. The less likely it becomes that any advantage is to be derived from his life in the world, the less pressing becomes the necessity on the part of the Institute to advise him freely to return to the world.[23]

Maroto states that not all the cases of partial insanity are included in the response; *i. e.*, those mental diseases which are grave, sometimes impel men to insane acts, and so disturb the mind that the light of reason is truly extinguished but only for certain periods of time. Not all such diseases were included because from their symptoms a skilled physician can gather that a person is only temporarily demented. Such a religious can, in the periods in which he is sane, freely ask for a dispensation, or freely leave if the period of his vows has expired. He may even be advised to do so by appropriate arguments showing that he is not fit to bear the burdens of the religious life. If he wishes to remain, however, he cannot solely because of his mental illness be dismissed or denied the right to a renewal of temporary or to eventual perpetual profession.[24]

Cases of temporary or partial insanity are not always easily solved. A medical question is involved and expert physicians should be consulted; on their decision will rest the outcome of the case. If

[23] Maroto, *art. cit.—CpR,* VI (1925), 177; "Annotazioni"—*Il Monitore,* Series IV, VII (1925), 75; Creusen, *art. cit. NRT,* LII (1925), 333.

[24] Maroto, *art. cit. CpR,* VI (1925), 171, note 1; G. Lardone, "Proroga della professione religiosa"—*Perfice Munus,* VII (1932), 275.

they are of the opinion that the affliction is a real mental illness, so that the religious will never recover though he be permitted to live outside the Institute, or even in his own home, it seems that he cannot be dismissed. If, however, the experts state that the mental quirks and vagaries are due rather to a character and temperament which cannot stand the strain of a rigid daily schedule of duties and religious exercises in a religious community or, for that matter, in any type of school, academy, etc. where the day is marked out with clocklike precision and does not allow for much freedom, then the ailment cannot be called a sickness in the sense of canons 647 and 637. It is comparable rather to a levity of spirit than to a neurasthenia. It is "cured" by the sole fact of departure from the Institute and not by any medical means. This "cure" shows plainly that the subject was not fit for the religious life in view either of his mental or nervous state, or of a constant condition of his temperamental or physical constitution, or of a latent defect brought to the fore only in certain conditions. This ineptitude is not always apparent in the novitiate. If it is manifested only in the additional period of probation provided by the period of the temporary vows, the religious can be dismissed for it is not a sickness or pathological condition.

In either case the Institute could give him permission to live outside the house, and if his parents wish it, at home. If the trial period (not to last more than six months according to canon 606, §2, without the permission of the Holy See) bears out the physican's report that it is a real illness or sickness, he may not be dismissed. If he is "cured," *i. e.,* if the removal of the circumstances which affect his temperament show that in their absence, he is completely normal, he may be dismissed, since he was not really insane or sick, but merely unfit for the religious state. He should be persuaded, if possible, to ask for a dispensation by arguments showing him that he has no religious vocation inasmuch as he is not capable of bearing the burdens of the religious life. If, however, the physician's report is not certain, *i. e.,* if the report does not state that there certainly is no mental illness, the religious cannot be dismissed. The religious has a right to remain in the Institute and until it is proved certainly that he is not sick and further that he is unfit for the religious life, he cannot be dismissed.[25]

Prior to the Code the Sacred Congregation of Religious decided the case of a religious whose nerves were so weakened from the study necessary for his state that in the judgment of the physicians there was grave danger that if he persevered in his studies he would become insane. In the decision, the Sacred Congregation decided that this ineptitude for study was not mere ineptitude but was in effect a true and real sickness and, as a result, the religious could not be dismissed.[26] The same reasoning holds in the present law, for canon 647, § 2, 2° states that "ill health is not a sufficient cause for dismissal." Inasmuch as his neurasthenia renders him incapable of acquiring the knowledge necessary to fulfill his clerical duties, the superiors can propose to him and even impose on him a transfer from the clerical to the lay class of the Institute. In fact, since grave illness will come upon him as a result of the continuance of his studies, the superior is bound in charity to keep him from study. The religious may make this transfer or, if it seems too hard for him, he may leave when his vows expire, or he may seek a dispensation immediately from the Holy See. If he transfers he has the obligation of making a year's novitiate, for canon 558 rules that a novitiate made for one class of religious life does not avail for another. He is not bound after this novitiate year to live another full three years in that class before his perpetual vows; the time spent in the clerical class will count, and he needs only to fill in the remaining time of the full three-year period.[27]

[25] Canon 538; Jombart, "Le renvoi au cours des voeux temporaires"—*RCR*, V (1929), 200; "Maladie de la volunté"—*RCR*, VII (1931), 189-191.

[26] S. C. Ep. et Reg., *Ordinis S. Benedicti*, 3 maii 1904—*ASS*, XXXVII (1904-1905), 445-450; see especially the annotation on pp. 448-450.

[27] Goyeneche, "Consultatio" *CpR*, III (1922), 11, 15, 82-84; V (1924), 163; VI (1925), 90; *CpRM*, XVII (1936), 80; XIX (1938), 13; Schäfer, *De Religiosis*, p. 942. It would seem at first sight that a neurasthenic condition could be considered as an ineptitude for study and thus constitute a cause for dismissal. But in order to be a true cause for dismissal this ineptitude for study, as will be seen, must arise not from illness but from intellectual slowness or incapacity, a totally different thing. The neurasthenia developing from application to study cannot be considered the equivalent of light-mindedness which results in a frequent infringement of the rules and a repeated disturbance of

Just as it cannot permit for a reason of health that a religious be dismissed, so the Institute cannot drive him out equivalently by exercising over him a moral pressure which, practically, will constrain him to leave. Such a procedure is manifestly unjust. One cannot tell a religious that he has a duty to leave when the Code expressly gives him the right to remain. This does not mean the kind and charitable presentation to him by the Superior of the difficulties which he will encounter by remaining in the Institute in his present condition. This is allowed and may be demanded by charity if the subject has not considered the question from all angles in making his judgment. What is forbidden is the moral pressure constraining him to leave.[28]

Physical, like mental, ill health is not a sufficient cause for dismissal. If a novice openly reveals a physical ailment and is accepted notwithstanding, that ill health cannot be made a cause for his dismissal. Such a candidate should not be admitted to profession, since canon 538 demands fitness to bear the burdens of the religious life as a condition for entrance to an Institute. It is licit for the superior to admit him only if it is sure that this ailment will not get worse or hinder the work of the religious in the future. In doubt the candidate should not be accepted. At most he can be accepted on the condition that the Institute may send him away at the end of or during the time of his temporary vows, but only if the subject freely agrees to this condition.[29] Even if the sickness which comes on him

the good order and the peace of the community. The latter is a defect of character, an inability to be serious-minded, whereas the former is a sickness. It is true that both are "cured" by a return to the world. But neurasthenia can also be cured by a cessation of the mental effort needed in study. Hence it does not demand a return to the world for its cure and there are many other useful occupations in the Institute which the afflicted religious can fulfill. On the other hand the light-mindedness is only brought to the fore more vividly in the rather difficult routine of regular order and spiritual exercises; it is not cured by a return to the world, only the occasion of its manifestation is removed.

[28] Jombart, "Conseil de quitter l'institut"—*RCR,* XI (1935), 197-199; Lardone, "Proroga della professione religiosa"—*Perfice Munus,* VII (1932), 275.

[29] Berutti, *De Religiosis,* p. 325. Against this opinion are: Coronata, *Institutiones,* I, 854, note 3; Palombo, *De Dimissione Religiosorum,* p. 202; Creusen, *Religious Men and Women in the Code* (First translation by Edward F.

during the period of his temporary vows renders impossible the fulfillment of a fourth vow demanded by the rule; *e. g.*, the vow to observe the lenten fare, he may make perpetual profession with the understood phrase "when I am able," since the rule itself exempts the religious when they are sick.[30]

b. Other Negative Causes

(1) Cases Reserved to the Holy Office

Canon 501, § 2, strictly forbids all Superiors to interfere in causes pertaining to the Holy Office. While these causes may be and often are sufficient for dismissal, they are placed under negative causes because, as far as the superior is concerned these causes are not sufficient for him to effect a dismissal. He may not interfere in the least, for the case is taken from his hands when the Holy Office or its delegate has taken direct cognizance of it. What are these causes and what is to be the superior's conduct toward the delinquent?

The cases reserved to the Holy Office are especially those which involve matters of faith and morals, whether in writing or in preaching together with the crimes of heresy, apostasy, schism and all other

Garesché. Third English edition, revised and edited to conform with the fifth French edition, by Adam Ellis, Milwaukee: Bruce, 1940), p. 252; Jombart, "La sortie de religion a l'expiration des voeux temporaires"—*RCR*, V (1929), 163. The argument adduced by these authors is that such a profession would be against the mind of the Code, because the time for experiment is the time of the novitiate. Against this it can be said that, as was seen in the first chapter (p. 70), the time of temporary vows was instituted expressly as a time of further trial. In the matter of health it cannot always be judged in the novitiate whether the health of the novice will be able to stand up under the hardships of the life led under a particular religious rule. Possibly the only fair trial of a candidate whose health gives rise to such a doubt could be found in an experiment in which the actual work of the Institute is to be performed by one while he is under vows. A profession made with the condition of dismissal if his health failed to stand up under the rigors of the religious life would in the circumstances not be against the mind of the Code, for the temporary period of vows is one of further probation. Neither would it fail against justice inasmuch as it is presupposed that the novice has freely agreed to abide by the stipulated arrangement.

30 Goyeneche, "Consultatio"—*CpR*, XII (1931), 361-364.

acts which generate a suspicion of or connection with heresy.[31] Also reserved to the Holy Office is the case of religious who join the Masons or other such societies; these are to be denounced to the Holy Office.[32] Specially reserved to the Holy Office are the extreme cases of abuse of the sacraments.[33] Other cases reserved to the Holy Office are the violation of the oath against Modernism [34] and the violation of the secret of the Holy Office, especially regarding knowledge obtained in regard to persons being promoted to or considered for promotion to the Episcopacy.[35]

In all these matters the religious superior is totally incompetent; the case is taken out of the superior's hands whether he be a major or even a supreme superior. He may not interfere on his own authority, but only as a delegate of the Holy Office; to do otherwise would be to act invalidly.[36] The decree of the Holy Office of 1901 which

[31] Canon 1325, § 2: apostasy, heresy and schism. Acts which generate a suspicion of heresy: canon 2316, *communicatio in sacris*; canon 2320, the tossing about or throwing away of consecrated Hosts, the disposing or retaining of Them for a bad purpose; canon 2332, the appealing from the reigning Pope to a General Council; canon 2340, § 1, the obdurate persevering in a state of excommunication for a year; canon 2371, the simoniacal ministration or reception of the sacraments. Acts connected with heresy: canon 2317, pertinaciously defending a doctrine condemned by the Holy See or a General Council (even though it is not formally condemned); canon 2318, the editing of books of apostates, heretics or schismatics which defend apostasy, heresy or schism, and the defending or the reading, knowingly and without permission, or the retaining of these books or of books *nominatim* prohibited by Apostolic Letter; canon 2325, grave delicts of superstition, sorcery, sacrilege, etc.

[32] Canon 2336, § 2.

[33] These are mentioned in canons 904 and 2367: the crime of solicitation; canons 889, 890, 2369: the direct as well as the serious indirect violation of the seal of confession; and canon 2322: the simulation of the saying of Mass or of the hearing of confessions by one who is not a priest.

[34] Pius X, motu propr. *Sacrorum Antistitum,* 1 sept. 1910—*AAS,* II (1910), 669.

[35] S. C. Consist., dubium, 1 maii 1917—*AAS,* IX (1917), 232; Lega, Michael Cardinalis, *Praelectiones in Textum Iuris Canonici,* Liber II, Vol. IV, *De Iudiciis Ecclesiasticis in Genere et in Specie De Delicitis et Poenis Praemisso Tractatu* (Romae: 1901), pp. 533-545; 549 sq.; Lega, M. Card.—Bartoccetti, V, *Commentarius in Iudicia Ecclesiastica Iuxta Codicem Iuris Canonici* (3 vols., Romae: Anonima Libraria Cattolica Italiana, 1938-1941), I, pp. 28-31.

[36] Canons 247, § 1; 1555, § 1. All other tribunals besides the Holy Office,

is still in force [87] directs that if any religious knows that any of his subjects, confrères, or even superiors is guilty of or suspect of any of these crimes (especially those which regard the abuse of the sacrament of penance), he is strictly bound without communicating the matter to anybody else, getting nobody's permission, and passing over all fraternal correction or admonitions to denounce him immediately to the Holy Office or to the local Ordinary. The purpose of the secrecy is twofold: to safeguard the accused if the suspicion is unfounded and, secondly, to prevent the spread of the knowledge of such a crime if it is true, lest the common good be harmed and the Institute defamed.

Coronata notes that these matters must be sent by the superiors and chapters to the Holy Office. But, he warns, they should not be sent immediately if there is only a suspicion of the delict. In the case of suspicion, the superior should proceed with great prudence and charity to an investigation of the matter. If he finds out that it is a matter reserved to the Holy Office, he then reports it to the Holy Office directly or through the medium of the local Ordinary.[88] A subject who has merely a suspicion should act in the same way; *i. e.*, he should investigate and until he is sure in his mind that it is a fault reserved to the Holy Office, he should use the rules of fraternal correction. Once he is sure that it is a case reserved to the Holy Office, then he must report it.

Once this has been done, the Holy Office alone is competent. It corrects and punishes the delinquent with just rigor. The superior can correct and punish only if he is made a delegate by that Congregation. For this purpose the Sacred Congregation of Religious ruled that the crime of solicitation be expunged from a Rule as a cause of dismissal.[89] The superior is not forbidden, indeed, to do

or the inferior tribunals delegated by it or by the law, are incapable of acting in matters reserved to the Holy Office; having no competence, their acts are null. Ried-Brig, *Manuale Practicum Juris Disciplinaris et Criminalis Regularium ad usum Ff. Minorum Capuccinorum* (Romae: 1902), pp. 10, 165, 166.

[87] S. C. S. Off., decr. *In congregatione*, 15 maii 1901—*ASS,* XXXIV (1901-1902), 383.

[88] Coronata, *Institutiones,* I, 648; Augustine, *Commentary,* III, 111.

[89] S. C. de Relig., 11 iun. 1911—*apud* Larraona, "Commentarium Codicis—Canon 501"—*CpR,* VII (1926), 96, note (188).

what he can without using his jurisdictional power; in fact, he can do all that which does not pertain properly to the canonical judgment of the case. He cannot inquire into the matter, receive denunciations, interrogate witnesses, punish the guilty one, institute a trial, pass sentence or in any way intervene with jurisdiction in these matters. He could, though, by still observing the secret, change the religious from one house to another, shield him from danger by forbidding him to hear confessions, or by taking away the faculties which he is able to take away, as stated in canons 874, § 1, and 880, § 1. He could even, in the case of grave and imminent danger to the Institute, dismiss him in the provisory manner described in the second chapter of this work.[40]

(2) Causes Which Effect a Dismissal by Their Very Existence

A case also taken out of the superior's power is the case in which, according to canon 646, dismissal follows immediately upon the commission of certain specified delicts. In this case the superior, on ascertaining and proving the fact of the delicts, solely declares the fact of their commission. The superior does not dismiss, the law does so by stating that the dismissal of religious is effected by the very fact of the commission of one of the delicts. This canon applies to religious in temporary vows equally as well as to religious in perpetual vows. A doubt might arise if this type of dismissal applies to religious in temporary vows at least as regards all the effects of dismissal. Canon 648 in giving some of the effects of dismissal during the time of temporary vows lists the effects as applying to those religious dismissed "ad normam can. 647." Still it does not seem to restrict the effects solely to those dismissed by superiors according to canon 647. In canon 646 the law takes the place of the superior and, on the commission of any of the delicts mentioned in canon 646, the law immediately dismisses them and they are held to be dismissed religious with all the effects which the law lays down for dismissed religious. Since in the case here treated the religious is in temporary vows, all the effects of dismissal incurred during the time of temporary vows are applied to him.[41]

[40] Larraona, *art. cit.*—*CpR,* VII (1926), 93-96; Schäfer, *De Religiosis,* pp. 223, 224; *supra,* pp. 101-104.

[41] Tabera, "De dimissione religiosorum"—*CpR,* XI (1930), 413.

(3) Mutual Consent—Consent of the Superior and His Council Only

The mutual consent of both the religious to be dismissed and the proper superior with the consent of his Council is *in itself* not a sufficient cause for dismissal during the period of temporary vows. It does not satisfy *in itself* the general requirement that the cause be external. If there is an external cause, then the case considered here (mutual consent *alone*) is not verified. In the case of mutual consent alone, the subject should either wait for his vows to expire or ask for a dispensation.[42]

This case differs from the case considered above[43] in which a religious who is in ill health admitted on the condition that he can be dismissed if his health gets worse or if he cannot perform the duties of the Institute. There is mutual consent, it is true, but not solely that; the mutual consent is about an external cause the validity of which would not be present were it not for the mutual consent.

(4) Failure to Receive Holy Communion Daily

The failure of a religious to receive Holy Communion every day in itself and considered alone cannot be a sufficient cause for dismissal. Canon Law enacts no obligation of daily Communion and authors have warned against the allowing of failure to receive daily Holy Communion to become a cause for wonderment or uncharitable talk.[44] The Instruction of the *S. Congregatio de disciplina Sacramentorum* directed, in part, that, in seminaries and other such institutes in which at stated times the superiors give their judgment about every student as to his piety, study and discipline, when these superiors are furnishing their judgment as to the progress of a student in piety, they shall not take account of the student's greater or lesser assiduity in receiving the Holy Eucharist.[45] Surely included is the

[42] Schäfer, *De Religiosis*, p. 996; Goyeneche, *De Religiosis*, p. 211; Jombart, "De dimissione ex mutuo consensu"—*Periodica*, XII (1924), (58)-(60).

[43] *Supra*, p. 122.

[44] Canon 595, § 2; Vermeersch-Creusen, *Epitome*, I, 551; Berutti, *De Religiosis*, p. 253.

[45] S. Cong. de Disciplina Sacramentorum, instructio reservata, 8 dec. 1938—*CpRM*, XX (1939), 203-210; *Periodica*, XXVIII (1939), 317-324; Schäfer, *De Religiosis*, p. 823.

vote taken in houses of studies in clerical Institutes,[46] and also the vote taken before admission to profession in those Institutes in which the constitutions provide for such a vote. Immediately before this, the Instruction directed the superior to inform his subjects in express words that, in general, he is pleased by their frequent approach to Holy Communion, but, on the other hand, that he does not in any way find fault with any individual who does not go to Communion every day, but that he sees in his conduct only an indication and sign of liberty and of a delicate and tender conscience. The actions of the superior were not to belie his words, *i. e.*, by finding fault with those who do not go to Communion every day and by praising those who do. These directions of the Instruction clearly show that *in itself* and dissociated from any other fault the failure to go to daily Communion is not in any way a fault and cannot in itself be a cause for dismissal.

(5) Other Causes

Obviously the judgment of the superior alone in a cause known to him alone and not capable of proof is not enough cause to dismiss a religious, for the consent of his Council is necessary for the validity of the act of dismissal. Not even his judgment together with the consent of his Council is sufficient. There must be an external, grave and sufficient cause on which to pass judgment. Their own judgment alone is not sufficient.[47] Solely the often and tenaciously repeated assertion that he has lost his religious spirit is not cause enough, *in itself,* to dismiss a religious in temporary vows.[48] Nor is loquacity alone without other adjuncts as, for instance, the grave violation of fraternal charity, etc., a sufficient cause for dismissal.[49]

[46] S. C. de Relig., instr. 1 dec. 1931, n. 14—*AAS,* XXIV (1932), 74 sq.

[47] Schäfer, *op. cit.*, p. 997; S. C. super statu Regularium, 7 febr. 1862, n. 2—*Fontes,* n. 4387.

[48] S. C. Ep. et Reg., resp. 19 nov. 1886—*apud* Vermeersch, *De Religiosis,* II, 275.

[49] S. C. Ep. et Reg., 12 aug. 1891, ad 8—*apud* Battandier, *Guide Canonique,* p. 271; Angelus a SS. Corde, *Manuale Juris Regularium,* I, p. 221, q. 200; Schäfer, *op. cit.*, p. 1005.

2. *Positive Causes*

All the positive causes for dismissal (*i. e.*, causes which *are* sufficient for the dismissal of a religious) have one note in common: the subject does not offer the qualities or necessary aptitude to render to the Institute the services which it has a right to expect.[50]

a. *In the Moral Order*

Under this heading are contained all the moral defects in a religious who is to be dismissed.

(1) Absence of the Religious Spirit—Scandal—Warning

> " . . . Defectus spiritus religiosi qui aliis scandalo sit, est sufficiens dimissionis causa, si repetita monitio una cum salutari poenitentia incassum cesserit, . . . " [51]

This cause, the absence of the religious spirit, is the only one mentioned in the Code. It has two conditions attached to it: (1) it must be a cause of scandal to others and (2) the religious must be proved to be in some way contumacious or incorrigible inasmuch as warnings and penances have not effected the necessary change. *Absence of the religious spirit* is a wide term. It covers a good deal. The doctrine of the authors and the prescriptions of the Rules and Constitutions approved by the Holy See will now be examined to see what in particular can be called an absence of the religious spirit.

First of all comes a carelessness, a manner of acting which shows no love for the religious life, but manifests that in place of the supernatural motives which should direct his life there are only natural motives. This is shown clearly in the transgressions of the Rules and Constitutions and of the precepts of the superiors whenever such violations spring from laziness and perverse will rather than from human frailty. It is shown, too, in the lack of a sincere striving for the interior life, in the state of relaxation which shows itself in his

[50] Battandier, *op. cit.*, p. 272.

[51] ". . . The absence of the religious spirit which is a cause of scandal to others, is a sufficient motive for dismissal, when a repeated admonition together with a salutary penance has produced no effect; . . ."—Canon 647, § 2, 2°.

constant desire to be out of the house and among lay people, and in his missing of the common prayers, exercises and meditations, and, if he does come to them, in his inattentiveness and constant disinterestedness, and finally, in his making no attempt to correct or amend his actions.[52]

Faults against the vows also may show this lack of a religious spirit. Thus the frequent and constant violations of poverty betray, especially if they involve large amounts, a guilty conscience or a totally incorrect motive for his life, and, even if they involve small amounts, a disregard for the constitutions and the superior's power. All faults against purity including bad morals, incontinence, sensuality, immodesty, are evidence either of a total lack of comprehension of the duties of his state or, what is worse, of a will not at all in accord with the religious spirit. This holds above all for any actions which are grave matter in themselves but also for actions which though not grave in themselves, violate modesty and pave the way to the sin which will cast the greatest disrepute on the religious life: impurity. Faults against obedience are manifold: the unwilling or grudging obedience given to superiors and their commands, the habitual murmuring against or criticizing of the superiors, negligence in fulfilling the duties assigned by the superiors, habitual insubordination or a grave exterior fault against the vow of obedience, and the non-observance or contempt of the constitutions.[53]

[52] Schäfer, *De Religiosis*, p. 993; Vermeersch-Creusen, *Epitome*, I, 598, 599; Tabera, "De dimissione religiosorum"—*CpR*, XII (1931), 372; Palombo, *De Dimissione Religiosorum*, p. 179; *Regulae et Praescriptiones pro Congregatione Presbyterorum a Sacro Corde* (Romae, 1934), p. 115, n. 299; p. 116, n. 300, 1°, 6°; *Constitutions of the Congregation of the Resurrection of Our Lord Jesus Christ* (Rome: Typographical Institute, 1937), p. 57, n. 172.

[53] Vermeersch-Creusen, *op. cit.*, I, 599; Prümmer, *Manuale Iuris Canonici*, q. 258, p. 346; Palombo, *op. cit.*, 178, 179; Berutti, *De Religiosis*, p. 342; Schäfer, *op. cit.*, p. 993; *Constitutions of the Congregation of the Resurrection of Our Lord Jesus Christ*, p. 57, n. 172; *Constitutions of the Brothers of Christian Instruction* (Jersey, 1936), p. 44, n. 68, 1°; *Declarationes et Statuta Sive Constitutiones Congregationis Ottiliensis O.S.B. Pro Missionibus Exteris* (Typis Archiabbatiae SS. Cordis Jesu Ad Ottiliam, 1925), p. 28, n. 66; *Regulae et Praescriptiones pro Congregatione Presbyterorum a Sacro Corde*, p. 116, n. 300, 4° and 6°; *Manual of the Clerics of St. Viator*, pp. 21, 151; *Regula Primitiva et Constitutiones Fratrum Discalceatorum Ordinis Sanctissimae Trinitatis Re-*

Accumulated faults against the virtues in general may also furnish causes for dismissal. One can fail gravely against charity by being very disagreeable and caustic with his confrères; by sowing discord and contentions either by his own actions and conduct or by the relating and magnifying of words spoken by one confrère about another or by lying about a confrère. One can sin gravely against charity also by being very quarrelsome, by defaming a confrère, by violating secrets revealed to him, by grave fits of anger. Faults against sobriety, if they be grave and frequent, can be a cause for dismissal, as also grave dishonesty (however, except for the lying involved, this would come under faults against poverty) and too great levity.[54]

All these listed faults truly come under the term *absence of religious spirit,* for they are all contrary to the very spirit and purpose of the religious life and show, therefore, a lack either of knowledge or of appreciation of the religious life. Human nature is weak and frail, however, and one cannot expect perfection in a subject who has vowed to spend his life striving for that perfection. That this lack of knowledge or appreciation be verified and be grave enough for dismissal the Code presupposes that these faults be a cause of scandal to others and that the religious first be warned and made to amend by means of punishments. Only when it is evident that no effort at amendment has been made can the superior be sure that this absence of the religious spirit constitutes a cause grave enough and sufficient for dismissal.

Scandal, theologically considered, is a word or deed, evil in itself or having the appearance of evil, which gives rise to the spiritual ruin of another.[55] Not every scandal is, however, a sufficient motive for dismissal. It must arise from one of the causes listed above and be apt to lead others into the same fault or to a loss of the religious spirit.[56] The subject has the right in this matter to be informed of

demptionis Captivorum (Isola Del Liri: A. Macioce & Pisani, 1933), nn. 223, 224, 225.

[54] Schäfer, *op. cit.*, p. 993, and the authors and rules cited in note 53.

[55] St. Thomas, *Summa Theologica,* IIa, IIae, q. 43, art. 1; Aertyns-Damen, *Theologia Moralis* (13. ed., Taurini: Marietti, 1939), I, 283.

[56] *Manual of the Clerics of St. Viator,* p. 150; Prümmer, *Manuale Iuris Canonici,* q. 258, p. 346.

the faults by warnings and punishments. The reason for this is clear. For the absence of the religious spirit there is needed some incorrigibility or contumacy, and not the ordinary human frailty or levity. This contumacy or incorrigibility can be proved only by means of these warnings and punishments, since continued transgressions after a warning show contumacy, whereas without these warnings there would be no certainty that the contumacy was present. These warnings are not canonical warnings in the strict sense,[57] but rather paternal.

These paternal warnings may be of the kind that is styled *secret; i. e.*, they may be exhortations, friendly and paternal, which are made by the superior out of benevolence or even in virtue of his pastoral office, directly for the correction of the subject and only indirectly for the welfare of the Institute without any diminution of the rights of the subject. Penances may or may not be used as will seem appropriate; they should be the ordinary ones found in the constitutions. These paternal warnings may on the other hand be of the kind that is styled *public; i. e.*, they may be given to the subject not privately but before two witnesses or by a legitimate document; they intend directly the good of the Institute and indirectly the good of the subject. The law in no way makes this distinction between secret and public warning nor does it require that the paternal admonition be public. While it is not necessary for validity, still the superior should use the public admonition if he thinks it more effective.[58]

[57] A canonical warning in general always presupposes a delict or danger of delict, neither of which is necessary in order to dismiss a religious in only temporary vows.

[58] Palombo, *op. cit.*, pp. 115-117; 180, note 2; Bastien, *Directoire Canonique*, p. 131, note 3. Palombo believes the superior will act more securely by using public paternal warnings. This is true since the Code demands warnings, and public warnings are the only ones which can be proved afterwards (in case of recourse if the subject will object that he had not been sufficiently warned). These public warnings will also furnish proof of the superior's justness and fairness in case of recourse. Cf. Beste, *Introductio in Codicem* (Collegeville, Minn.: St. John's Abbey Press, 1938), p. 441. Still, if he believes that a private paternal warning will be effective, he should try it in order to safeguard as far as possible the subject's good name. Cf. Creusen, "Le renvoi au cours de voeux temporaires"—*RCR*, V (1929), 192; Larraona, "Consultatio"—*CpR*, III (1922), 15.

There is no need, either, for these warnings to threaten dismissal. In itself all that is needed is that the subject be warned to be more observant of the duties of his state. The object of these warnings is then obtained, for when the subject has been warned and punished there can be no reasonable doubt as to the presence of some kind of contumacy or incorrigibility, and not only of human frailty. Palombo correctly states that the superior will act more securely if he threatens dismissal when he warns the delinquent because such a threat acquaints the latter more impressively with the force of the admonition and he will know definitely in just what particulars he fails. Further, the form of the subsequent dismissal, although administrative, will more closely approach the judicial process.[59]

In regard to number there must be at least two admonitions, for the Code has the phrase *repetita monitio.* The warning, then, must be at least twofold. This preserves the superior from hasty action on the one hand, and, on the other hand, the subject's rights are much better guarded.[60] There is no need that the major superior give these warnings. The Code does not specify this as it does in canons 649 and 659. Hence the local superior may give these warnings and punishments.[61]

(2) Delicts and Graver Causes

(a) Delicts

If the absence of the religious spirit can be a cause for dismissal once it has been proved, so too, *a fortiori,* can be any graver deficency in the moral order. Thus a grave delict can be the cause of dismissal; [62] *e. g.*, a grave external fault against chastity,[63] a grave

[59] Palombo, *op. cit.*, p. 181.

[60] Schäfer, *op. cit.*, pp. 993, 994; Goyeneche, *De Religiosis*, p. 211; Blat, *De Religiosis*, p. 571.

[61] Goyeneche, "Consultatio"—*CpR,* XIII (1932), 100 sq.

[62] Goyeneche, "Consultatio"—*CpR,* XIV (1933), 184.

[63] Tabera, "De dimissione religiosorum,"—*CpR,* XII (1931), 371; *Manual of the Clerics of St. Viator,* pp. 21, 149; *Regulae et Praescriptiones pro Congregatione Presbyterorum a Sacro Corde,* p. 46; *Rules of the Brothers of the Christian Schools* (Lembecq-Lez-Hal, 1925), p. 47; *Constitutions and Rules of the Institute of the Brothers of the Sacred Heart* (Metuchen, N. J.), p. 171; *Constitutiones Ordinis Fratrum Beatissimae Virginis Mariae de Monte Carmelo,*

and public scandal committed in the community or outside of it together with a grave suspicion that he may commit it again,[64] or formal contempt of authority.[65] They are not causes which effect the dismissal by the very fact of their commission, rather, as in all other causes listed here, they give the superior sufficient reason and motive for the dismissal which must take place according to the formalities of law.

(b) Fugitives and Quasi-Apostates

A fugitive (one who without the permission of his superior deserts the religious house, but with the intention of returning to the Institute) gives the superior a cause sufficient to dismiss him.[66]

A religious in temporary vows who unlawfully leaves the house without the intention of returning or who, although lawfully outside the house, fails to return to it with the intention of withdrawing himself from religious obedience, is not an apostate since he has not perpetual vows, nor is he a fugitive because he does not fit under the definition of a fugitive. This unlawful leaving (or unlawful remaining out of the house, if the leaving was lawful) is of itself a cause for dismissing a religious who is in temporary vows.[67]

(c) Causes Sufficient to Dismiss a Religious in Perpetual Vows

Every cause sufficient to dismiss a religious while he has perpetual vows is *a fortiori* sufficient for dismissing him while he has

art. 287, p. 105. For the confessor's role in this matter, confer: Salsmans, "Vocation et Chastete"—*Nouvelle Revue Théologique,* LX (1933), 401-413; Creusen, "Role du confesseur dans l'admission en Religion"—*NRT,* LV (1928), 444-447.

[64] Tabera, *loc. cit.*; *Regulae et Praescriptiones pro Congregatione Presbyterorum a S. Corde,* p. 116, n. 300, 7°; *Manual of the Clerics of St. Viator,* p. 21.

[65] Tabera, *loc. cit.*, Cappello, *Summa Iuris Canonici* (3 vols., Vol. II, 3. ed., Romae: apud Aedes Universitatis Gregorianae, 1939), II, 259.

[66] Goyeneche, "Consultatio"—*CpR,* XIV (1933), 183, 184; 258, 259; Larraona, "Quaestio Canonica"—*CpR,* IV (1923), 176; Creusen, *Religieux et Religieuses,* n. 281, 3; Coronata, *Institutiones,* I, 862; Raus, *Institutiones Canonicae* (ed. altera, Lugduni-Parisiis: Typis Emmanualis Vitte, 1931), n. 204, p. 334.

[67] Vermeersch-Creusen, *Epitome,* III, 310; Berutti, *De Religiosis,* p. 336; Creusen-Garesché-Ellis, *Religious Men and Women in the Code,* p. 261.

only temporary vows. In regard to men such a cause would be three delicts with a double warning and failure to amend.[68] The delict meant here is the delict properly so called as defined in canon 2195. The repeated delicts must be of the same species, *i. e.*, against the same virtue, though they be perpetrated perhaps in different circumstances. Thus three delicts against chastity are sufficient, though they may be specifically different kinds of sin.[69] These delicts must be grave, *i. e.*, they must constitute matter for a mortal sin, and they are measured according to the norms of canon 2196.[70] These delicts must also be external; *i. e.*, they must have the special note which make it possible that they be proved in the external forum in a trial to be grave delicts. Thus canon 656 gives *external* a particular shade of meaning, namely, that the delict be known by so many persons that it can be proved in a trial.[71] These grave external delicts can be committed either against the common law or the special laws for religious, *i. e.*, the laws of the Code which bind them equally with clerics or lay people, or the laws which bind them specifically as religious or are enacted specially for them in the constitutions or in the laws and the precepts of the Institute.[72]

For the dismissal of religious women in perpetual vows there are also required grave external causes, according to the wording of canon 651. These causes must be more grave than the causes which are required for dismissing a woman in temporary vows for the bond of perpetual vows creates a fixed, certain and permanent right as contrasted with the unstable, uncertain and temporary bond created

[68] Canons 649 and 656.

[69] Blat, *De Religiosis*, p. 559; Coronata, *Institutiones*, I, 879.

[70] Blat, *op. cit.*, p. 594. Creusen, however (Vermeersch-Creusen, *Epitome*, III, 184), says that the delicts here are not delicts properly so called but rather *crimina*. He argues first that there would be no need for the words *gravia* and *externa* of canon 656 if *delicta* were used in the proper sense, inasmuch as all delicts are grave and external. The words are taken from the decree *Quum singulae* (*Fontes*, n. 4409), he says, which uses the words *delicta* and *crimina* indiscriminately; the word should be translated in the sense of the decree *Auctis Admodum* (*Fontes*, n. 2020) which had: "nisi ad *culpam* gravem externam et publicam."

[71] Blat, *op. cit.*, pp. 594-596.

[72] Coronata, *op. cit.*, I, 880; Blat, *op. cit.*, p. 595.

by temporary vows.[73] These causes, however, need not be theologically grave, *i. e.*, they need not be mortal sins.[74] such causes in particular are: a manner of living which brings notable and grave spiritual or temporal harm to the Institute, the disturbance of the domestic peace by murmuring, etc., the undermining of domestic charity and the nurturing of insubordination to superiors, frequent violations of poverty even in matters not grave in themselves, the frequent making public her complaints against the superioress or the faults of the Sisters, the not infrequent temporal loss to the Institute caused by her grave negligence, and the giving or receiving of small gifts without permission of the superioress.[75]

When a religious has been in temporary vows for more than six years in an Institute which has only temporary vows, it seems that for his dismissal there are needed causes sufficient to dismiss a religious in perpetual vows. It does not seem that the causes sufficient to dismiss a religious in temporary vows are adequate. In all other phases: the superior to dismiss the religious, the procedure, and the effects, the dismissal of that religious is ruled by all the prescriptions of the law concerning the dismissal of religious in temporary vows. The reasons for this statement will be treated fully in Chapter Five.[76]

(d) Extraordinary Causes of Canons 653 and 668

Included also under the causes which are sufficient for dismissing a temporarily professed religious, as was seen in the former chapter, are those grave and urgent cases which are outlined in canons 653 and 668. These must be of such a nature as to cause grave external scandal, *i. e.*, the acts must have been committed in such circumstances that discreetly earnest and serious people would suffer a truly grave scandal[77] and that the acts were to the knowledge of others

[73] Coronata, *op. cit.*, I, 873, 874, note 8, against Vermeersch-Creusen, *Epitome*, I, 600.

[74] Chelodi, *Ius De Personis*, p. 453; Wernz-Vidal, *Ius Canonicum*, III, 480; Palombo, *op. cit.*, pp. 209, 210; Schäfer, *De Religiosis*, p. 1004, against Coronata, *op. cit.*, I, 873; Pejska, *Ius Canonicum Religiosorum*, p. 195.

[75] Wernz-Vidal, *op. cit.*, III, 480; Bastien, *Directoire Canonique*, p. 138; Berutti, *De Religiosis*, p. 347.

[76] Cf. *infra*, pp. 171-175.

[77] Palombo, *op. cit.*, p. 164; Bastien, *op. cit.*, p. 141.

committed outside of the religious house or that the knowledge about them became general among outsiders even though the acts were committed within the religious house. It suffices consequently that factual infamy have occurred.[78] The cause must also be one which begets a grave and imminent danger for the house.

First, the threatened harm must be most grave. This could be verified, for instance, if there were present a serious fear that the retention of the religious would cause a tumult of the people against the Institute; if the religious himself should propose to inflict a grave damage on the Institute; if grave loss of temporal goods were feared; if criminal action in court against the guilty religious impended; or if the scandal itself gravely undermined the Institute.[79] Among such faults could be enumerated the seduction of another to external violations against chastity; the lapse of one into such a sin with an accomplice; the commission of a crime which can be punished by the civil power with defaming penalties; the machination against ecclesiastical, religious or civil superiors and their commands; attempts to incite others against these authorities; the publication of the internal affairs of the Institute with consequent grave danger to it or with grave scandal to externs, or, indeed, the communication of the Institute's private business to outsiders of any kind without canonical justification.[80] Secondly, the cause which threatens this grave harm must affect not only an individual religious, but the house, province, or Institute.[81] Finally, the cause must be one which is threatening or imminent, *i. e.*, according to the judgment of prudent men the damage will soon come upon the community unless the religious is

[78] Coronata, *op. cit.*, I, 876; Chelodi, *op. cit.*, p. 455; Wernz-Vidal, *op. cit.*, p. 489; Vermeersch-Creusen, *op. cit.*, I, 601; Schäfer, *op. cit.*, p. 1008; Palombo, *op. cit.*, 164.

[79] Blat, *op. cit.*, p. 584; Coronata, *op. cit.*, I, 876; Palombo, *op. cit.*, p. 165.

[80] *Regulae Et Praescriptiones pro Congregatione Sacerdotum a S. Corde*, n. 311, p. 120, 121. Note what Vermeersch says: the purpose of each Institute must be taken into consideration. Thus, even if there is no fear of a judicial trial because of the quality of the person harmed, still it can easily happen that, in an Institute which educates young people, the Institute cannot defend or shelter such a delinquent without grave danger of infamy if many know of the delict. (*Epitome*, I, 602; confer: Palombo, *op. cit.*, p. 165).

[81] Berutti, *op. cit.*, p. 349; Coronata, *op. cit.*, I, 876.

dismissed in order to avert the disaster. This imminent harm can arise from even one delict. It could be present when the accusation of an innately defaming delict (which is now occult) is foreseen to follow soon.[82]

b. In the Physical Order

In regard to corporal causes, it was noted that sickness of any kind could not be a reason for dismissal from temporary vows, unless the knowledge of it was hidden deceitfully from the Institute before temporary profession. If knowledge of this sickness was deceitfully hidden during the postulancy and before admission to the novitiate, the novitiate is invalid according to canon 542, 1°, and the consequent profession is invalid according to canon 572, § 1, 3°. All that is needed in this case is proof of fraud in the concealing of the condition of sickness. If the sickness came upon the religious during the novitiate and knowledge of it was deceitfully hidden from the Institute at the time of temporary profession, then it seems that the profession was valid, for canon 572, § 1, 3°, unlike canon 542, 1°, has placed no invalidating sanction on fraud which is exercised on the superior.[83] This opinion holding that the profession is valid even if fraud has been practiced on the superiors seems true also because canon 647 allows it as a motive for dismissal. If fraud practiced on the superior rendered the profession invalid, there would be no need

[82] Blat, *op. cit.*, pp. 584, 607; Coronata, *op. cit.*, I, 877; Wernz-Vidal, *op. cit.*, p. 489. Vermeersch-Creusen (*Epitome*, I, 602) note that the civil external forum often punishes less grave sins against chastity much more severely than even some consummated sins against the same virtue which they leave almost totally unpunished.

[83] Schäfer, *De Religiosis*, pp. 574, 5; 580; Vermeersch-Creusen, *op. cit.*, I, 519; Cappello, *Summa Iuris Canonici*, II, p. 217, n. 611; Coronata, *op. cit.*, I, 754; Biederlack-Führich, *De Religiosis*, n. 90; Chelodi, *Ius De Personis*, p. 442; Bastien, *Directoire Canonique*, p. 94; Creusen-Garesche-Ellis, *Religious Men and Women*, p. 173; Berutti, *op. cit.*, p. 197, note 2; Cervia, *De Professione Religiosa*, p. 93; Bouuaert, "De metus influxu"—*Ius Pontificium*, VI (1926), 105-111, esp. p. 110; 138; Larraona, "Commentarium Codicis—Canon 542"—*CpRM*, XVII (1936) 12; Goyeneche, "Consultatio"—*CpRM*, XVI (1935), 233, 234. Against this opinion and holding that fraud practiced on the superior will invalidate the profession are: Wernz-Vidal, *op. cit.*, III, 270; Craisson, *Manuale Totius Iuris Canonici*, n. 2694; Frey, *Religious Profession*, p. 95; Palombo, *op. cit.*, p. 176.

for dismissal but only for proof of the fraud and the consequent invalidity of the profession. From canon 647, though, it can be gathered that after proof of the fraud has been obtained there still is needed the act of dismissal on the part of the superior.[84] The Code states clearly those cases in which the act is invalid when the one who acts does so by reason of fraud practiced on him: canon 103, § 2. Canon 572 does not clearly say that fraud practiced on the superior by the subject renders the profession invalid; and canon 647 seems to indicate clearly that the mind of the legislator in canon 572, 1°, was that the profession is not invalid but that the fraud, if proved, can be the reason for dismissal and the rescinding of the contract even without the recourse to canons 1684-1689 provided for in canon 103, § 2.

c. In the Intellectual Order

A lack of necessary talent is cause enough for the dismissal of a religious in temporary vows from a clerical Institute or even from a lay Institute the purpose of which lies in the field of education. The reason is that there is nothing more just and reasonable than to demand the talent which is necessary for those studies without which one cannot perform the duties which derive from one's membership in the Institute. This is a particularization of a general cause: the ineptitude to fulfill the duties either common to all religious or special to the members of the Institute. Ineptitude consequent upon illness has already been ruled out as a cause. Ineptitude caused by levity of spirit or lack of ability to control oneself has been listed under the absence of religious spirit. The lack of talent as a cause for dismissal was not universally received before the Code as a sufficient cause for dismissing a religious who had temporary vows; it was, however, the better opinion as was seen in the historical conspectus.[85] Canon 647 followed the old law in regard to

[84] Goyeneche, "Consultatio"—*CpRM*, XVI (1935), 234. In this consultation, Goyeneche states that the fraud which invalidates the entrance to the novitiate or the profession is viewed as the fraud by force of which the one on whom fraud is committed acts (*vi cuius operatur; re vera actus ex dolo ponatur*); whereas the fraud of canon 647 is viewed on the part of the one who commits the fraud (*quem operando quis committit*).

[85] Cf. *supra*, pp. 60-61.

the gravity and nature of the causes sufficient for the dismissal of religious in temporary vows; hence this ineptitude should be accepted as a sufficient cause.[86]

Several conditions are necessary in order that this cause be grave enough for the effecting of a dismissal. First, it must surely be so grave that the religious is deemed unable or unfit to study or to fulfill the requirements of his Institute, *e. g.*, the work of preaching, of hearing confessions, of teaching, etc. Secondly, it must not have been detected before the first profession. If this lack of ability was fully known before the making of the first profession then the contract in regard to this point was absolute and not conditional. Thirdly, the lack of talent need be only grave enough to render the religious less apt even for the minor offices of the Institute.

This cause is often discovered only during the philosophy and theology courses. If before profession the superior doubts whether the subject is apt he shall lay before the novice the condition under which it is accepted, *i. e.*, that he may be dismissed if he prove not to be fit for the duties of his state, so that the novice can choose freely either to leave or to stay and to attempt to better himself by more diligent study. If after profession the doubt arises as to whether he has sufficient talent, the subject's right to remain prevails in the case, and he cannot be dismissed until it is certain that he has not sufficient knowledge. The superior should then wait until the end of the period of temporary vows.[87]

In Institutes which have two classes of religious, the professed can in this case be allowed the choice either of asking for a dispensation, of being dismissed, or of joining the lay class. In Institutes which have no lay class strictly so called but still have need of members to take care of duties which do not require any specific intellectual ability for teaching, etc., the superiors cannot dismiss the subject because *de facto* the latter is not inept to perform the duties of a member in the Institute.

[86] Prümmer, *Manuale Iuris Ecclesiastici* (ed. altera, Friburgi Brisgoviae: Herder & Co., 1920), p. 331; Chelodi, *op. cit.*, p. 452; Schäfer, *op. cit.*, pp. 646, 905; Palombo, *op. cit.*, p. 182; Goyeneche, *De Religiosis*, pp. 210, 211; "Consultatio"—*CpR*, I (1920), 231-236; III (1922), 82; V (1924), 214, 215; XIV (1933), 183, 184.

[87] Goyeneche, *art. cit.*, *CpR*, I (1920), 234; Palombo, *op. cit.*, p. 184.

Somewhat similar is the case of a religious in temporary vows in a clerical Institute who does not wish to receive orders even though he is judged capable and worthy of them. He cannot be forced to take orders. He can be persuaded to transfer to the lay class or he may be dismissed from temporary vows, for in relation to the Institute there can be no more reasonable cause for the dismissal of a religious than the refusal, culpable or inculpable, of a subject to fit himself for the work of the Institute.[88]

d. Causes Sufficient for Dismissal from a Seminary

In clerical Institutes, by analogy of law, canon 1371 can be applied to religious in temporary vows. The only objection possible to this application is that the religious are bound both by vows and contract, whereas no such obligations are on the seminarian, and hence causes of less moment are needed to dismiss the seminarian. Be that as it may, every cause noted in canon 1371 has already been considered and judged a cause sufficient for dismissal. The causes mentioned in canon 1371, then, are sufficient causes for the dismissal of a religious in temporary vows, especially, if he is in a clerical Institute and intends to go on to the priesthood. Such causes are: disorderliness and an attitude of intolerance regarding discipline; the manifestation of a notable lack of docility; [89] obstinate disobedience; the promotion or fostering of rebellion; unsuitability of character and conduct for the ecclesiastical State; [90] such little display of pro-

[88] Wernz-Vidal, *op. cit.*, III, 478; Palombo, *op. cit.*, p. 172; Goyeneche, "Consultatio"—*CpR,* III (1922), 82; *CpR,* VI (1935), 90.

[89] S. Poenit., 8 mart. 1927, dubium II—*AAS,* XIX (1927), 158.

[90] Pius X, motu propr. *Sacrorum Antistitum,* 1 sept. 1910—*AAS,* II (1910), 166, 167. Blat (*op. cit.*, III, 351, 352) says that the prescriptions of Pius X are still to be kept. These demand that the moderator of a seminary watch for signs of lack of vocation in the seminarians. If he notices these signs he shall frequently warn the seminarians and try them for a year. If they fail to amend he shall expel them in such a way that they will not be received by any bishop in the future. Such signs are the lack of virtues, viz., of docility to obey, of due dispositions to piety and humility, of love for discipline, or of the right intention. Other bad signs are the performance of duty or the keeping of discipline with a servile fear and the neglect of duty or the breaking of discipline through levity of mind or out of contempt.

ficiency in study that the attaining of sufficient knowledge for the priesthood practically appears hopeless. There should be dismissed immediately those who fail against good morals, *e. g.*, by such delicts as are mentioned in canons 2350-2359, but especially by sins against the sixth commandment; and those who fail against faith, *i. e.*, by such delicts as are recounted in canons 2314-2319. All of these causes should be proved in some way in the external forum before the superiors proceed to dismissal or ejection. Regarding the causes which can be known only in the internal sacramental forum, the confessor shall follow the rules given by the moralists to persuade the delinquent to amend, or, failing this, he shall strive to induce the delinquent to leave of his own accord, threatening the refusal of absolution if such a means prove necessary.[91]

II. Causes in Relation to the Institute

Considered here are causes which will bring to the Institute grave harm or notable damage from the mere fact of its keeping a certain member, *e. g.*, economic inability which will deprive the Institute of the ability to sustain its members, dispersion of the Institute or its suppression; hatred, infamy, or persecution. If such calamities come to the Institute from the government or from the people because of a member in temporary vows, even though he is guilty of no crime, he may be dismissed. Moreover, economic incapacity is a sufficient cause for dismissing all or any number of those who are in temporary vows.

As can be seen from this list of causes there can be no adequate division of causes into those which arise on the part of the religious and those which relate to the Institute on the basis of the cause being found in the religious or outside of him. Rather the basis must be somewhat nearer to the involvement of culpability in these causes, but even this is not adequate, for the inability to perform the

[91] Canon 1371; Pius XI, litt. encycl. *Ad catholici sacerdotii*, 25 dec. 1935—*AAS*, XXVIII (1936) 40, 41; Blat, *op. cit.*, III, 351, 352; De Meester, *Compendium*, III, pars I, 223; Cocchi, *Commentarium*, III, 110, 111; Ayrinhac, *Administrative Legislation in the New Code of Canon Law* (New York: Longmans, 1934), pp. 259, 260; Vermeersch-Creusen, *op. cit.*, II, 489, 490. Cf. also: S. C. De Prop. Fide, instr. 18 oct. 1883, IV, 4—*Fontes*, n. 4903.

duties of the Institute may exist on the part of the religious and, in a certain degree, in relation to the Institute but it is a cause which is inculpable in the religious. Despite this lack of an adequate basis for a division, it can be said that these causes for dismissal are based on the primacy of the common good over the individual good.

It may be noted that the cases listed under the causes in relation to the Institute which could not be remedied by some other means than dismissal are indeed rare. Such a remedy could be provided by the transfer of the religious to another house of the Institute (in cases of infamy resulting from calumny, etc.). The inability of the Institute to support its members seems to be a cause rather for exclaustration than dismissal from temporary vows. The Institute is bound to furnish him with sufficient food and clothing. If, due to circumstances beyond its control, the Institute cannot support the religious, it may obtain for him a decree of exclaustration and when the temporary vows lapse they have the just and sufficient reason required by canon 637 to refuse to admit him to perpetual vows until they are able to support him.[92] Infamy which the Institute would suffer without culpability in the religious, because of the religious or of his parents, could be, in circumstances rarely verified, a sufficient cause for dismissal, *e. g.*, in view of peculiar local circumstances, as in mission lands or in very bigoted sections of a country. Here, too, the remedy would be found rather in his transfer to another house of the Institute.[93] The necessity of his parents is again a cause which can very rarely become a cause for dismissal. The Institute should help them, or obtain for the religious a decree of exclaustration so that he can help them and be able to return to the Institute when their necessity ceases.[94]

[92] Biederlack-Führich, *De Religiosis*, p. 299; Oesterle, *Praelectiones Iuris Canonici*, I, 371; Coronata, *Institutiones*, I, 869; Vermeersch-Creusen, *Epitome*, I, 599; Fanfani, *De Iure Religiosorum*, p. 497; Schäfer, *De Religiosis*, p. 993. Palombo (*De Dimissione Religiosorum*, p. 175) allows dismissal because of the inability of the religious Institute to support its members only if there is no solid hope that they will be able to support him in the future; Raus (*Institutiones Canonicae*, p. 341) says this case will only very rarely be a sufficient cause for dismissal.

[93] Schäfer, *De Religiosis*, p. 993.

[94] Goyeneche, *De Religiosis*, p. 210; Schäfer, *op. cit.*, p. 481.

CHAPTER IV

THE PROCEDURE AND EFFECTS OF DISMISSAL OF RELIGIOUS IN TEMPORARY VOWS. RECOURSE AGAINST THE DECREE OF DISMISSAL

Article 1. The Procedure for Dismissal

In regard to the form or method of dismissal, the Code states:

> ". . . non est tamen necesse ut formali iudicio comprobentur. At religioso semper manifestari debent, data eidem plena respondendi licentia; eiusque responsiones Superiori dimittenti fideliter subiiciantur . . . "[1]

If the religious who is to be dismissed dwells in the house or in the vicinity of the house in which the superior resides, the form of dismissal is not a complicated one. After the superior has warned and punished the subject at least twice for a fault which constitutes matter for a just judgment that he is lacking in the religious spirit or, in the case of a delict or grave fault, even immediately after the commission of such a delict or fault, or, if the cause is one which involves no fault on the part of the religious, as soon as the cause becomes evident, the superior shall summon the delinquent and lay before him the motives which are regarded as sufficient for his dismissal. The religious may ask and must be given time to consider these charges and causes and to formulate an answer against them if he sees fit to do so. These answers may be sent in writing, or the subject may himself appear to answer the charges and defend himself. The superior shall then consider the whole case (with his Council when the Code or constitutions require him to have their consent), and proceed to dismissal if he thinks that this is the only

[1] ". . . it is not necessary, however, that they (the causes) be proved by a judicial process. But they must always be manifested to the religious, and full liberty to reply given him; and his replies must be faithfully submitted to the Superior effecting the dismissal; . . . "—Canon 647, § 2, 3°.

course open for him to follow. This procedure will be used in a number of cases, *e. g.*, if the subject lives in the house or in the immediate vicinity of the house of the superior general (in Institutes of pontifical approval) or if he lives in the city or in the vicinity of the local ordinary (in Institutes of diocesan approval). This will frequently be the procedure when the Abbot effects a dismissal, for his subjects will be in the house with him.

The most frequently used procedure will be that of the case in which the subject cannot himself talk with or meet the superior who may have to dismiss him. In this case, since the superior who dismisses the religious must know certainly the causes for his dismissal, the local superior or the major superior may hold an investigation to collect proofs and then may send them either to the superior general (in Institutes of pontifical approval), to the local ordinary or to the regular superior (in the case of *moniales*), or to the ordinary of the locality of the house in which the religious who is to be dismissed is stationed (in Institutes of diocesan approval). The superior who has gathered these proofs shall make them known to the subject either by word or in writing. It should be noted that there is nothing which requires that the superior reveal the names of witnesses or read to him their testimony *verbatim*. It suffices that he tell the subject plainly what is held against him and that the procedure to dismiss him has begun. Time must be allowed for the accused to answer the charges. These answers may be made either orally or in writing. In either case they should be signed by the religious but, if he refuses to sign, this must be noted.[2] The proofs of the causes for dismissal and the answers of the religious to them are then sent to the superior who is empowered to effect his dismissal. This superior (and his Council, if the Code or constitutions demand that he obtain its consent) then considers the whole case and decides whether or not the causes and circumstances are such as to warrant giving a decree of dismissal.[3]

In view of the possibility of recourse, prudence demands that

[2] Schäfer, *De Religiosis*, p. 996; Bastien, *Directoire Canonique*, p. 131, note 2. If he makes his answers orally they should be taken down in writing, read to the religious, changed in any points which do not suit him, and signed by him.

[3] Palombo, *De Dimissione Religiosorum*, pp. 184-186, 189.

there be preserved the proofs of the facts and all the documents and testimony which have been consigned to writing as well as the written record of the verbal process of the interrogatory which was signed by the religious.[4]

The decree of dismissal issued by the superior is in the form called commissory and necessary; *i. e.*, the decree needs an intermediary for execution and this executor has no choice in the matter but must execute the decree. Since the execution of this decree concerns the external forum it should be done in writing. The religious should remain in the house or in some house of the Institute until the decree has come and has been executed.[5]

Once the decree of dismissal has been executed, the effects take place immediately. If the subject believes he has been treated unfairly or unjustly there is always open to him the remedy of recourse. The next two considerations shall be, in order, the effects of dismissal and the recourse against the decree of dismissal.

Article 2. The Effects of Dismissal

In general, when the decree of dismissal has been executed, its effect is that the religious in temporary vows ceases to be a religious. He is deprived of all the rights and privileges of a religious and he is freed from all the obligations of the religious state.

A. Cessation of Vows

The first and principal effect of the dismissal of a religious in temporary vows is the cessation of his vows and, consequently, of the obligations flowing from these vows, regardless of whether the obligations are indicated in the Code or in the constitutions. The religious is freed *ipso facto* and no special dispensation is needed.[6] It should be noted that if the vows have their source from any other fact than religious profession they do not cease at the moment of

[4] Jombart, "Le renvoi au cours des voeux temporaires"—*RCR*, V (1929), 201.

[5] Battandier, *Guide Canonique*, p. 282.

[6] Canon 648; Schäfer, *De Religiosis*, p. 999, note 59; Coronata, *Institutiones*, I, 871.

dismissal. Thus the private vows of the religious, if they were taken while he was in the Institute, remain. If they were taken before religious profession and then became suspended by that profession, they revive. So, too, the vows and duties annexed to major orders remain.[7]

B. Minor Orders

A religious in temporary vows and simultaneously in minor orders is by the very fact of dismissal reduced to the lay state. When he is reduced to the lay state he by that very fact loses the offices, benefices, rights and privileges of clerics, and is forbidden to wear the ecclesiastical garb and the tonsure.[8]

Most of the authors merely repeat the wording of the Code in treating of this effect of dismissal.[9] Others make a distinction. They state that if the religious was ordained to minor orders while he was in the Institute, the reduction to the lay state follows in accordance with the principles of the Code and is altogether equitable. However, they say, if a religious had already been in minor orders before he entered the Institute, he is not by his dismissal reduced to the lay state.[10] Reduction to the lay state after dismissal for a religious who was ordained to minor orders while he was in the Institute follows the principles of the Code governing ordination. A cleric must be either affiliated with a religious Institute or incardinated in a diocese. The cleric who was ordained while he was in the Institute became affiliated with that Institute. When he is dismissed he loses that affiliation. Since the law does not admit of vagrant or unattached clerics,[11] it is clear that his reduction to the lay state as indicated in

[7] Canon 1315; Schäfer, *loc. cit.* and p. 583; Damen, "De irritatione et suspensione votorum"—*Apollinaris,* III (1930), 286.

[8] Canons 213, § 1; 123.

[9] Canon 648; Coronata, *op. cit.*, I, 871; Blat, *De Religiosis,* p. 574; Fanfani, *De Iure Religiosorum,* p. 515; Battandier, *Guide Canonique,* p. 273; Berutti, *De Religiosis,* p. 344; Mothon, *L'État Religieux,* p. 372; De Meester, *Compendium,* II, p. 485, n. 1058, III; Cappello, *Summa Iuris Canonici,* II, 261; Jombart, "Le renvoi au cours des voeux temporaires"—*RCR,* V (1929), 202.

[10] Goyeneche, "Consultatio"—*CpRM,* XIX (1938), 163-166; Schäfer, *De Religiosis,* p. 1000.

[11] Canon 111, § 1.

canon 648 follows as a corollary from Canon 111, § 1.[12] Such a reduction to the lay state has not the character of a penalty but is a mere privation of the clerical state as demanded by the principles which govern ordination; it is, however, a privation of rights and hence, as a *lex odiosa,* it demands a strict interpretation.[13] It is equitable, too, since a religious who was ordained while he was a religious was certainly ordained for the utility of the Institute; it is clear that when he ceases to be a religious his utility for the Institute has also vanished. On the other hand, the ordinary of the place of his origin and domicile (or his proper ordinary according to canon 956) should not be forced to accept a cleric about whom he knows nothing and who, possibly, would not be necessary for the service of the churches of his diocese. The ordinary had no intention of employing this religious in his diocese, even though he may have ordained him himself.[14]

The case is entirely different, these same authors say, with a religious who was ordained to minor orders before he entered the Institute. He is incardinated into the diocese and he does not lose this incardination until his perpetual profession.[15] There is no question here, then, of the *clericus vagus* of Canon 111, § 1, and hence there is no reason for his reduction to the lay state, since, as stated above, this reduction has no penal character attached to it. Besides, this reduction to the lay state would put him in as bad a condition as the cleric in minor orders who is dismissed while he has perpetual vows, which dismissal, according to canon 669, § 2, presupposes three delicts. Indeed, he would be in a worse condition, since for a less grave cause he would suffer the same effects and even be deprived of

[12] Moeder, *The Proper Bishop for Ordination and Dimissorial Letters,* The Catholic University of America Canon Law Studies, n. 95 (Washington, D. C.: The Catholic University of America, 1935), p. 106.

[13] Canon 19; Goyeneche, "Consultatio"—*CpRM,* XIX (1938), 165; *CpR,* XIV (1933), 146 sq. Not all causes for dismissal are culpable on the part of the religious. Yet those who claim that every dismissal has the character of a penalty: Palombo (*De Dimissione Religiosorum,* p. 257) and Schaaf ("Episcopus proprius ordinationis religiosorum"—*Ecclesiastical Review,* XC [1934], 495—henceforth cited as *ER*) would have to attach an element of penalty even to dismissals inflicted for causes which are inculpable on the part of the religious.

[14] Canon 964; 965; Schaaf, *art. cit.,* pp. 491-509.

[15] Canon 585.

more benefits. The religious in perpetual vows has already lost his diocese by perpetual profession so at his dismissal he is only reduced to the lay state, whereas the religious in temporary vows at dismissal is both reduced to the lay state and loses his diocese. Finally it would seem very strange that by the action of a superior alone a bishop should lose a cleric.[16]

This opinion postulates a distinction made in the law which, because it is not clearly there, must be arrived at by argumentation. One can agree with the opinion only if it is proved by the arguments adduced for it, otherwise the principle *"ubi lex non distinguit, nec nos distinguere debemus"* imposes the presumption that the lawgiver had not intended the distinction. The wording of the law does not seem, in itself, to admit of this distinction; it states merely: "a cleric who is in minor orders is reduced by such a dismissal to the lay state." As to the arguments adduced, the first argument, namely, that canon 648 is a corollary of canon 111, § 1, can be countered with the argument that it is rather a parallel and particularized statement of canon 211, § 2: *"Clericus minor ad statum laicalem regreditur . . . ipso facto ob causas in iure descriptas."* This is one of the causes described in law.[17] It does not follow strictly that the one who was dismissed while he was in temporary vows is in a worse state than the one who was dismissed while he was in perpetual vows. Reduction to the lay state does not imply an excardination for the religious in temporary vows at his dismissal, for canon 212 states that if for any cause he returns to the clerical state, then in order to be admitted again among clerics he needs the permission of the ordinary of the diocese to which he was incardinated by his earlier ordination. With regard to the argument that the Code does not wish the bishop to lose his cleric by the action of the superior alone, it can be answered that he does not really lose his cleric. He lost the services of the cleric when the latter entered the Institute, and he can easily regain the cleric by returning him to the clerical state.

In conclusion, it seems that the wording of the canon does not admit of the proposed distinction, nor do the arguments adduced

[16] Goyeneche, "Consultatio"—*CpRM,* XIX (1938), 165, 166; Schäfer, *op. cit.,* p. 1000.

[17] Wernz-Vidal, *Ius Canonicum,* II, 384.

seem to have legal force sufficient to overthrow the literal meaning of the canon. Therefore it seems that, until more cogent arguments can be brought forth, canon 648 refers to all religious in minor orders whether they were ordained before or during their temporary vows.

C. Ineligibility to Certain Benefices, Offices, Etc.

Canon 642 renders certain religious ineligible for specified benefices, offices, etc., all clearly enumerated in the canon. The canon will be considered first to see who are the religious rendered ineligible to offices by this law and secondly to see which are the benefices, etc., to which they are ineligible.

Regarding religious in temporary vows who are dismissed, the term *"quilibet regressus"* of canon 642 can refer only to those who were professed in Institutes which take only temporary vows, oaths, or special promises. And even in such an Institute the term can refer only to one who is in major orders and who has been in temporary vows for at least six years.[18] Several authors state this explicitly. Goyeneche [19] and Nevin [20] state that canon 642, § 1, is a codification of the decree *Quum minoris,* which did not apply to religious dismissed during their period of temporary vows.[21] Goyeneche further appeals to canon 6, 2° and 4°, to strengthen his recourse to the *Quum minoris.* He further states that the context of canon 642 is proof of this opinion. The argument from the context will be elaborated below. A writer in *Jus Pontificium* indirectly holds this opinion since he states that canon 642, § 1, refers to religious in solemn vows, and to those religious who have been bound by temporary vows, oaths, or promises for at least six years. These are all he

[18] Canon 642, § 1: "Quilibet professus, ad saeculum regressus, licet valeat, ad normam can. 641, sacros ordines exercere, prohibetur tamen sine novo et speciali Sanctae Sedis indulto. . . ." Canon 642, § 2: "Haec valent quoque de iis qui vota temporaria, vel iuramentum perseverantiae, vel peculiares quasdam promissiones ad normam suarum constitutionum ediderunt et ab eisdem dispensati fuerunt, si per sex integros annos eisdem ligati fuerint."

[19] Goyeneche, "Consultatio"—*CpR,* V (1924), 26-28.

[20] Nevin, "Offices prohibited to secularized religious"—*ACR,* XII (1935), 163-166.

[21] S. C. de Religiosis, decr. 15 iun. 1909—*AAS,* I (1909), 523.

enumerates as bound by the law.[22] On the other side is Battandier,[23] who says the Code has changed the provisions of the *Quum minoris*.

The context of canon 642 and an analysis of all the possible cases to which the canon could refer will show the impossibility of the canon's referring to any other religious in temporary vows than the religious who has been bound by temporary vow, oath, or promise for at least six years in Institutes whose members take only temporary vows, oaths, or promises.

Canon 642, § 1 cannot refer to the members of the Institutes mentioned in canon 574, *i. e.*, to those professed with temporary vows in orders of solemn vows and in congregations of perpetual vows, in which the perpetual vows, whether solemn or simple, must be preceded by a profession of temporary simple vows. In such Institutes, it cannot refer to one who has been ordained to major orders, either before or after he enters the Institute. If ordained before entering, he is not included in the prescriptions of canon 642, § 1, even though, when dismissed, he is by that very fact dispensed from his vows. The first part of the canon can refer only to those in perpetual vows.[24] If the *"quilibet regressus"* refers to religious in temporary vows at all, § 2 of the canon is rendered useless. The word *"quoque"* shows that the law refers *also* to religious in temporary vows and major orders only when they have been bound by those vows for a period of six years.[25] If the Institute refuses to admit him to perpetual vows after his temporary vows have expired he is not dismissed or dispensed from his vows mediately through any act of dismissal. This latter case is not the case treated here. It will be dealt with in the next chapter. Suffice it to say here that a religious who is refused admission to perpetual profession is not comprehended in canon 642, § 2. The only other thinkable case, a religious being ordained to major orders while still a religious in temporary vows, is an impossibility, since no one in such Institutes can be ordained to sacred orders while he is still in temporary vows.[26]

[22] Responsum 46, *Jus Pontificum,* III (1923), 119, 120.

[23] Battandier, *Guide Canonique,* p. 468.

[24] Cf. *supra,* the authors cited in notes 19 and 20.

[25] D'Ambrosio, "Consultatio"—*Apollinaris,* IV (1931), 127.

[26] Canon 964, 3°, 4°; S. C. de Relig., instr. 1 dec. 1931, n. 15—*AAS,* XXIV (1932), 80.

The only cases in which religious in temporary vows would be bound by the ruling of canon 642 are those which are mentioned in second paragraph of that canon with reference namely to Institutes which have only temporary vows, or oaths, or special promises. These may not be ordained to major orders until they have been in the Institute for at least three years. One, then, who has been in such an Institute for at least six full years and who has received major orders, either before he entered or during his time as a religious, is bound by the prescriptions of canon 642.[27]

Such a religious is forbidden without a new and special indult of the Holy See to obtain certain offices and benefices. The terms used in this canon are to receive a strict interpretation, since they imply restrictions of rights. Such a religious cannot obtain a *benefice* in a major or minor *basilica* or *cathedral* church. A *benefice* strictly is a juridical entity constituted or erected in perpetuity by competent ecclesiastical authority. It consists of a sacred office and of the right to receive the fruits of the dowry which is annexed to the office. The religious who has returned to the world is not forbidden to exercise a simple office in such a place, *e.g.*, that of *econome*, sacristan, chaplain, etc., since these offices are not constituted as benefices.[28] *Basilica* strictly refers only to a church which has that title, whether major or minor, by apostolic concession or immemorable custom.[29] *Cathedral churches* refer, strictly only to those which are truly such at the present time. Not included under the term are those which are cathedral churches only by honorary title, but are such no longer in fact. Also excluded from the term are all other collegiate

[27] "Can ex-religious become pastors?"—*ER*, LXXXIX (1933), 431, 432; Goyeneche, "Consultatio"—*CpR*, V (1924), 26-28; *Jus Pontificium*, XI (1931), 110.

[28] Canon 1409; Piontek, *De Indulto Exclaustrationis Necnon Saecularizationis*, p. 239.

[29] Canon 1180. There are four major basilicas in Rome: St. John Lateran, St. Peter, St. Paul, St. Mary Major. There are nine minor basilicas in Rome and many others throughout the world. For a list of many of these minor basilicas, cf. Wetzer und Welte's *Kirchenlexicon* (2. ed., 12 vols., Freiburg im Breisgau, 1882-1901), II, 22.

churches.[30] Benefices in the cathedral churches of the United States are included under this term.[31]

The dismissed religious is also forbidden to teach or hold office in major or minor seminaries or colleges in which clerics are educated; or in Universities and Institutes which by apostolic privilege grant academic degrees. The term *college* is used often in the United States to describe the preparatory seminaries of religious, but it matters not whether they be called juvenates, scholasticates, or colleges, they are all contemplated in the text of canon 642 as long as the students therein are educated with a view to advancing to the clerical state. The academic degrees referred to in this canon are only those which are conferred by apostolic privilege and enjoy full canonical effect, *i. e.*, the degrees conferred in the schools of philosophy, theology, and canon law. The dismissed religious would also be forbidden to teach or hold any office in the Pontifical Biblical Institute or on the Pontifical Biblical Commission.[32] Not included in this prohibition would be the teaching or holding of offices in Universities or Institutes which give degrees in other sciences. If the religious received the doctorate from his own Institute according to the norms of the constitutions in virtue of a faculty conceded to that Institute by the Holy See, he loses it on his return to the world.[33]

The dismissed religious is forbidden to obtain any office or charge [34] in episcopal curiae and in religious houses whether of men or women, even in diocesan congregations. Such a religious cannot

30 Blat, *Commentarium,* II, 713.

31 Piontek, *op. cit.*, p. 239, against Augustine, *Commentary,* Vol. III (1. ed., 1919), 379. Augustine wrote before it was absolutely certain by declaration of the Apostolic Delegate that all parish churches of the United States were benefices. Cf. Bouscaren, *Canon Law Digest,* I, 149-151.

32 Canons 1377, 1380; Pius XI, Ap. const., *Deus Scientiarum Dominus,* 24 maii 1931, art. 10, §§ 2, 3—*AAS,* XXIII (1931), 241; Piontek, *op. cit.*, p. 240.

33 S. R. C., *Bahien in Brasilia,* 23 maii 1846, ad 4—*Fontes,* n. 5935.

34 *Office* (*officium*) is a narrower term than *charge* (*munus*). In a wide sense an office is any charge exercised for a spiritual purpose. In the strict sense (and this is the sense in which it is always used in the Code unless the wide meaning is apparent from the context) an office is a charge firmly established by divine or ecclesiastical ordinance, to be conferred according to the norms of the canons, and bearing with it a participation of ecclesiastical power, whether of orders or of jurisdiction. Cf. canon 145.

be a vicar general, an *officialis,* a chancellor, a promoter of justice, a defender of the bond, a synodal judge or examiner, a parish priest consultor, an auditor, a notary, a *cursor,* an *apparitor,*[35] a member of a cathedral chapter,[36] or a diocesan consultor.[37] He also cannot assume the charge of a confessor, a spiritual director, a chaplain, a rector, a preacher, or a curate in any religious Institute.[38]

D. Entrance in Another Religious Institute or in a Seminary

A religious who is dismissed while he is still in temporary vows cannot enter another Institute or return to his own without an apostolic indult, because canon 542, 1 ° states that those who are or have been bound by the bonds of religious profession are invalidly admitted to the novitiate. This profession must have been truly juridical, else the religious will not come under the prescriptions of this canon. One who during his novitiate had made profession in danger of death becomes again a novice at his recovery. If he leaves before profession he needs no apostolic indult to enter the novitiate of another religious Institute or even to re-enter the novitiate he has left. The prescription of canon 542, 1 ° does not bind those who once lived in a society in which vows are not taken since such persons are not properly religious nor did they make nor were they bound by the bond of religious profession properly so called.[39] In

[35] Canon 363, § 2.

[36] Canon 363, § 1 compared with canon 391, § 1.

[37] *PCI,* 29 ian. 1931: "An sub nomine *sacerdotes* de quibus in canone 423 veniant etiam religiosi vel religiosi saecularizati? Responsum: Negative"—*AAS,* XXIII (1931), 110; compare canon 423 with canon 368, § 1. Confer also: Oesterle, *Praelectiones Iuris Canonici,* I, 364; Nevin, "Religious cannot be diocesan consultors"—*ACR,* XII (1935), 69, 70, and "Offices prohibited to secularized religious"—*ACR,* XII (1935), 163-166.

[38] Piontek, *op. cit.,* p. 241; Schäfer, *De Religiosis,* pp. 966, 967. Note that the Code uses the words *"officio vel munere"* which denote not a mere act but a status. It is not forbidden him to preach an occasional sermon. He may also act as confessor, in accord with the rules contained in canons 519 and 522, in such cases wherein the religious may approach him for the sake of tranquillity of conscience, or when a woman religious who is gravely ill seeks his service as confessor in accord with the right which canon 523 grants her. *A fortiori,* he can hear the confessions of any and all religious in the case provided for in canon 882, namely, when they are in danger of death.

[39] Schäfer, *op. cit.,* p. 472; Goyeneche, "De egressu a religione"—*CpR,* V

regard to the subject of this dissertation there is bound by this law only that religious who during the time of his temporary vows has been dismissed from a religious Institute which is properly such in the sense of 488, 1°. On the other hand, although it is not the religious profession, but simply the oath or the promise, that establishes the bond between any person and the Institute to which he belongs (if the Institute be one in which vows are not taken by rule) nevertheless anyone who is or was bound by the profession of religious vows cannot validly enter the novitiate of such an Institute, for canon 677 expressly states that the rule of canon 542 must be observed in the admission of subjects to such an Institute.[40]

A religious who is dismissed during the time of his temporary vows (included here is he who is dismissed from an Institute in which no profession of vows is made according to canon 681) cannot enter a seminary in order to become a diocesan priest until the bishop has received secretly from the superiors or others information regarding the causes of dismissal and regarding his habits, natural qualities and intellectual abilities, and has moreover found out for certain that there is nothing in him which will not suit the sacerdotal state. Superiors are gravely bound in conscience to supply this information truthfully.[41] A recent decree issued jointly by the Congregation of Religious and the Congregation of Seminaries and Universities rules that if a candidate for the seminary has in any way at all belonged to a religious community the ordinary must confer with the Sacred Congregation of Seminaries and universities before such a one can be admitted to the seminary.[42]

E. The Cession of the Administration of Property; The Disposition of the Use and Usufruct

Regarding any assignment or disposition in the matter of the administration of his own property which was made by the dismissed

(1924), 338; Larraona, "Commentarium Codicis—Canon 542, 1°"—*CpRM*, XVII (1936), 75.

[40] Schäfer, *op. cit.*, p. 1032.

[41] Canon 1363, § 3; Blat, *Commentarium*, Lib. III, partes II-VI, 339, 340.

[42] S. C. de Religiosis atque de Seminariis et Studiorum Universitatibus, decr. 25 iul. 1941—*AAS*, XXXIII (1941), 371.

religious before the time of his simple profession, the following legal course of acting will obtain. The commitment of this administration to whomsoever he chose and the disposition which he made concerning the use and usufruct accruing from the property during the period of the temporary profession will automatically cease to have any further effect once the act of dismissal has effectively intervened in accordance with the law of the Code. If by the disposition of the person's will his goods and property were held and administered by the Institute, they shall be returned to him except for the accrued fruits and revenues which have already been consumed or expended.[43]

F. Remuneration for Services

There is no obligation whatsoever for the Institute to pay the religious for any of the services which he rendered while he was a religious. As was seen in the consideration of temporary profession in its nature of a bilateral contract (in the first chapter of the commentary), obligations arose on each side: the religious vowed to obey and to fulfill his duties, and the Institute contractually agreed to support the religious. Canon 643, § 1 is very just in stating that whoever has been dismissed cannot seek compensation for services rendered by him to the Institute. By the same token the Institute cannot demand reimbursement for special or extraordinary expenses it has made in his behalf unless it can be proved beyond doubt that he had entered the Institute solely to complete a course of studies or to learn an art with the intention of leaving the Institute afterwards.[44] This provision holds even if after the dismissal of the religious there is proof that his profession was invalid, for if he could sue for services rendered to the Institute, then the Institute could in turn sue for the expense of his support. The two claims would probably cancel each other.[45] Many Institutes have the prudent practice—and it should be made a practice in all Institutes in order to avoid all difficulties in this matter—to draw up a document which

[43] Canons 580, § 3; 569, § 2; Schäfer, *op. cit.*, pp. 598, 599, 969.

[44] Goyeneche, "Consultatio"—*CpR,* V (1924), 210 sq.; Schäfer, *De Religiosis*, p. 946.

[45] Goyeneche, "Consultatio,"—*CpR,* XII (1931), 134, 135; Schäfer, *op. cit.*, p. 951.

shall have legal force even in the civil courts and which shall embody the prescriptions of canons 580, § 2, and 643, § 1, namely, that whatever he acquires by his own industry or with relation to his Institute belongs to the Institute, and, further, that he cannot seek compensation for services rendered by him to the Institute whenever he leaves it, whether it be at the expiration of his vows, whether it be upon his dismissal from the Institute, or whether it be upon the granting of a decree of secularization.[46]

G. Restoration of the Dowry

Canon 551, § 1, states that if a professed woman religious in either solemn or simple vows leaves the Institute for any cause whatsoever, her dowry must be returned to her intact, but not the interest already derived therefrom. In the case of a religious who was dismissed while she was in temporary vows the dowry must be returned to her, for her dismissal is surely a factor which is comprehended in the phrase, "If, *from whatever cause*, a professed religious . . . leave the Institute," etc.[47] It does not seem that the dowry should be restored to those who are dismissed only provisorily according to canons 653 and 668. These dismissals are not true dismissals. They are acts of but a temporary and provisory character. No obligation arises for the Institute to return the dowry until the religious has been permanently dismissed.[48]

The Code states that the *entire dowry* must be returned. A dowry is a definite sum of money, or its equivalent, paid by a postulant to a convent in which she wishes to make her profession, so that the interest from this capital sum is destined primarily for her support as long as she remains in the Institute.[49] Obviously this does

[46] Schäfer, *op. cit.*, pp. 557; 971; Berutti, *De Religiosis*, p. 333.

[47] Schäfer, *op. cit.*, p. 507, note 319, and p. 1001; Berutti, *op. cit.*, p. 163; Cappello, *Summa Iuris Canonici*, II, 204; Larraona, "Commentarium Codicis—Canon 551"—*CpRM*, XXI (1940), 146.

[48] Larraona, *art. cit.*, p. 147, note (784), against Tabera "De dimissione religiosorum"—*CpR*, XIV (1933), 59.

[49] Kealy, *Dowry of Women Religious*, The Catholic University of America Canon Law Studies, n. 134 (Washington, D. C.: The Catholic University of America Press, 1941), p. 1. This section of the effect of dismissal on the dowry is taken in the main from Kealy's thesis. It may profitably be consulted for a

not include the gifts made freely to the Institute before her profession by the later dismissed religious.

But what is meant by the *entire dowry?* This dowry, from the definition, can consist of a definite sum of money or its equivalent, *i. e.*, of securities, titles, mortgages, etc., or of movable or immovable goods such as houses, land, etc. If the dowry consisted of investments or securities which are still retained by the Institute, these investments or their cash equivalent must be returned regardless of their change of value.[50] If the dowry was paid in cash which later was invested or if it was paid in securities which later were reinvested, then a distinction must be made. If each individual dowry is placed in a correspondingly individual investment, these securities or their cash equivalent must be returned to the religious regardless of any change in value.[51] If several of the dowries have been invested cumulatively and have thus been converted into a single investment, the regular procedure is to return the same amount of money as the cash or the cash equivalent of the investment which constituted her dowry.[52] Larraona favors another method which seems to be more in conformity with law and justice. The current value of her proportionate share of the investment should be returned. Since the Institute has not acquired irrevocable title to the capital of the dowry, and since the entire dowry must be returned, the Institute seems to lack any title which could justify the withholding for itself the increase in the value of the investment. On the other hand, if through no fault of administration the proportionate share of the combined capital sum has decreased in value with the other shares, the Institute is not obliged to bear the loss. There is no reason for assuming that the Institute should bear the loss for acts which the

fuller treatment of this matter. Cf. also: Wernz-Vidal, *Ius Canonicum,* III, 221; Vermeersch-Creusen, *Epitome,* I, 497; Augustine, *Commentary,* III, 224; Schäfer, *op. cit.*, p. 501.

[50] Schäfer, *op. cit.*, p. 507; Creusen, "Restitution d'une dot"—*RCR,* I (1925), 151; Coronata, *Institutiones,* I, 727; Larraona, *art. cit.*, p. 149, note (788).

[51] Larraona, *art. cit.*, p. 150; Creusen, *art. cit.;* Jombart, "Les dots"—*RCR,* III (1927), 56.

[52] Coronata, *op. cit.*, I, 727; Larraona, *art. cit.*, p. 151, nn. 5, 6, and note (792).

law itself imposes or for acts which are placed in accordance with the law.[53] These rules all presuppose that the law of canon 549 regarding the investment of the dowry has been observed. The Institute must make up for any loss of the dowry which results either from maladministration or from a manner of administration which runs contrary to the requirement of canon 549.[54]

Finally, the entire dowry must be restored, but not the interest already derived therefrom. Since the income produced by the investment of the capital of the dowry is destined for the support of the religious during her life in the community, the Institute acquires the free and absolute title of ownership to the income from the invested dowries. At her departure the religious has no claim at all on the interest which has matured at the time of her departure. If the securities bear interest which is payable only on a certain date annually (*e.g.*, January first), and the religious is dismissed on a day other than that date (*e.g.*, May 23rd), the interest for that year to be divided *pro rata temporis* between the Institute and the departing religious.[55]

H. Charitable Subsidy

> Si tamen religiosa sine dote recepta fuerit nec ex propriis bonis sibimet providere valeat, religio ex caritate eidem dare debet ea quae requiruntur ut modo tuto ac convenienti domum redeat, ac providere ut, naturali aequitate servata, per aliquod tempus, mutuo consensu vel in casu dissensus ab Ordinario loci determinandum, honeste vivere possit.[56]

Contemplated in canon 643, § 2, are: the religious of simple vows who have been dismissed from those Institutes in which no dowry is required, the individual religious who have received from the Insti-

[53] Larraona, *art. cit.*, p. 149, note (789); Jombart, *art. cit.*, p. 56.

[54] Larraona, *loc. cit.*

[55] Wernz-Vidal, *Ius Canonicum*, III, 225; Vermeersch-Creusen, *Epitome*, I, 499; Fanfani, *De Iure Religiosorum*, p. 191; Vromant, *De Bonis Ecclesiae Temporalibus* (Louvain: Desbarax, 1927), p. 270.

[56] "In the case of a female religious who has been received without a dowry, and who cannot provide for herself out of her own resources, the Institute should in charity give her what is necessary for her to return safely and becomingly to her home, and provide her for a certain period with the means, to be determined by mutual consent, or, in case of disagreement, by the local Ordinary, of an honest livelihood, in accordance with natural equity."—Canon 643, § 2.

tute a condonation in regard to the fixed amount of the dowry, and the religious who have indeed furnished the dowry in the amount which is required by the constitutions, but not in an amount which suffices to cover the needs for which the law of canon 643, § 2, seeks to provide for properly.

If the dowry which must be restored in justice does not equal the amount which is demanded in canon 643, § 2 (called by the authors *the charitable subsidy*), then the Institute is obliged in charity to add to the dowry the amount which is wanting to make up a fitting charitable subsidy.[57]

The amount of the help to be given to a religious who has either no dowry or not a sufficient dowry depends greatly upon circumstances of person, time and place. It would be futile to try to establish a set sum which absolutely could be considered as a sufficient charitable subsidy in each case or, for that matter, to set an absolute minimum amount for the charitable subsidy, so that the Institute would have to be considered at fault in not providing at least that sum. The futility of trying to determine the amount can best be illustrated by examples. There is a very great difference, on the one hand, between the help to be given to a young girl who has been professed only a year and who lives in the same city, or even only a few blocks away from the convent, especially if her family is of comfortable means or if she can immediately secure a position, and, on the other hand, the help to be given to one who has perhaps spent many years in an Institute in which the members profess only temporary vows and who when she leaves the convent is far removed from home or even from her homeland, especially if her parents have died and she has no home to which she can return. The subsidy depends too much on circumstances to permit one to set a fixed sum as being adequate. It depends on the constitutions to determine whether the house to which she is attached, the province, or the Institute as such shall pay her this charitable subsidy.[58]

The Code by positive law deals only with the Institutes of religious women in the matter of this charitable subsidy, but natural

[57] S. C. de Relig., resp. 2 mart., 1924—*AAS,* XVI (1924), 165, 166; Schäfer, *op. cit.,* pp. 970, 971; 997; Maroto, "Annotationes"—*CpR,* V (1924), 320-323.

[58] Battandier, *Guide Canonique,* p. 272, n. 320, 5; p. 284, n. 328; Berutti, *De Religiosis,* p. 334.

equity demands that the same prescription of law be applied also in Institutes of religious men if the dismissed religious really needs such charitable help.[59]

In some Institutes the constitutions state that those things which pertain to personal use (clothing, etc.) or which are of small moment are presumed either to have been left to the Institute or to have been used up or expended (and this latter is generally the case unless the religious is dismissed immediately after profession, for the time spent in vows plus that of the postulancy and the novitiate is normally such that clothing, etc., which the religious brought with him has become worn out or is used up). If the constitutions state nothing on this point then these effects are to be returned to the departing member in the state in which they are.[60]

Jombart, however, states that the Code demands this return only in the case of novices leaving the Institute. He says that unless the constitutions provide otherwise there is no obligation in justice to return such clothing though there may be an obligation in charity if the religious or his parents are convinced that they have a right to such clothes or to a return of the money they gave to buy the material for a habit, etc., and will cause trouble or spread tales as to the avarice of religious, etc.[61] Practically the question is not of much importance since the charitable subsidy covers the need of clothing as well as the need of transportation and either the clothing must be given back or new clothing bought or provided for.

Article 3. The Recourse Against the Decree of Dismissal

The Code grants to every religious who has been dismissed during the time of his temporary vows a recourse against the decree of dismissal:

> Contra dimissionis decretum est religioso facultas recurrendi ad Sedem Apostolicam; et pendente recursu, dimissio nullam habet iuridicum effectum.[62]

[59] Coronata, *Institutiones*, I, 861; Jansen, *Ordensrecht*, p. 281; Jombart, "Le renvoi au cours des voeux temporaires"—*RCR*, V (1929), 202.

[60] Goyeneche, "Consultatio"—*CpR*, V (1924), 99; Fanfani, *De Iure Religiosorum*, p. 481; Battandier, *op. cit.*, p. 283.

[61] Jombart, "Restitution de trousseau"—*RCR*, VI (1930), 190-191.

[62] "The religious has the right to appeal to the Apostolic See against the

Thus, even if the religious has already left the Institute, the recourse made within the proper time limit will halt the effect of the decree of dismissal and he should return to the Institute.

How much time is allowed for the placing of this recourse which connotes a suspension of the effect of dismissal? This was indeed a knotty question, for the Code had stated no express time-limit in the matter of interposing an extrajudicial recourse. There was need of an official statement [63] and the Sacred Congregation of Religious did give the desired statement with additional explanatory remarks.[64] The reply stated that the available time (*tempus utile*) for the interposing of this recourse with a suspensive effect was ten days according to the norm established for similar cases in canons 1465, § 1, and 2153, § 1.

In order to remove all doubt regarding the limit of time and certain consequences following from it, the Sacred Congregation observed that the following points should be attended to: [65]

"1. The religious may interpose a recourse from the decree of

decree of dismissal; and, pending the appeal, the dismissal has no juridical effect. . . ."—Canon 647, § 2, 4°. Note that the official English translation uses the phrase "the right to *appeal*" and "pending the *appeal*." This is a less correct wording. Strictly an appeal may be made only in a judicial process and only against an unjust sentence. Canons 1879, 1880, 1601; cf. Noval, *Commentarium Codicis Iuris Canonici,* Vol. IV, *De Iudiciis* (Romae, 1920), n. 642. The Code no longer speaks of "extrajudicial appeal" against the decrees of a superior or of a judge, but designates this remedy as "recourse" (*recursus*). On Canon 1601, cf. Noval, *loc. cit.*; Vermeersch-Creusen, *Epitome,* III, p. 98, n. 237; Wernz-Vidal, *Ius Canonicum,* IV, n. 600, note 9; Connolly, *Appeals,* The Catholic University of America Canon Law Studies, n. 79 (Washington, D. C.: The Catholic University of America, 1932), p. 4; and Roberti, "De recursu ad reiectionem libelli"—*Apollinaris,* I (1928), 73, 74. The dismissal, as was seen, is of an administrative and not of a judicial character. Therefore the word "recourse" is a more fitting term for the extrajudicial redress which is sought.

[63] Thus Bastien (*Directoire Canonique,* p. 132) before the answer of the Sacred Congregation of Religious stated that three months was the maximum time that could be allowed for the interposing of this recourse.

[64] S. C. de Relig., resp. et declar., 20 iul. 1923—*AAS,* XV (1923), 457.

[65] The English translation of the text of these declarations will be given in quotation marks and the commentary will follow each declaration. The English translation is from Bouscaren, *Canon Law Digest,* I, 328, 329.

dismissal, either immediately by a letter sent to this Sacred Congregation, or mediately through the person who communicated to him the decree."

"2. To prove the fact that the recourse has been made, an authentic document, or at least the testimony of two trustworthy persons, is required and sufficient." This authentic document is the letter of the religious to the Sacred Congregation or to the superior who communicates to him the decree of dismissal. In the latter case the religious can have a duplicate copy of the letter of recourse made, and have the superior attest on that copy that he has received it and have him note the date in writing. If the letter is lost or cannot be found the testimony of two trustworthy persons suffices.[66]

"3. The available time of ten days from notice of the decree given to the religious, is to be computed according to c. 34, § 3, 3°; and according to c. 35 it does not run if the dismissed religious does not know he has a right to make the recourse, or if he is unable to do so. Hence, it is well that the Superior inform him of his right and of the limit of time for its exercise, at the same time when he notifies him of the decree of dismissal." This provision protects the Institute and the superior as well as the religious. The Institute is saved from further uncertainty and protected from future claims once the time-limit has been made known to the religious; the superior by his action shows that he is acting with sincerity and prudence; the religious is protected against his own ignorance and against the negligence or bad faith of a superior.[67] No mode of informing the religious of his right is specified, but it would be better if it were given in writing rather than orally, and preferably affixed to the decree of dismissal.[68] Since the decree of dismissal will not coincide with the beginning of the day, the day on which it was communicated to the religious is not counted. Thus if the decree was communicated on May 14th, the ten day period begins running on May 15th.[69] *Tempus utile* implies that the time for the exercise or prosecution of one's rights does not

[66] Maroto, "Annotationes"—*CpR,* IV (1923), 355; Geser, *The Canon Law Governing Communities of Sisters,* p. 368.

[67] Creusen-Garesché-Ellis, *Religious Men and Women,* pp. 268, 269.

[68] Maroto, *art. cit.,* p. 355.

[69] Canon 34, § 3, 3°.

lapse if one is ignorant of one's rights, or unable to act at the time.[70] The use of this right of recourse can be impeded by ignorance or by some other impediment. But not any and every kind of ignorance is admitted as an impediment. Any continued ignorance on the part of the religious relative to his right of making recourse is definitely prevented if the superior informs him concerning the possible use of this right at the very time that the decree of dismissal is intimated to him. Since, however, the superior could possibly and imprudently omit it (inasmuch as the declaration states merely that "it is well" to do so), the lack of knowledge on the part of the religious must be of the kind which a responsible man would be apt to have.[71]

As to the impediments, the words "agere non valenti" of canon 35 are broad and indefinite and can be rendered by "impeded" or "hindered by some impediment." The impediment to the interposing of recourse is normally a physical impediment, such as illness. There

[70] Cicognani, *Canon Law,* Authorized English Version by J. O'Hara and F. Brennan (Philadelphia: Dolphin Press, 1934), p. 691.

[71] Dubé, *The General Principles for the Reckoning of Time in Canon Law,* The Catholic University of American Canon Law Studies, n. 144 (Washington, D. C., The Catholic University of America Press, 1941), pp. 130, 131. Dubé appeals to several authors (Toso, *Commentaria Minora,* I, 113; Cicognani, *op. cit.,* p. 692; Michiels, *Normae Generalis,* II, 158; Van Hove, *Commentarium Lovaniense in Codicem Iuris Canonici,* Vol. I, Tomus III, *De Consuetudine, De Temporis Supputatione* [Mechlinae: Dessain, 1933], n. 320) for his statement that if the person does not know what is obvious to all, he himself is responsible for the loss of his rights. A difficulty, however, could arise with regard to the interpretation of the phrase "what is obvious to all." On the one hand the dismissed religious could argue that, even though the constitutions clearly stated the rule of the ten-day period for the interposing of a recourse, his ignorance of that particular provision of the constitutions was not so culpable that he sacrifice the benefit of still being able to make recourse; in other words, just because the matter was stated in the constitutions, that fact does not make the prescription of the constitutions "obvious to all" the religious of that Institute. On the other hand, the superior could maintain that with all the time given to the reading and studying of the rule such a provision of the constitutions would be a fact "obvious to all" the members of the Institute and that as a result the ignorance of the religious was culpable enough so that he lost the right to have his time of recourse be suspended until his ignorance ceased. This possible difficulty could readily be avoided by means of the timely warning given him concerning the ten-day period available to him for placing a recourse.

cannot be any legal impediments, for excommunication, suspension, etc., do not forbid anyone to supply this recourse. The day on which the continued impediment has eventually ceased is not counted; the time begins to run on the next day. Any discussion as to what portion of the day constitutes it as an available day seems out of place here. Any hour of the day may constitute a time at which the interposing of a recourse can be considered as available. Unlike an appeal which must be brought to the attention of a court during the hours within which the court received pleas, a recourse can be interposed at any hour of the day. To pass by on any given day a substantial opportunity for the interposing of recourse implies the loss of one of the ten available days which are granted.[72] In case of dispute, if, for instance, a religious having recourse after the ten days, maintains that he was impeded for the greater part of several of the days in this period of time and that these days should not count, the plea must be heard unless certainly untrue or unfounded in fact. In case of dispute it would be for the Sacred Congregation of Religious to decide the merits of the case; even then, if the plea were proved to be true it would be useless since that Congregation will by that time be judging the merits of the causes for dismissal and will send back a confirmation or rejection of the decree of dismissal rather than a decision of the truth of the plea of the religious about the availability of the time.

"4. The recourse duly made has a suspensive effect; hence, until the decree of dismissal is confirmed by the S. C. Rel., and until the Superior who did the dismissing has been notified of its confirmation by an authentic document from the Sacred Congregation, the decree of dismissal is ineffective and cannot be put into execution." In other words, the recourse forestalls the immediate effect of the dismissal. The superior must wait for authentic information from the Sacred Congregation and he cannot proceed to action until he gets the authentic document from the Congregation and recognizes its authenticity and integrity; no other knowledge suffices for definitive action.[73]

"5. While the recourse is pending, the person dismissed remains

[72] Dubé, *op. cit.*, pp. 231-240.

[73] Canon 53; Maroto, *loc. cit.*

a religious, and hence has the same rights and obligations as other religious, in exactly the same way as before his dismissal. Hence, he has the right and obligation of dwelling in the religious house, and remains under the obedience of Superiors, without prejudice to the provision of c. 2243, § 2." Until the confirmation or repudiation of the recourse, the religious has all the rights and duties he had before dismissal. If he is out of the house when he makes the recourse, he must return to the house of the Institute assigned to him by the superior and must remain there under obedience to the superior. If, however, there were any penalties or censures incurred, the recourse against the dimissal will have no suspensive effect on them.[74]

If the available time of ten days has elapsed, there is always open to the religious the right to interpose a recourse *in devolutivo*. In such a case the decree of dismissal stands with full legal effect until it is reversed. This recourse is always open to him since it is an extrajudicial matter which never becomes a *res iudicata*. This recourse leaves matters in the state in which they are and does not suspend the effects of dismissal. Therefore the religious has no right or obligation of returning to a house of the Institute. If the Holy See finds that the dismissal took place unjustly or without the observing of the law, it can recall the decree of the superior and restore the religious to his status as a member of the Institute. [75]

As to the practice in the matter of recourse *in devolutivo*, Woywod warns against too sanguine hopes for the success of such a recourse. The presumption is that the superiors have made a conscientious judgment. He states that only in the case in which it can be proved that the religious has been dismissed because of illness contracted after profession is there any hope of obtaining reinstatement.[76]

[74] Canon 2243, § 2; Creusen-Garesché-Ellis, *Religious Men and Women*, p. 269; Maroto, *loc. cit.*

[75] Maroto, *loc. cit.*

[76] Woywod, "Answers to questions"—*HPR*, XXXVII (1936-1937), 419, 420.

CHAPTER V

EXCLUSION FROM PROFESSION

As was pointed out in Chapter One,[1] the exclusion of a religious from perpetual vows or from a renewal of temporary vows cannot strictly be called a dismissal. In the case of dismissal there is presupposed as a note proper to itself that the religious shall still be bound to the Institute by the bond of profession.[2] It has, however, a great similarity with dismissal; yet, it is governed in so many points by a different legislation that it merits a separate treatment under the various heading of: the superior authorized for the act of excluding from profession; the causes for which the exclusion is effected; the time at which the exclusion is effective; the form, the effects and the recourse from the exclusion. For the sake of brevity, the word *exclusion* will be employed in this chapter to refer to the act of a competent superior by which the subject, when the time of his preceding temporary profession is at an end, is refused permission to renew his temporary profession or to take perpetual vows.

A. The Superior Authorized for the Act of Exclusion

In regard to the superior who is authorized to exclude a religious from the Institute the Code is silent. It merely states that " . . . religio . . . eundem potest a renovandis votis temporariis vel ab emittenda professione perpetua excludere. . . . [3] The Code, then, leaves it to the constitutions to designate the superior who will be competent to exclude the religious.[4] Usually this will be a major superior but

[1] Cf. *supra*, p. 74.

[2] Canon 637; Schäfer, *De Religiosis*, p. 947, note 10, p. 984; Chelodi, *Ius De Personis*, p. 450; Jombart, "La sortie de la religion a l'expiration des voeux temporaires"—*RCR*, V (1924), 161. Schäfer calls it *egressus passivus*.

[3] " . . . the Institute . . . can exclude the religious from renewing the temporary vows or from making profession of perpetual vows. . . ."—Canon 637.

[4] Cervia, *De Professione Religiosa*, p. 116; Palombo, *De Dimissione Religiosorum*, p. 200; Goyeneche, "Consultatio"—*CpR*, I (1920), 235; Vermeersch, "De conscribendis constitutionibus congregationis votorum simplicium vel de iisdem ad codicem aptandis"—*Periodica*, XVI (1927), 162*.

it need not necessarily be the Supreme Moderator.[5] Nor need it necessarily be a major superior; the constitutions could give this power to a local superior.[6] It will usually be the major superior, the same one to whom is given the right to admit the novice to temporary profession.[7] The authors all seem to be of the opinion that, if the constitutions are silent on the matter, the competent superior is he who admits the postulant to the novitiate and the novice to the first profession.[8] Among the major superiors is to be numbered the *Antistita* of an independent house of nuns (*moniales*); in the matter of excluding from profession she is not subject to the local ordinary or regular superior, as she is in the matter of executing a true dismissal according to canon 647, and she can herself exclude a religious from the Institute unless there is some provision in the constitutions contrary to this.[9] Nowhere is it provided in the Code that the local ordinary is a major superior.[10] If in an Institute of diocesan approval the constitutions are silent, the competent superior is that major superior who is authorized to admit candidates to the novitiate or first profession.

As to the consent or advice of the Council, the Code leaves it to the constitutions to determine whether the intervention of the Council is needed at all and, if it is, whether its consent or merely its advice is needed.[11] Some hold that if the constitutions are silent, no in-

[5] Larraona, "Consultatio"—*CpR,* V (1924), 100-102; Schäfer, *op. cit.*, p. 948.

[6] Palombo, *op. cit.*, p. 200.

[7] Coronata, *Institutiones,* I, 854, note 1; Bouuaert-Simenon, *Manuale,* I, 413.

[8] Canon 543; Palombo, *loc. cit.;* Cervia, *op. cit.*, p. 87, note 1; p. 116; Schäfer, *loc. cit.;* Beste, *Introductio,* p. 430; Vermeersch, "De exclusione a renovandis votis ex c. 637"—*Periodica,* XIII (1925), (70)-(71); Goyeneche, "Consultatio"—*CpR,* I (1920), 235; *CpRM,* XIX (1938), 8-12; "Ad varias quaestiones responsa brevissima"—*Jus Pontificium,* VIII (1928), 150; Jombart, "La sortie de religion a l'expiration des voeux temporaires"—*RCR,* V (1929), 163; Creusen, "Admission au renouvellement des voeux"—*RCR,* V (1929), 167.

[9] Canon 504; Vermeersch-Creusen, *Epitome,* I, 595; Cervia, *op. cit.*, p. 87, and note 1; Vermeersch, *art. cit.*—*Periodica,* XIII (1924), (71); Jombart, "La sortie de religion a l'expiration des voeux temporaires"—*RCR,* V (1929), 163.

[10] Cervia, *op. cit.*, p. 58; Goyeneche, *De Religiosis,* p. 80.

[11] Mothon, *L'État Religieux,* p. 370, note 13; Berutti, *De Religiosis,* p. 324; Bastien, *Directoire Canonique,* p. 130.

tervention of the Council is needed, for, while the Code demands it for the admission of the subjects, it does not demand it for their exclusion.[12] Others admit that the major superior can exclude from profession for secret causes known only to himself and not to the Council.[13] Palombo [14] and Schäfer [15] maintain that the vote is consultative only. Goyeneche [16] says that there is needed at least a consultative vote. He contends that admission and exclusion are integrally related or, at least double correlative matters; *i. e.*, exclusion is the mere denial of admission and is the same but correlative power as that of admission[17] He argues that since, at least a consultative vote of the Council is demanded by the Code for the admission of a religious to perpetual profession,[18] so, too, it is required for the exclusion of the professed religious. It seems, however, that if the constitutions are silent, the silence of the Code coupled with the diversity of opinion among authors, leaves uncertain the question of the necessity of at least a consultative vote of the Council for the exclusion of a religious. Because of the probability of the opinion of Goyeneche, Schäfer, and Palombo, the omission of this consultation could be alleged as an additional defense in recourse based on an alleged injustice or arbitrariness of the superior in excluding the candidate from profession. Therefore, practically, it is safe for the superior to ask the advice of his Council in the matter of excluding a religious even though the constitutions do not demand the seeking of such advice.

B. The Causes Sufficient for the Act of Exclusion

The meaning of the words *just and reasonable* were considered in Chapter III. Suffice it to say here that a just cause connotes a

[12] Cervia, *op. cit.*, p. 116; Beste (*op. cit.*, p. 430) states that the intervention of the Council is not necessary, but that it would be safer and more fitting to have it.

[13] Vermeersch-Creusen, *op. cit.*, I, 595; Coronata, *op. cit.*, I, 883, note 1; Goyeneche, "De egressu a religione"—*CpR,* V (1924), 216; Vermeersch, *art. cit.—Periodica,* XIII (1925), (70).

[14] *Op. cit.*, p. 199.

[15] *Op. cit.*, p. 948.

[16] *De Religiosis,* p. 194, note 10.

[17] Canons 543; 575, § 1; 637.

[18] Canon 543.

proportionate cause; *i. e.*, the cause (or harm to the Institute) must outweigh or balance the right of the religious to remain in the Institute. The determination of the causes is left to the judgment of the superiors who should have the Institute chiefly in mind when forming their judgment. In general, it can be said that those who will prove more harmful than useful to the Institute should be excluded.[19] The greater number of the causes for exclusion are contained under this very general cause: the superior foresees that the religious will not give honor to the Institute because he is a very mediocre, if not bad, religious. This mediocrity or lack of goodness is caused by the deficiency in the required qualities whether this be involuntary on his part or because of his lack of good will.[20]

A cause which is not enough to dismiss a religious during the time of his temporary vows can be a cause sufficient to keep him from perpetual profession or from renewing his temporary vows, for, as has been seen, a cause of less magnitude is needed.[21]

Therefore all the causes sufficient for dismissal from temporary vows are sufficient here; indeed, if the superior should have grave doubts as to the sufficiency of the causes to dismiss, he may wait until the time of temporary profession has elapsed. The causes may then appear to be just and reasonable enough to exclude the religious from the Institute. The authors in their commentaries on canon 637 list a great number of causes in the moral, intellectual and physical order but all the causes they mention have been treated in the Third Chapter under the causes for dismissal. Note that although these causes are the same in species they may be less in degree when it is a case of exclusion rather than dismissal.[22]

[19] Palombo, *op. cit.*, pp. 201-203.

[20] Jombart, "La sortie de religion a l'expiration des voeux temporaires"—*RCR*, V (1929), 162.

[21] Goyeneche, *De Religiosis*, p. 214; Schäfer, *op. cit.*, pp. 646, 947; Palombo, *op. cit.*, p. 201; Vermeersch-Creusen, *Epitome*, I, 595.

[22] Palombo, *op. cit.*, pp. 202, 203; Goyeneche, *op. cit.*, pp. 193, 194; Schäfer, *op. cit.*, p. 947; Coronata, *Institutiones*, I, 874; Fanfani, *De Iure Religiosorum*, pp. 480, 481; Berutti, *De Religiosis*, p. 324; De Meester, *Compendium*, II, 479, n. 1051, note 5; Beste, *op. cit.*, p. 430; Goyeneche, "Consultatio"—*CpR*, I (1920), 234; V (1924), 215; *Constitutiones Congregationis Presbyterorum a Sacro Corde Jesu. Regulae et Praescriptiones* . . . (pro hac congregatione), p. 115, n. 299.

If after careful consideration, the superior cannot decide whether or not to admit a religious to perpetual profession, the decision must be made in favor of the Institute and against the admission of the religious. If the spiritual, mental or physical qualifications of the religious are such that the superior is doubtful whether the religious has a vocation to the life of the respective community, the religious should be excluded from perpetual vows because the common good of the Institute is to be preferred to the welfare of individuals. Further, the candidate for a religious Institute must give positive and satisfactory proof that he has a divine vocation for a particular community. One cannot say that he has a divine vocation for a certain form of life when he cannot show for certain that he has the required spiritual, mental and physical qualifications.[23] At most, the superior can prolong the period of temporary vows. If at the end of these extra three years of probation the vocation of the religious is still in doubt, he should be excluded.

One question of grave importance in regard to causes sufficient for exclusion, raised first by D'Ambrosio and supported by several authors,[24] concerns the case of a religious in an Institute whose members take only temporary vows which are to be renewed at stated intervals. When the religious has been in the Institute for six years or more, are just and reasonable causes enough to dismiss him at the expiration of a period of temporary profession? It seems that they are not enough but that grave causes with incorrigibility are needed —though this incorrigibility need not be proved by a formal trial; *i. e.*, there are needed the same causes, but without the process, which are needed to dismiss a religious of perpetual vows in either a clerical non-exempt or a lay Institute.

This opinion holds that there is a lacuna in the Code which must be remedied by a recourse to canon 20; *i. e.*, to laws made in similar cases, to canonical equity and general principles of law, and to the style and practice of the Roman Curia. The cases here are similar;

[23] Woywod, "Answers to questions"—*HPR*, XXVII (1936-1937), 418, 419.

[24] D'Ambrosio, "De causis exclusionis religiosi a renovatione professionis in institutis votorum temporariorum"—*Apollinaris*, IV (1931), 124-128; Schäfer, *op. cit.*, p. 948; Vermeersch-Creusen, *Epitome*, I, 595; Creusen-Garesché-Ellis, *Religious Men and Women*, p. 252; Jombart, "La sortie de religion a l'expiration des voeux temporaires"—*RCR*, V (1929), 162.

the religious in temporary vows for more than six years and the religious in perpetual vows both have an acquired right to support based on their years of service to the Institute. It was presumably, such a right which made the lawgiver lay down such stringent provisions as to the causes for dismissal and the proved incorrigibility of the subject who had made perpetual profession. It is true that the religious who has been bound by temporary vows has not the same acquired right as the religious in perpetual vows because the latter's right is based on the stability effected by his vows and a perpetual contract. Another reason, arising out of the similarity of the cases applies equally to both; namely, the hardship in returning to the world arising from the difficulty in making proper adjustment and in finding remunerative employment. For these two reasons general principles of law and equity demand an equalization of causes in regard to the exclusion of the religious who has been in temporary vows for more than six years and the dismissal of a religious in perpetual vows. The argument is confirmed by canon 642, § 2, which regards those who have been bound for six years by temporary vows, oaths, and promises as juridically in the same category as those perpetually professed. Vermeersch-Creusen assert that it is the practice of the Sacred Congregation of Religious, when it concedes a long or indefinite deferring of perpetual vows, not to allow a sister whose perpetual profession has been thus deferred to be dismissed except for causes which would be necessary to dismiss a religious in perpetual vows. They infer that this rule can be applied to those Institutes which even without indult permit perpetual profession to be deferred for more than six years.[25] D'Ambrosio states that he knows of such a case. A few years after the promulgation of the Code the Sacred Congregation of Religious, after consulting the Holy Father, handed down the decision that the exclusion of a religious who had been in temporary vows for more than six years could be effected only by those causes demanded for the dismissal of a religious in perpetual vows. From this practice of the Sacred Congregation, he infers a norm is available for judging the mind of the Holy See in regard to these cases.

Reviewing the arguments set forth, one observes, first a weakness

[25] Vermeersch-Creusen, *Epitome,* I, 595.

in this that the cases are not parallel and are not strictly the *leges latae in similibus* demanded by canon 20. D'Ambrosio himself admits this, as was seen above. Then, as to the practice of the Curia, it is not so evident that the few cases cited can constitute a practice.

Though the cases are not strictly parallel, due, in one case, to the expiration of the obligation of the vows and contract at the end of the period of temporary vows, still there is a similarity, if not parallelism in this: the religious in temporary vows who spent the whole time of more than six years in the Institute worked just as hard, was bound by his obligations just as firmly, was viewed just as equally as a religious by the Code in the section *De Religiosis* as was the religious in perpetual vows. The ties binding him to the Institute grew stronger and his adaptability to the life outside the Institute lessened with the years; in other words, his claim to stay in the Institute, based on his services rendered to and his dependence on the Institute, give him a right to stay in the Institute, a right much stronger than that of a religious professed only a few years. It is not, it is true, a right based on justice arising from a contract freely entered upon but it is based on a claim arising in equity, which cannot be ignored by the ecclesiastical legislator in regulating human relations.

General principles of law seem to persuade one to accept D'Ambrosio's opinion. When canon 637 was compared with canon 647, it was seen that the difference in gravity of the required causes was a result of the difference of status; in canon 637 the contract was regarded as ended, in canon 647, as still binding. Now, if canon 647 is compared with canons 649-652, one, noting another gradation of causes, might easily ask the reason for the difference of the gravity of the causes required by each. Essentially a contract is the same whether it binds perpetually or only for a time. The parties to the contract cannot justify the rescinding a contract which binds only for a specified period of time for any less of a cause than is demanded for the rescinding a perpetual contract. On the other hand, in view of the stability engendered by the perpetual profession and the sureness of each other felt by both parties of the contract which is based on that contract, one can easily see why graver causes are needed to rescind it. On the basis of this proved stability the Institute gives more trust and confidence to a religious in perpetual vows than to a religious in temporary vows; positions of trust and special training for certain positions or offices will be given by the Institute if it can feel sure of the permanence and stability of the relationship between the religious and itself. There is no strict parallel between this case and the other case of a religious who has been in temporary vows for more than six years in an Institute whose members profess only temporary vows. General principles of law seem, however, to make them almost parallel. There is no way provided either in the Code or particular law by which this permanent stability can be adequately supplied in Institutes with only temporary vows, but it can be said that *ex communiter contingentibus* when a religious has been professed six years in the Institute, both he and the Institute have tried each other thoroughly and have accepted each other. It is by this longer trial in the absence of perpetual profession, that this type of Institute can reach a reliable judgment as to the particular religious' permanence and stability. It is a valid ground for the judgment though less certain than that based on perpetual profession. It seems that on the basis of this similarity in regard to permanence and the effects of permanence, *i. e.*, trust and confidence, one could judge that much weightier reasons would be needed by the Institute to exclude a religious, professed for six years than to exclude one in the Institute only a short while. These reasons, it would seem, should approach in gravity those demanded to dismiss a religious whose permanence is assured by perpetual vows.

Since canon 20 does not demand that *all* four criteria for filling in *lacunae* of the Code be used in the same case, the opinion advanced is tenable because, first, it is warranted by the argument based on canonical equity and general principles of law; secondly, it is supported by the equalization, in canon 642, § 2, of religious who have spent six full years bound by temporary vows, oaths, or promises, and a religious bound with perpetual vows; finally, it is not opposed by any dissenting voice among the few authors who treat the case. It is to be noted, as it has already been,[26] that if this is true of causes needed for exclusion at the expiration of the obligation of the vows, it holds *a fortiori* for the same type of religious (*i. e.*, one who has actually spent more than six years in temporary vows, oaths, or

[26] *Supra*, p. 136.

promises in Institutes which have only a temporary bond) when the superiors wish to dismiss him while his vows still bind him.

C. Time at which the Exclusion May Be Effected

When may a religious leave the Institute if he has been refused perpetual profession or the renewal of temporary profession? Is that time governed by the rules which govern the renewal of vows so that, just as he can renew his vows on any day of the anniversary of his profession, he can leave at any time of that day? The dispute centers on canon 34, § 3, 5°: "Si agatur de actibus eiusdem generis statis temporibus renovandis, ex. gr., *triennium ad professionem perpetuam post temporariam,* . . . tempus finitur eodem recurrente die quo incipit, sed novus actus per integrum eundem diem poni potest."

One group of canonists maintain that either the professed religious (if he leaves on his own accord) or the Institute (if it, through the superior, should command the religious to leave at a certain time that day) is free to determine the exact moment of the day when the vows cease to bind. This group views the interval of time (the *triennium* of temporary vows) as expiring at the moment the religious chooses to leave or the Institute chooses to request his departure. This group stresses the words of the canon *tempus finitur*; this section of the canon, they say, is a special instance where the old rule would hold: "dies inceptus pro completo habetur." [27]

Another group of canonists insists on the words: *renovandis* and *actus eiusdem generis.* This number 5 in section 3 of canon 34 aims at avoiding the difficulties that would arise either from an interval arising between the renewal of such acts or, conversely, from the overlapping of two supposedly successive acts. Without this canon the

[27] Vermeersch-Creusen, *op. cit.,* I, 525; Chelodi, *Ius De Personis,* p. 424, note 4; Cappello, *Summa Iuris Canonici,* I, n. 181, 7, 3°; II, n. 613; Coronata, *Institutiones,* I, 759; Blat, *Commentarium Textus Codicis,* I, 123; Cervia, *De Professione Religiosa,* pp. 109-112; Berutti, *De Religiosis,* p. 324; Creusen-Garesché-Ellis, *Religious Men and Women,* 251-253; Vermeersch, "A quonam momento estne professo a votis temporariis integrum religionem deserere ad normam c. 637?"—*Periodica,* XXII (1933), 34*-39*; Creusen, "Terme des voeux et cloture"—*RCR,* XIV (1938), 155; Caviglioli, *Manuale di Diritto Canonico,* p. 120, note 4. Vermeersch-Creusen (*loc. cit.*) mention many others holding this opinion.

time covered by the vows would frequently overlap since the first day of the vows is not counted. Unless the vows were renewed at midnight the temporary vows would last all through the anniversary day no matter at what time of the day the perpetual vows are taken. Number 5 of section 3 leaves intact numbers 2 and 3 of the same section of this canon; but it does make lawful the effective renewal of vows or the taking of perpetual vows at any moment throughout the day. In the case which is being considered, that of departure, there is no question of renewal of vows or an act of the same species; rather it is an act of an opposite nature. The vows taken for three years on August 15, 1940, will expire on midnight between August 15th and August 16th, in 1943, and only from this point can the religious measure his freedom to leave or the Institute its freedom to exclude him. The renewal, on the other hand, may take place at any time on August 15, 1943.[28] This seems the better opinion.

D. The Procedure for the Act of Exclusion

There is no form or procedure prescribed for the proof of causes and the presentation of them to the superior in the case of exclusion of a religious from the Institute. It is not a juridic dismissal in the sense of the Code and in the execution of it there is demanded not even the minimum requirements of procedure which the Code prescribes for the dismissal of a religious during the time of his temporary vows. All that is needed is that the major superior, or the local superior at the command of the former should inform the religious in

[28] Dubé, *Reckoning of Time*, pp. 224-229; Maroto, *Institutiones*, I, 259, d; Michiels, *Normae Generales*, II, 156. Confer the review of an article by Schweigman ("De geldingsduur eener tydelyke professie" [Quousque ligat professio temporarie]—*Nederlandsche Katholieke Stemmen*, 1929, pp. 148-151), in "Excerpta ex ephemeridibus"—*Apollinaris*, III (1930), 58; Frey, *Religious Profession*, p. 110; Cance, *Le Code de Droit Canonique* (6. ed., Paris: Libraire Lecoffre, J. Gabalda et fils, 1930), p. 78; Geser, *The Canon Law Governing Communities of Sisters*, pp. 341, 342; Cicognani, *Ius Canonicum* (2 vols., Romae: Ex Officina Typographica Ausonia, 1925), II, 197; Cicognani-O'Hara-Brennan, *Canon Law*, p. 690. Cicognani seems to hold this opinion for, in commenting on canon 34, § 3, 5°, he says: "Si professio temporaria ad triennium facta fuerit d. 20 Jan. 1920 ab incipiente die 21 Jan. 1923 expleta computanda esset." The later English translation has the same doctrine, changing only the dates in the example given.

writing or orally that he is excluded from the Institute and must return to the world.

The constitutions should make provisions for the gathering of the proof of the causes for exclusion in the case in which the superior competent to decide on this exclusion is far distant from the house; *i.e.,* the constitutions shall decide whether the local superior is to do this alone, when and in what manner he is to send the case to the superior, etc. In the absence of any prescription of the constitutions, recourse must be had to general principles of law. It would seem best to follow the procedure outlined in Chapter Four for the dismissal of religious during the time in which he is bound by temporary vows. The local superior (if he is not himself the superior competent to exclude) should gather the proof of the just and reasonable causes and send them to the legitimate superior. The latter investigates all the facts and circumstances and, having made his judgment, sends the decision either directly to the religious in question or to his superior; or he may even send it by his delegate.[29]

Must the superior make known to him the causes for which he is being excluded? Several authors deny this. They say that all the superior need do is to declare the fact of exclusion, because of an analogy to dismissal from the novitiate, as stated in canon 571, § 1.[30] Others demand that the causes be made known to the religious. The legal reason justifying this view is that the religious has a right to recourse *in devolutivo* against the decree of the superior. In order, then, to make his right of recourse effective, the reasons for his exclusion should be made known to him.[31] One should adopt this as the better opinion. The superior then should tell the religious the causes for which he was excluded.

Should the excluded religious be given the canonical admonitions? There is no express mention of them in the Code nor do the authors treat this question. If the constitutions are silent, by an analogy of law it seems that the paternal admonitions demanded for a dismissal of a religious in temporary vows are required and sufficient. In the

[29] Schäfer, *De Religiosis,* pp. 947, 948; Palombo, *De Dimissione Religiosorum,* p. 203.

[30] Goyeneche, *De Religiosis,* p. 194; Palombo, *loc. cit.*

[31] Schäfer, *op. cit.,* p. 948; Beste, *Introductio in Codicem,* p. 430.

examination of the causes for exclusion it was seen that they were the same in kind, though less in degree, as for dismissal, of religious bound by temporary vows. Causes in the physical or intellectual order demand no warning since they would be necessarily ineffective; warned or not the religious can do nothing about it. For grave faults and delicts in the moral order no warning is needed; one fault is enough to exclude or dismiss the religious. As to those faults which can be placed under the heading, *defect of the religious spirit*, the warnings should be given, otherwise the punishable contumacy is not present, and the superior would run the risk of excluding a religious for causes which are not just and reasonable.[32] For similar reasons the superior should in equity, in charity to the religious, and in loyalty to his Institute, threaten exclusion for lack of amendment. The purpose of exclusion is to weed out unworthy members; the purpose of the warning is to correct the subject, to make him amend and thus to benefit both the subject and the Institute. Hence a threat of exclusion will help the subject because it will render the warning much more efficacious. It will also protect the superior from a charge of unreasonableness and injustice should the subject have recourse. However since it is not positively certain that the threat of exclusion must be given the superior may deem it advisable not to give them. If he is quite sure that such a warning may make the subject amend only exteriorly but not interiorly, it would be better to omit the threat of exclusion from the warnings and thus more surely test the good will of the religious. His response to such a warning will more clearly show what type of character he is, than will his response to a warning with a threat of exclusion.

E. Effects of the Act of Exclusion

Several effects of exclusion are identical with the effects of dismissal in the case of religious bound by temporary vows; they are merely enumerated here, for they have been treated in the preceding chapter. There is no dispensation from the vows because they have ceased to bind.[33] The religious cannot demand any remuneration for

[32] Jombart, "Le renvoi au cours des voeux temporaires"—*RCR*, V (1929), 198.

[33] Palombo, *De Dimissione Religiosorum*, p. 259.

services rendered to the Institute; [34] the dowry must be restored; [35] if there is no dowry or if it is insufficient, a charitable subsidy must be given to women religious and in cases also to men religious; [36] the ceding of the administration of property ceases to have effect; [37] the religious canot enter the novitiate of another Institute or reenter his own, unless he was in an Institute in which he had been bound only by oaths or promises; [38] nor, finally, can he enter a seminary.[39]

In regard to the disabilities listed in canon 642, § 2, the merely excluded religious is not subject to them. Even if he had been in the Institute for six years and had been ordained to major orders either before his profession or during his religious life, the manner of his exclusion does not fullfill the requirements of canon 642, § 2, which states *"et ab eisdem (votis) dispensati fuerunt."* He is not dispensed from his vows even by the law itself, as is the one who was dismissed while he was in temporary vows.[40] A religious in major or minor orders who was ordained before he entered the Institute should return to his diocese and be received by his bishop, if he is excluded from the Institute [41]

[34] Schäfer, *De Religiosis,* p. 949.

[35] Kealy, *Dowry of Women Religious,* p. 109.

[36] Palombo, *loc. cit.*; Fanfani, *De Iure Religiosorum,* p. 481.

[37] Canons 589, § 1; 580, § 3.

[38] Vermeersch-Creusen, *Epitome,* I, 607.

[39] Canon 1365, § 3. Palombo (*op. cit.*, p. 281) states that from the text and context of this canon the case implied in the phrase *dimissi . . . ex aliqua religione* stands in contradistinction to the case in which one left freely. The religious who has not been allowed to make profession does not leave freely. Cf. S. C. de Religiosis atque de Seminariis et studiorum Universitatibus, decr. 25 iul. 1941—*AAS,* XXXIII (1941), 371. This decree rules that if a candidate for the seminary has *in any way* at all belonged to a religious community the ordinary must confer with the Sacred Congregation of Seminaries and Universities before he can admit the student to the seminary.

[40] Raus, *Institutiones Canonicae,* p. 338, note 1; Blat, *De Religiosis,* p. 555; Beste, *Introductio,* p. 436; Cappello, *Summa Iuris Canonici,* II, 253; Palombo, *op. cit.*, p. 260; Schäfer, *op. cit.*, pp. 949, 950; Chelodi, *Ius De Personis,* p. 449; Wernz-Vidal, *Ius Canonicum,* III, 464; Vermeersch-Creusen, *op. cit.,* I, 607; De Meester, *Compendium,* III, 481, note 3; Goyeneche, "De egressu a religione"—*CpR* (1924), 339-341.

[41] Canons 115; 585; 641, § 1; Blat, *op. cit.*, p. 552; Schäfer, *op. cit.*, p. 949; Palombo, *op. cit.*, p. 261.

If he were ordained while in the Institute, it is an entirely different case, since he is by profession ascribed to the Institute. The question now arises: What is his juridical status when he is excluded from the Institute. Is he still in orders, and, if so, to which bishop does he belong?

Ordinarily, the question involves only religious in minor orders. In Institutes in which temporary vows are taken in preparation for perpetual profession, religious can be ordained at most to minor orders, even if it is an exempt Institute.[42] In Institutes whose members take only temporary vows, oaths or promises, the religious can be ordained to major orders only after a three year profession of temporary vows.[43]

If the religious is in a non-exempt clerical Institute it seems, by the requirements of the Code, that he is to be ordained by his proper bishop; *i. e.*, by the bishop in whose diocese he had his domicile before he entered the Institute.[44] If the religious is in a clerical exempt Institute, he is ordained, with dimissorial letters from his superior, by the ordinary of the place in which is situated the house in which he is stationed.[45]

As has been stated, the religious is by profession ascribed to the Institute. Still, canon 585 states that a religious does not lose his proper diocese until the day of his *perpetual* profession. Canon 115, without further specification as to the type of profession, states merely that by religious profession one is excardinated from his proper diocese according to canon 585. If then a religious who was promoted to minor orders while still in temporary vows is excluded

[42] Canon 964, 3° and 4°.

[43] S. C. de Relig., instr. 1 dec. 1931, n. 15—*AAS*, XXIV (1932), 80. Their status when dismissed or excluded has been considered in Chapter Four. Cf. *supra*, pp. 147-150.

[44] Canons 964, 4°; 956; Schaaf, "Episcopus proprius ordinationis religiosorum"—*ER*, XC (1934), 500-504; Moeder, *The Proper Bishop for Ordination and Dimissorial Letters*, p. 103; Pejska, *Ius Canonicum Religiosorum*, pp. 303-306. Against this opinion are: Oesterle, "De domicilio religiosorum"—*CpR*, V (1924), 167-178, especially pp. 177, 178; Vermeersch, "De domicilio religiosorum"—*Periodica*, IX (1919), (8).

[45] Canons 964, 2° and 3°; 965; Schaaf, *art. cit.*, pp. 493-497. Abbots can confer minor orders themselves on their subjects.

from the Institute at the end of his term of those temporary vows, what is his juridical status in regard to incardination?

There are three opinions current as to his status on departure from the Institute. The first holds that the religious by exclusion is made a vagrant or unattached cleric. Affiliation with the Institute is not strict but at most only equivalent incardination.[46] His keeping of his diocese until perpetual profession [47] is not a suspended incardination. It is surely not such in the case of exempt religious who are not ordained by their proper bishop. Nor is such the case of those religious (*i. e.*, members of non-exempt Institutes or of exempt Institutes whose members do not take vows) who are ordained by their proper bishop, because by that ordination conferred on them as religious there is no incardination into the diocese of the ordaining bishop.[48] When they are excluded from the Institute, their affiliation with the Institute is broken. Since they are not incardinated into any diocese, it seems that they are vagrant and unattached clerics (*clerici vagi vel acephali*).[49]

A second solution states that such a religious is reduced to the lay state. The reason adduced is this: since the premises based on the prescriptions of the Code lead to the conclusion that this cleric is a vagrant cleric (*clericus vagus*), he is to be reduced to the lay state, for the Code demands either his affiliation with an Institute or his incardination in a diocese, and in no other way can this prescription of the law be fulfilled.[50]

[46] Piontek, *De Indulto Exclaustrationis Necnon Saecularizationis*, p. 226; Maroto, *Institutiones*, I, 577, 578, note 3.

[47] Canon 585.

[48] Beijersbergen, "De transitu religiosi de una classe ad alteram eiusdem religiosi instituti"—*Periodica*, XXVI (1937), 36; Ellis, "De religiosi minoristae saecularizati incardinatione"—*Periodica*, XXV (1936), 54*.

[49] Coronata, *Institutiones*, I, 203, note 3; 204, 210, 4; Chelodi, *Ius De Personis*, pp. 174, 175, note 1. Note that Chelodi applies this reasoning only to exempt religious; the non-exempt religious, he says, are to return to their proper diocese and bishop.

[50] Canon 111, § 1. Wernz-Vidal, *Ius Canonicum*, II, 76; Palombo, *De Dimissione Religiosorum*, p. 261; Oesterle, *art. cit.*—*CpR*, V (1924), 169; Moeder, *Proper Bishop for Dimissorial Letters and Ordination*, pp. 105, 106. Schäfer holds that if the religious was in minor orders before entering the Institute he should, at his exclusion, be reduced to the lay state in one of the three

A third solution offered is that which is based on an analogy with canon 641, § 1, and a recourse to the general principles of law. By this argument, the conclusion is reached that the religious is at his ordination incardinated in the diocese of his proper bishop.[51] These authors contend that there can be no question of reduction to the lay state on the part of the excluded religious, since reduction to the lay state is a restriction of the exercise of his rights.[52] He remains a cleric with all the rights and obligations of a cleric and is incardinated in the diocese of his proper ordinary according to the general rules of canons 90, 92, 93, § 2, 94, § 1. This bishop can reduce him to the lay state for a just cause, which could be considered as present if there were a lack of any place for him in the diocese.[53] This opinion seems the most acceptable of the three proposed. It must be admitted, however, that it, too, is not entirely satisfactory, because of the strength of the first opinion.

F. *Recourse Against the Act of Exclusion*

The Code does not grant recourse *in suspensivo* to a religious who is excluded from making a new profession of vows at the end of his temporary profession. Recourse *in suspensivo* is available only when

ways described in canon 211, § 2; *i. e., ipso jure,* at his own request, or by the decision of the bishop. Since this is not the case of reduction to the lay state *ipso jure,* it is hard to see why Schäfer quotes the canon in its entirety; nor is it evident why the opinion is credited to him especially when immediately afterwards he says that a religious ordained to minor orders while in temporary vows is, when he is excluded from the religious Institute, a cleric incardinated in his proper diocese.

[51] Schäfer, *De Religiosis,* p. 949; Goyeneche, "Consultatio"—*CpR,* IV (1923), 146, 147; VII (1926), 449, 450; XIV (1933), 352-354; Ellis, "De religiosi minoristae saecularizati incardinatione"—*Periodica,* XXV (1936), 53*-55*; Schaaf, *art. cit.*—*ER,* XC (1934), 495, 496; 501, 502; 508, 509. Goyeneche (*CpR,* XIV [1933], 354) quotes Coronata (*Institutiones,* I, n. 649) for his opinion. He does so incorrectly. In the place cited, Coronata rejects the view holding for the reduction of the exempt religious to the lay state, but he does not affirm that he is incardinated in the diocese of his proper bishop. He holds, rather, that he is a *clericus vagus.* Cf. *supra,* note (49).

[52] Canon 19; cf. Goyeneche, "Consultationes"—*CpR,* IV (1923), 146; VII (1926), 449; *CpRM,* XIX (1938), 165.

[53] Canon 212, § 2; 117.

the Code grants it expressly and it is not granted in this case. There remains the recourse open to all who believe they have been injured, namely, recourse *in devolutivo,* which leaves matters as they are until the decision concerning them is reversed. The excluded religious must put off the habit and leave the religious house. All the effects of exclusion are applied to him even during the time in which his recourse is pending.[54] Schäfer maintains that equity seems to suggest *(convenit)* that the Institute do not send the religious into the world until the Holy See had answered the recourse by its definitive decree.[55] Woywod warns the excluded religious not to be too sanguine as to the results of this recourse *in devolutivo.* The reason is that the Code requires just and reasonable causes for the refusal to admit a religious to perpetual profession. In this case, as in the case of the dismissal of religious during the course of temporary vows, the superior and the Council are given large discretionary powers. Their judgment is presumed to be a conscientious one and ordinarily the Holy See will not force an Institute to accept a religious against the vote of the superior and the Council. He states that only in the case in which it can be proved that the religious is refused admission to perpetual vows because of illness contracted after profession is there much hope to obtain reinstatement.[56]

G. Appendix: Military Service Cases

There is a special provision in the law for the dismissal or exclusion of those religious who, in the fulfillment of the law of their country in regard to compulsory military service are stationed in army camps or in other camps in one of the branches of the service. As long as the religious are in temporary vows and live in their religious house, they are subject to all the provisions of dismissal already outlined. But when they are in military service they are in a different status than any other religious—a status which on examination seems to be more like that of the religious which was reviewed

[54] Palombo, *op. cit.,* p. 203; Coronata, *Institutiones,* I, 854; Prümmer, *Manuale Iuris Canonici,* q. 258, 1, p. 347.

[55] Schäfer, *De Religiosis,* pp. 948, 949.

[56] Woywod, "Answers to questions"—*HPR,* XXXVII (1936-1937), 419, 420.

in Chapter Five in the commentary on canon 637.[57] The question of their dismissal or exclusion will be considered in this order: a short historical background of the law will be given; then there will follow an explanation of what is meant by military service and of the question as to who are bound by the ecclesiastical law which is enacted for religious who are subject to military service; this will be followed by a description of the manner in which they take their vows; finally, an inquiry will be made to reveal who dismisses or excludes them and what are the causes for that exclusion or dismissal.

The Sacred Congregation of Religious, deploring the great harm done to individuals and to religious Institutes by laws compelling religious to render military service, issued a decree in 1911 to remedy the situation. The decree, among other things, legislated that in orders of regulars, young men who are not certainly known to be exempt from military service cannot be promoted to orders or make solemn profession until they have completed their military service and thereafter have remained in simple vows for a year, and that in Institutes of simple vows they can be admitted only to temporary vows before their military service and on their return are required to spend another year in temporary vows before they can take perpetual vows. If during their military service or after it, before taking either solemn vows (in orders) or perpetual vows (in Institutes in which the members take simple vows), they falter in their vocation; if they do not follow the rules laid down for them during military service; or if they have turned away from the right way of faith and morals, the superior general with the consent of his consultors shall dismiss them and they shall be released from their vows by the very fact of the dismissal. These prescriptions applied also to those societies in which the members do not take vows but make only promises.[58]

In a declaration which was made to clear up doubts about the matter, the Sacred Congregation stated that the temporary vows of the religious do not cease at their entry into military service, but that they cannot be renewed when they expire during military service. They can be renewed only after a year's trial in temporary vows after

[57] Cf. *supra*, pp. 167-183.

[58] S. C. de Relig., decr. *Inter reliquas*, 1 ian. 1911—*AAS*, III (1911), 37; Bouscaren, *Canon Law Digest*, I, 106, ff.

the completion of the military service. Even if in good faith a religious in an order has made solemn profession against the prescriptions of the decree, and a religious in an Institute of simple vows has, to the neglect of that decree, made perpetual profession, then the profession is invalid. If during military service or for one year afterwards one wishes a dispensation from his vows, he may ask it from the superior general in clerical Institutes and from the superior in lay Institutes, these superiors being empowered to act as delegates of the Holy See in this matter.[59]

These provisions were made as temporary law and were not embodied in the Code. Consequently it was asked whether the decree still held after the promulgation of the Code, and if so, were novices who were bound to render military service permitted to take their vows according to canon 574, *i. e.*, for three years. The Sacred Congregation answered that the decree was still in force, inasmuch as in many places the religious were subject to military service and that the novices were to take vows which were to be effective until they actually enlisted in the service and became subject to military discipline, or until the moment at which they had been declared absolutely and permanently unfit for military service.[60]

What is military service and which religious are bound by the decree which was specifically enacted for such religious as were engaged in military service? It matters not what is the type of service, whether it be the actual bearing of arms, kitchen duty, tasks of cleaning or sanitation, or the acting as internes and nurses in hospitals; the essential note which makes these duties fall under the classification of military service in the sense of the decree is that, by force of law, the religious are taken out of their religious houses and away from the direct care of their superiors and are placed in camp with soldiers and under obedience to military officers.[61] Ministry per-

[59] S. C. de Relig., declar., 1 febr. 1912—*AAS*, IV (1912), 246, 247; Maroto, "Annotatio"—*CpR*, I (1920), 322.

[60] S. C. de Relig., resp., 15 iul. 1919—*AAS*, XI (1919), 321.

[61] Frey, *Religious Profession*, pp. 151, 152; Cervia, *De Professione Religiosa*, pp. 184, 185; Goyeneche, "Consultatio"—*CpRM*, XVI (1935), 124; Coronata, *Institutiones*, I, 750; Fanfani, *De Iure Religiosorum*, pp. 277, 278; Schäfer, *De Religiosis*, pp. 622, 627, 628. Vermeersch (*Epitome*, I, 528) says that religious doing works of mercy in army hospitals, etc., do not fall under

formed as a chaplain, if the religious is under the *Episcopus Castrensis* and not under the military authorities, is not considered military service.

If a religious has already complied with the stated time of military service (ordinary service), but still remains subject to that type of military service (extraordinary service) which is imposed on all the citizens of the country in war time, he can be admitted to his final vows. If a war occurs before he makes his final profession, or if the law is changed, so that in both cases he again becomes subject to a period of ordinary service, he cannot make his final profession.[62]

In those Institutes which take only annual vows the novices may take their vows for a year, but these vows cease when the religious are effectively enlisted in the service, even if the complete year is not finished. Since the response of the Sacred Congregation of Religious on July 15, 1919, there are no possibilities whereby one can be in military service while still bound to his vows, except in two cases: that in which military service was introduced after vows were taken for three years and the religious becomes subject to military service, and that in which the vows were taken for three years in good faith even though the novice was subject to military service.[63]

For what period do these novices take their vows? They pronounce temporary vows to be effective until they enter military service. These vows will cease the day on which the religious becomes actually enlisted in the service and subject to military discipline, or on which he is declared absolutely and permanently unfit for service. Two things are needed to fulfill the first condition: the inscription of his name in the military records, and his subjection to

this law. This is true only if they are there by the appointment of their superiors, but not if they are there by civil law decree and cannot be changed or moved by their superiors.

[62] Coronata, *op. cit.*, p. 750, n. 595, note 3; Vermeersch-Creusen, *op. cit.*, I, 680; Fanfani, *op. cit.*, n. 244; De Meester, *Compendium*, II, 449, b; Pejska, *Ius Canonicum Religiosorum*, p. 108; Maroto, "Annotatio"—*CpR*, I (1920), 329, VII; Goyeneche, "Consultatio"—*CpR*, XII (1931), 133.

[63] S. C. de Relig., resp. 30 nov. 1919—*AAS*, XII (1920), 73; Maroto, "Annotatio"—*CpR*, I (1920), 329; Larraona, "Consultatio"—*CpR*, V (1924), 220-222; Frey, *Religious Profession*, p. 153.

military discipline. Military service has not begun until a religious has left his religious house as a soldier or member of the armed forces of the country. His vows cease to bind only at this time.[64]

During the period of his military service the religious, although he is not bound by his religious vows, still continues to be a member of his religious Institute and under the authority of his superiors. He may freely leave the Institute, according to canon 637, and the superiors may for just and reasonable causes exclude him from the Institute. He cannot, then, be said to be dismissed in the strict sense of the word, since he is not bound by his vows, but he can be excluded from the renewal of his vows. If, after having been excluded from the Institute, he asks to be received again he must, if he is accepted, begin his novitiate anew.[65] Since he is excluded from vows rather than dismissed the measurement of the causes for exclusion will be that of the causes needed in canon 637; the effects will also be the same as for an excluded religious.[66]

Religious in the United States are not subject to military service in the sense described above.

[64] S. C. de Relig., resp., 15 iul. 1919—*AAS,* XI (1919), 321; P. G. R., "Consultatio"—*CpR,* VII (1926), 104; Goyeneche, "Consultatio"—*CpRM,* XVI (1935), 123.

[65] S. C. de Relig., *loc. cit.*; Maroto, "Annotatio"—*CpR,* I (1920), 131; Schäfer, *De Religiosis,* p. 949.

[66] Cf. *supra,* pp. 178-182.

CONCLUSIONS

1. The superior to dismiss in an independent house of sisters of pontifical approval is the ordinary of the place in which is situated the house at which the dismissed religious is stationed (pp. 84-87).

2. The reason that the causes for dismissing a religious *during* the time of his temporary vows must be more grave than the causes for excluding him at the *expiration* of the period of his temporary vows is the fact that included in the dismissal is an implicit dispensation from the vows which is not present in the act of excluding him from a new profession of vows. The reason for the difference is not, as is often stated, the fact that the contract is still binding while the vows retain their binding force, but no longer exists at the expiration of the temporary vows (pp. 111-113).

3. A defect in character or temperament which cannot stand a rigid daily schedule of duties and religious exercises characteristic of a religious community cannot be called an illness in the sense of canons 647 and 637. It is comparable rather to a giddiness or levity of spirit than to a neurasthenia, for it is "cured" by the sole fact of departure from the Institute and not by any medical means. It is a *state* or constant condition of his temperament or physical makeup, a defect which is brought to the fore only in certain conditions. It is not a sickness or pathological affliction in the sense of canons 647 and 637 (pp. 119-121).

4. Under the causes for dismissal and especially under "the defect of the religious spirit" there are listed in the present study all the causes given by the authors and by the Rules and Constitutions which were available to the writer (pp. 129-143).

5. A cause listed in the Rule or Constitutions of one Institute as sufficient for the dismissal of a religious in temporary vows can validly be applied to another Institute as sufficient for dismissing one of its members in temporary vows (p. 114).

6. The opinion that those who have received minor orders before their entry into the Institute are not reduced by the very fact of the

dismissal to the lay state does not seem probable enough to be held (pp. 147-150).

7. A religious who has been bound for six years by temporary vows, oaths, or promises in an Institute in which the members are bound only by temporary vows, oaths, or promises can be *dismissed* or *excluded* only for the same causes that are required for the dismissal of a religious in perpetual vows (pp. 136; 171-175).

BIBLIOGRAPHY

SOURCES

General Sources

Acta Apostolicae Sedis, Commentarium Officiale, Romae, 1909—

Acta et Decreta Sacrorum Conciliorum Recentiorum, Collectio Lacensis, 7 vols., Friburgi Brisgoviae, 1870-1890.

Acta Sanctae Sedis, 41 vols., Romae, 1865-1908.

Bullarum Diplomatum et Privilegiorum Sanctorum Romanorum Pontificum Taurinensis Editio, 25 vols., Augustae Taurinorum, 1857-1872.

Bullarii Romani Continuatio Summorum Pontificum, 19 vols., Prati, 1835-1858.

Codex Iuris Canonici Pii X Pontificis Maximi iussu digestus Benedicti Papae XV auctoritate promulgatus, Romae, Typis Polyglottis Vaticanis, 1917.

Canonical Legislation Concerning Religious, Authorized English Translation, Rome, Vatican Printing Office, 1919.

Codex Iuris Canonici Fontes cura Emi. Petri Card. Gasparri Editi, 9 vols., Romae (postea Civitate Vaticana): Typis Polyglottis Vaticanis, 1923-1939. (Vols. VII, VIII, et IX ed. cura et studio Emi. Iustiniani Card. Serédi.)

Collectanea in usum Secretariae S. C. Episcoporum et Regularium, 2. ed., Romae: ex typographia Polyglotta S. C. de Propaganda Fide, 1885.

Corpus Iuris Canonici, ed. Lipsiensis sècunda, post Aemilii Ludovici Richter curas—instruxit Aemilius Friedberg, 1879-1881; ed. anastatice repetita, 2 vols., Lipsiae: Tauchnitz, 1928.

Decretales D. Gregorii Papae IX, una cum Glossis Restitutae, Romae, 1582.

Mansi, Joannes, *Sacrorum Conciliorum Nova et Amplissima Collectio,* 53 vols. in 59, Parisiis, 1901-1927.

Migne, Jacques Paul, *Patrologiae Cursus Completus, Series Graeca,* 161 vols., Parisiis, 1857-1866.

———, *Patrologiae Cursus Completus, Series Latina,* 221 vols., Parisiis, 1844-1864.

Normae Secundum Quas S. Congr. Episcoporum et Regularium procedere solet in Approbandis Novis Institutis Votorum Simplicium, Romae: Typis S. C. De Propaganda Fide, 1901.

Rules and Constitutions

Butler, Cuthbert, *Sancti Benedicti Regula Monasteriorum,* Editio Critico-Practica, 3. ed., Friburgi Brisgoviae: Herder, 1935.

Common Rules of the Institute of the Marist Brothers of the Schools or the Little Brothers of Mary, Dumfries, Mount St. Michael, 1924.

Constitutiones Congregationis Missionariorum de Marianhill, Missionsdruckerei Reimlinger, 1936.

Constitutiones Congregationis Presbyterorum a Sacro Corde Jesu, Lovanii: Typis Fr. Ceuterick, 1938.

———, *Regulae Ac Praescriptiones a variis Capitulis praesertim a decimo exaratae accedit statutum pro Missionibus a S. Congr. de Propaganda Fide Approbatum et jussu Rm̃i. Superioris Generalis P. Jos. Laur. Philippe Editum*, Romae: apud Curiam Generalitiam, 1934.

Constitutiones Ordinis Fratrum Beatissimae Virginis Mariae de Monte Carmelo iussu Revm̃i. P. Eliae Magennis Prioris Generalis in lucem editae praemissa Regula S. Alberti, Romae: Typis Polyglottis Vaticanis, 1930.

Constitutiones Ordinis Fratrum Minorum Sancti Patris Francisci Conventualium, Romae, Ad SS. XII Apostolos, 1932.

Constitutiones Piae Societatis Missionum, Ratisbonae: Typis Friderici Pustet.

Constitutions and Rules of the Institute of the Brothers of the Sacred Heart, Metuchen, N. J., 1928.

Constitutions and Rules of the Sisters of Our Lady of Mercy in the Diocese of Charleston, S. C. (No date or place of publication given.)

Constitutions of the Brothers of Christian Instruction (of Ploermel), Jersey, 1936.

Constitutions of the Catholic Foreign Mission Society of America, 2. ed., Maryknoll, N. Y., 1938.

Constitutions of the Congregation of the Resurrection of Our Lord Jesus Christ, Rome: Typographical Institute of Pius X, 1937.

Constitutions of the Congregation of the Sisters Adorers of the Most Precious Blood, Ruma, Ill., Columbia, Pa., Wichita, Kans., 1935.

Constitutions of the Congregation of the Sisters Servants of the Immaculate Heart of Mary, Monroe, Mich., 1920.

Constitutions of the Franciscan Friars of the Atonement. (No date or place of publication given.)

Constitutions of the Institute of Mission Helpers, Servants of the Sacred Heart, Baltimore, Md.: St. Mary's Industrial School Press, 1923.

Constitutions of the Institute of the Marist Brothers of the Schools or the Little Brothers of Mary, Grugliasco, 1935.

Constitutions of the Pious Society of Missions, 1935. (No place of publication given.)

Constitutions of the Religious Congregation of Brothers of Mercy of Montabaur, Buffalo, N. Y., 1928.

Constitutions of the Sisters of Saint Joseph of Carondolet, St. Louis, Mo.: B. Herder Book Co., 1926.

Constitutions of the Sisters of the Presentation of the Blessed Virgin of Dubuque, Iowa, Dubuque: Mount Loretto, 1925.

Constitutions of the Society of Mary, Dayton, Ohio, 1937.

Constitutions of the Society of St. Joseph of the Sacred Heart, Baltimore, Vatican Polyglot Press, 1932.

Declarationes et Statuta Sive Constitutiones Congregationis Ottiliensis O.S.B. Pro Missionibus Exteris, Typis Archiabbatiae SS. Cordis Jesu ad Ottiliam, 1925.

Declarations on the Rule of Saint Benedict, St. Joseph. Minn.: St. Benedict's Convent, 1936.

Declarations on the Rule of Our Holy Father St. Benedict and Constitutions of the Congregation of Saint Scholastica, Atchison, Kans.: Abbey Student Press, 1932.

Franciscan Brothers of the Brooklyn Congregation of the Regular Third Order of St. Francis: Constitutions, Rules, Decrees, Rescripts, Traditions, History, 1924. (No place of publication given except: "Printed in the U. S. A.")

Institutum Societatis Jesu, 3 vols., Florentiae, 1892-1893.

La Règle De Saint-Augustin Et des Soeurs Dominicaines de la Congrégation des Saints-Anges-Gardiens De Korčula (Dalmatie), Grottaferrata: Scuola Tip. Italo-Orientale "S. Nilo," 1923.

Manual of the Clerics of Saint Viator, Jette-Saint-Pierre, Belgium, 1926.

Règle de Nostre Pere Sainct Augustin, Paris, 1658.

Règle De Saint Augustin et Constitutions des "Augustins de L'Assomption," Paris: Typographie Augustienne, 1935.

Regula Primitiva et Constitutiones Fratrum Discalceatorum Ordinis Sanctissimae Trinitatis Redemptionis Captivorum, Isola Del Liri: Soc. Tip. A. Macioce & Pisani, 1933.

Regula S. Patris Benedicti cum Constitutionibus Congregationis Angliae a Sancta Sede Approbatis una cum Directorium et Formularium, Stanbrook, Typis Abbatiae B. V. M., 1931.

Regulae et Constitutiones Congregationis Sancti Spiritus sub tutela Immaculati Cordis Beatissimae Virginis Mariae, Norwalk, Conn.: Holy Ghost Fathers, 1934.

Rules of the Brothers of the Christian Schools, Lembecq-Lez-Hal, 1925.

The Constitutions of the Oblates of Saint Francis de Sales, Childs, Md., 1929.

The Rule and the Constitutions of the Congregation of the Sisters of Saint Mary of the Third Order of Saint Francis in the City of Saint Louis, Mo., U. S. A., St. Louis: Dewes Printing Co., 1923.

The Rule and Constitutions of the Religious Called the Sisters of Mercy—for the use of the Sisters in the diocese of Philadelphia, Philadelphia: The Catholic Standard and Times, 1928.

The Rule and General Constitutions of the Friars Minor, Paterson, N. J.: St. Anthony's Guild Press, 1936.

The Rule of Our Holy Father Saint Augustine and the Constitutions of the Ursuline Nuns of the Congregation of Paris, Toledo, Ohio, Ursuline Convent of the Sacred Heart, 1931.

The Rule of Saint Augustine. Appendix of Statutes and Regulations of the Rule for the Ursuline Order in Chatham, Ontario, Cleveland, 1892.

The Rule of Saint Benedict, edited with an English translation and explanatory notes by D. Oswald Hunter Blair, M.A., Abbot of Dunfermline, 4. ed., Fort Augustus, Scotland: Abbey Press, 1934.

Reference Works

Acta Congressus Iuridici Internationalis . . . Romae, 1934, 5 vols., Romae: Libraria Pont. Instituti Utriusque Iuris, 1935-1937.

Aertnys, J.-Damen, C. C., *Theologiae Moralis,* 13. ed., 2 vols., Taurini-Romae: Marietti, 1939.

Aichner, Simon, *Compendium Juris Ecclesiastici Ad Usum Clerici Ac Praesertim Per Imperium Austriacum in Cura Animarum Laborantis,* 6. ed., Brixinae, 1887.

Albertus Magnus, St., *Opera Omnia,* 38 vols., Parisiis, 1890-1899.

Angelus a SS. Corde Jesu, *Manuale Juris Communis Regularium et Specialis Carmelitarum Discalceatorum,* 2 vols., Gandae, 1899.

Antonius a Spiritu Sancto, *Directorium Regularium,* Lugduni, 1675.

Appeltern, Victorius ab, *Compendium Praelectionum Juris Regularis,* Adm. R. P. Piati Montani ad recentissimas Leges Ecclesiasticas Redactum, Tornaci, 1903.

Appendix Ad Concilium Plenarium Americae Latinae Romae Celebratum Anno Domini MDCCCXCIX, Romae: Typis Polyglottis Vaticanis, 1910.

Arndt, Augustine, *Die Kirchlichen und Weltlichen Rechtsbestimmung für Orden und Kongregationen,* 2. ed., Paderborn, 1919.

Astrain, Antonio, *Historia de la Compañia de Jésus en la Asistencia de España,* 7 vols., Madrid, 1902-1925.

Ayrinhac, H. A., *General Legislation in the New Code of Canon Law,* New York: Longmans, 1930.

———, *Administrative Legislation in the New Code of Canon Law,* New York: Longmans, 1930.

[Bachofen] Charles Augustine, *Compendium Juris Regularium,* New York, 1903.

———, *A Commentary on the New Code of Canon Law,* 8 vols. Vol. III (Religious and Laymen), 1. ed., St. Louis: Herder, 1919; 5. ed., St. Louis: Herder, 1938. Vol. II (Persons), 4. ed., St. Louis: Herder, 1923.

Bastien, Pierre, *Constitution "Conditae a Christo" de León XIII sur les instituts à voeux simples,* Bruges, 1902.

———, *Directoire canonique à l'usage des Congrégations à voeux simples,* 3. ed., Bruges: Beyaert, 1923.

Battandier, Albert, *Guide Canonique pour les constitutions des Instituts à voeux simples,* Rome, 1898; 5. ed., Paris, 1911; 6. ed., Paris: Gabalda, 1923.

Benedict XIV, *Opera Omnia,* 17 vols., Prati, 1839-1847.

Berutti, Christophorus, *Institutiones Iuris Canonici,* 3 vols., Vol. III (*De Religiosis*), Taurinorum Augustae: Marietti, 1936.

Beste, Udalricus, *Introductio in Codicem,* Collegeville, Minn.: St. John's Abbey Press, 1938.

Biederlack, Joseph-Führich, Maximilianus, *De Religiosis,* Oeniponte, 1919.

Blat, Albertus, *Commentarium Textus Codicis Iuris Canonici,* 5 vols. in 6, 1921-1927. Liber II (partes II-VI), 3. ed., Romae: Apud "Angelicum," 1938.

Bondini, Aloisius, *De Privilegio Exemptionis,* Romae, 1919.

Bouix, Dominicus, *Tractatus De Jure Regularium,* 2 vols., Vol. I, Parisiis, 1857; Vol. II, 3. ed., Parisiis, 1883.

Bouscaren, T. Lincoln, *The Canon Law Digest,* 2 vols. and Supplement—1941, Milwaukee: Bruce, 1934-1937-1941.

Bouuaert, F. Claeys, *Selecta Capita Codicis Iuris Canonici,* Gandae, 1919.

——— —Simenon, G., *Manuale Iuris Canonici ad usum seminariorum,* 3 vols., Vols. I and III, 3. ed., Vol. II, 1. ed., Gandae et Leodii, 1930-1931.

Brandys, Maximilian, *Kirchliches Rechtsbuch für die religiosen Laiengenossenschaften der Brüder und Schwestern,* 2. ed., Paderborn: Schöningh, 1920.

Brucker, Joseph, *La Compagnie de Jésus,* Paris, 1919.

Cance, Adrien, *Le Code de Droit Canonique,* 6. ed., Paris: Libraire Lecoffre, J. Gabalda et fils, 1930.

Cappello, Felix M., *Summa Iuris Canonici in Usum Scholarum Concinnata,* 3 vols., Vol. I, 3. ed., 1938; Vol. II, 3. ed., 1939; Vol. III, 1936: Romae: apud Aedes Universitatis Gregorianae.

Cavagnis, Felix, *Institutiones Iuris Publici Ecclesiastici,* 4. ed., 3 vols., Romae, 1906.

Caviglioli, Giovanni, *Manuale di Diritto Canonico,* Societa Edetrice Internazionale, Torino, 1934.

Cervia, Eugenius P., *De Professione Religiosa*—Tractatus Iuridico-Canonicus, Bologna: Via Bellinzona, 1938.

Chelodi, J., *Ius De Personis Iuxta Codicem Iuris Canonici,* Tridentini, 1922.

Cicognani, Hamleto I., *Ius Canonicum,* 2 vols., Romae: Ex Officina Typographica Ausonia, 1925.

———, *Canon Law,* Authorized English Version by J. O'Hara and F. Brennan, Philadelphia: Dolphin Press, 1934.

Cocchi, Guidus, *Commentarium in Codicem Iuris Canonici Ad Usum Scholarum,* 5 vols. in 8, Liber II, Pars II, *De Religiosis,* 2. ed., 1926, Taurinorum Augustae: Marietti.

Connolly, Thomas A., *Appeals,* The Catholic University of America Canon Law Studies, n. 79, Washington, D. C.: The Catholic University of America, 1932.

Coronata, Matthaeus Conte a, *Institutiones Iuris Canonici,* 5 vols., Vol. I, 2. ed., Taurini (Italia): Marietti, 1939.

Corradus, Pyrrhus, *Praxis Dispensationum Apostolicarum,* Neapoli, 1641.

Craisson, D., *Manuale Totius Iuris Canonici*, 3 vols., 5. ed., Pictavii, 1877.

Creusen, J., *Religieux et Religieuses D'Après Le Droit Ecclesiastique*, 2. ed., Bruxelles et Paris, 1921.

Creusen, Joseph-Garesché, Edward F.-Ellis, Adam C., *Religious Men and Women in the Code*, Third English ed., Milwaukee: Bruce, 1940.

De Buck-Tinnebroeck, *Examen Historicum et Canonicum Libri R. D. M. Verhoeven*, Gandavi-Bruxellis, 1847.

De Meester, A., *Iuris Canonici et Iuris Canonico-civilis Compendium*, 3 vols. in 4, Vol. II, Brugis: Desclée, De Brouwer et Si, 1923.

Devoti, Joannis, *Institutionum Canonicarum Libri Quattuor*, ed. prima Romana post quintam, 3 vols., Romae, 1825.

Dubé, Arthur Joseph, *The General Principles for the Reckoning of Time in Canon Law*, The Catholic University of America Canon Law Studies, n. 144, Washington, D. C.: The Catholic University of America Press, 1941.

Eichner, Edward, *Lehrbuch des Kirchenrechts auf Grund des Codex Iuris Canonici*, 2. ed., Paderborn: Schöningh, 1926.

Fanfani, Ludovicus, *De Iure Religiosorum ad normam Codicis Iuris Canonici*, 2. ed., Taurini-Romae: Marietti, 1925.

———, *Il Diritto Delle Religiose conforme al Codice di Diritto Canonico*, Torino-Roma: Marietti, 1922.

Ferrari, Aloisio M., *De Statu Religioso Commentarium ad Usum Praesertim Clericorum Regularium S. Pauli*, Romae, 1899.

Ferraris, F. Lucius, *Prompta Bibliotheca, Canonica, Juridica, Moralis, Theologica necnon Ascetica, Polemica, Rubricista, Historica*, ed. Migne, 8 vols., Parisiis, 1860-1863.

Freriks, Celestine, *Religious Congregations in Their External Relations*, The Catholic University of America Canon Law Studies, n. 1, Washington, D. C.: The Catholic University of America, 1916.

Frey, Wolfgang, *The Act of Religious Profession*, The Catholic University of America Canon Law Studies, n. 63, Washington, D. C.: The Catholic University of America, 1932.

Gerster a Zeil, Thomas Villanova, *Ius Religiosorum in Compendium Redactum Pro Iuvenibus Religiosis*, Taurini (Italia): Marietti, 1935.

Geser, Fintan, *The Canon Law Governing Communities of Sisters*, St. Louis: Herder, 1938.

Goyeneche, Servus, *Iuris Canonici Summa Principia*, Libri II, Partes II et III, *De Religiosis et Laicis*, Romae: Tip. Pol. "Cuori Di Maria," 1938.

Haring, Johann B., *Grundzüge des katholischen Kirchenrechts*, 3. ed., 2 vols., Graz: Meyerhoff, 1924.

Heimbucher, Max, *Die Orden und Kongregationen der katholischen Kirche*, 3. ed., 2 vols., Paderborn: F. Schöningh, 1933-1934.

Hofmeister, Philipp, O.S.B., *Der Ordensrat*. Kanonischen Studien und Texte herausgegeben von Dr. Albert M. Koeniger, Band 13. Bonn: Ludwig Röhrscheid Verlag, 1937.

Hostiensis, Cardinalis (Henricus de Segusio), *Commentaria in Quinque Decretalium Libros*, 5 vols. in 3, Venetiis, 1631.

Jansen, Joseph, *Ordensrecht*, 2. ed., Paderborn: Schöningh, 1920; 3. ed., 1931.

Jardí, Antonio de la C., *El Derecho de Las Religiosas*, 2. ed., Vich: Editorial Seráfica, 1927.

Kealy, Thomas M., *Dowry of Women Religious*, The Catholic University of America Canon Law Studies, n. 134, Washington, D. C.: The Catholic University of America Press, 1941.

Keller, Émile, *Les Congrégations Religieuses en France*, Paris, 1880.

Kirchenlexicon, Wetzer und Welte, 2. ed., 12 vols., Freiburg im Breisgau, 1882-1901.

[Konings, Antoine], *De Jure Regularium*, Wittem, 1851.

Lega, Michael Cardinalis, *Praelectiones In Textum Iuris Canonici*, Liber II, Vol. IV, *De Iudiciis Ecclesiasticis in Genere et In Specie De Delictis et Poenis Praemisso Tractatu*, Romae, 1901.

——— —Bartoccetti, V., *Commentarius in Iudicia Ecclesiastica Iuxta Codicem Iuris Canonici*, 3 vols., Romae: Anonima Libraria Cattolica Italiana, 1938-1941.

Leitner, M., *Handbuch des katholischen Kirchensrechts auf Grund des neuen Codex*. 5 vols., Vol. III *Das Ordensrecht*, 2. ed., Regensburg: Pustet, 1922.

Lessius, L., *De Justitia et Jure*, Louvanii, 1605.

Leurenius, Petrus, *Forum Ecclesiasticum in quo Jus Canonicum Universum*, etc., 5 vols., Venetiis, 1729.

Lucidi, Angelus, *De Visitatione Sacrorum Liminum*. Instructio Sacrae Congregationis Concilii, 3. ed., ab innumeris mendis purgata et pluribus additionibus acuta per P. Josephum Schneider, Romae, 1883.

Matthaeucci, Augustinus, *Officialis Curiae Ecclesiasticae*, Venetiis, 1710.

Michelletti, A. M., *Commentarium in Decretum et Normas pro Reformatione Seminariorum*, Pars I, *De Ratione Pietatis*, ed. altera, Friburgi (B): Herder: Rome: Pustet, 1910.

———, *Jus Pianum*, Augustae Taurinorum, 1914.

Michiels, Gommarus, *Normae Generales Iuris Canonici*, 2 vols., Lublin: Universitas Catholica, 1929.

———, *Principia Generalia De Personis In Ecclesia*, Lublin: Universitas Catholica, 1932.

Moeder, John M., *The Proper Bishop for Ordination and Dimissorial Letters*, The Catholic University of America Canon Law Studies, n. 95, Washington, D. C.: The Catholic University of America, 1935.

Molitor, Raphael, *Religiosi Iuris Capita Selecta*, Ratisbonae: Pustet, 1909.

Mothon, Joseph Pie, *Traité sur L' État Religieux*, Paris: Desclée De Brouwer & Cie., 1922.

Navarrus (Martinus de Azpilcueta), *Opera Omnia*, 6 vols., Venetiis, 1618.

Nervegna, I., *De Jure Practico Regularium*, Romae, 1900.

———, *De Institutis Votorum Simplicium Religiosorum et Monialium*, Romae, 1904.

Noval, Joseph, *Commentarium Codicis Iuris Canonici,* Lib. IV, Pars II et III, Augustae Taurinorum: Marietti, 1932.

Oesterle, Gerardus, *Praelectiones Iuris Canonici,* Vol. I, Romae, in Collegio S. Anselmi, 1931.

O'Mara, William A., *Canonical Causes for Matrimonial Dispensations,* The Catholic University of America Canon Law Studies, n. 96, Washington, D. C.: The Catholic University of America, 1935.

Orth, Raymond, Clement, *The Approbation of Religious Institutes,* The Catholic University of America Canon Law Studies, n. 71, Washington, D. C.: The Catholic University of America, 1931.

Palombo, Joseph, *De Dimissione Religiosorum,* Taurini-Romae: Marietti, 1931.

Papi, Hector, *Religious in Church Law,* New York: Kenedy, 1924.

Passerinus, P. de Sextula, *De hominum statibus et officiis inspectiones morales ad ultimas 7 quaestiones 2ae 2ae D. Thomae Aquinatis,* 3 vols., Lucae, 1732.

Pastor, Ludwig Freiherr von, *The History of the Popes From the Close of the Middle Ages,* 29 vols. (translation, Vols. I-VI, ed. by Frederick I. Antrobus; Vol. VII-XXIV, ed. by Ralph F. Kerr; Vols. XXV-XXIX, ed. by Dom Ernest Graf), St. Louis: Herder, 1906-1938.

Pejska, Joseph, *Jus Canonicum Religiosorum,* 3. ed., Friburgi Brisgoviae: Herder, 1927.

Piatus Montensis, *Praelectiones Iuris Regularis,* 3. ed., 2 vols., Tornaci, 1906.

Petra, Vincentius, *Commentaria ad Constitutiones Apostolicas seu Bullas Singulas Summorum Pontificum in Bullario Romano Contentas Secundum Collectionem Cherubini Incipientes a divo Leono Magno,* 5 tomes, Romae, 1705-1726.

Piontek, Cyril, *De Indulto Exclaustrationis necnon Saecularizationis,* The Catholic University of America Canon Law Studies, n. 29, Washington, D. C.: The Catholic University of America, 1925.

Pirhing, Ernricus, *Ius Canonicum Novo Methodo Explicatum,* Dilingae, 1722.

Pourrat, Pierre, *La Spiritualité Chrétienne,* 4 vols., Vol. I, *Des Origines de l'Eglise au Moyen Age,* 6. ed., Paris: Libraire Lecoffre, J. Gabalda, 1921.

Prümmer, D. M., *Manuale Iuris Ecclesiastici,* 2 vols., Vol. I, *De Personis et Rebus Ecclesiasticis in Genere,* Friburgi-Brisgoviae, 1909; Vol. II, *Jus Regularium Speciale,* 1907.

———, *Manuale Iuris Ecclesiastici,* Ed. altera et secundum Codicem Jur. Can. Recognita, Friburgi-Brisgoviae, 1920.

———, *Manuale Iuris Canonici,* 4. et 5. ed., Friburgi-Brisgoviae: Herder, 1927.

Raus, J. B., *Institutiones Canonicae,* ed. altera, Lugduni-Parisiis: Typis Emmanuelis Vitte, 1931.

Reiffenstuel, Anacletus, *Jus Canonicum Universum,* 5 vols. in 7, Parisiis, 1864-1870.

Ried-Brig, Theodorus P. a, *Manuale Practicum Juris Disciplinaris Et Criminalis Regularium ad usum Ff. Minorum Capuccinorum exaratum,* Romae, 1902.

Rodericus, Emanual, *Quaestiones Regulares sive Resolutiones Questionum Regularium,* Lugduni, 1634.

Sanguineti, Sebastiano, *Iuris Ecclesiastici Privati Institutiones,* Romae, 1884.

Schaaf, Valentine Theodore, *The Cloister,* The Catholic University of America Canon Law Studies, n. 13, Cincinnati: St. Anthony's Messenger, 1921.

Schäfer, Timotheus, *Compendium De Religiosis ad normam Codicis Iuris Canonici,* 3. ed., Roma: S. A. L. E. R., 1940; ed. altera Münster, Ex Officina Libraria Aschendorff, 1931.

Schmalzgrueber, Franciscus, *Ius Ecclesiasticum Universorum,* 5 vols. in 12, Romae, 1843-1845.

Schönsteiner, Ferdinand, *Grundriss Des Ordensrechtes,* Wien: Ludwig Auer, 1930.

Sebastianelli, Gulielmus, *Praelectiones Juris Canonici quas in scholis pontificii seminarii romani traderat,* 2. ed., 2 vols., Romae, 1905.

Sipos, Stephanus, *Enchiridion Iuris Canonici,* Pécs: Ex Typographia "Haladás R. T.," 1926.

Soto, Dominicus de, *De Iustitia Et Iure,* Lugduni, 1569.

Stadtmüller, Raphael Maria, *Das neue Ordensrecht,* Dülmen i. W., 1919.

Suarez, Franciscus, *Opera Omnia,* in fol., 23 tomes, Venetiis 1740-1757; in 4°, 26 vols., Parisiis, 1856-1861.

Thévenot, *Le Noveau Droit Canonique des Religieuses,* 2. ed., Paris: Téqui, 1922.

Toso, Albertus, *Ad Codicem Juris Canonici Commentaria Minora,* Liber II, *De Personis,* Tome I, Taurini-Romae: Marietti, 1922.

Tyck, Charles, *Notices Historiques sur les Congrégations et Communautés Religieuses Du XIXme Siècle,* Louvain, 1892.

Van Hove, A., *Commentarium Lovaniense in Codicem Iuris Canonici,* 1 vol. in 5 tomes, Mechlinae-Romae: H. Dessain, 1928-1939. Tom. I, *Prologomena,* 1928; Tom. III, *De Consuetudine, De Temporis Supputatione,* 1933.

Verhoeven, Marianus, *De Regularium et Saecularium Clericorum Juribus et Officiis,* Lovanii, 1846.

Vermeersch, A., *De Religiosis Institutis et Personis,* 2 vols., Vol. I, ed. altera, Brugis, 1907; Vol. II, 4. ed., Brugis, 1909.

Vermeersch, A.-Creusen, J., *Summa Novi Iuris Canonici,* 4. ed., Mechlinae: H. Dessain, 1921.

———, *Epitome Iuris Canonici,* 3 vols., Vol. I, 5. ed., 1933; Vol. II, 5. ed., 1934; Vol. III, 4. ed., 1931, Mechlinae-Romae: H. Dessain.

Vromant, G., *De Bonis Ecclesiae Temporalibus ad Usum praesertim Missionariorum et Religiosorum,* Louvain: Desbarax, 1927.

Wernz, Franciscus, et Vidal, Petrus, *Ius Canonicum,* 7 tomes in 8 vols., Romae, Apud Aedes Universitatis Gregorianae, 1923-1938; Tom. II, *Ius De Personis,* 2. ed., 1928; Tom. III, *De Religiosis,* 1933.

Wernz, Franciscus, *Ius Decretalium,* 2. ed., 6 vols., Romae et Prati, 1905-1914.

Wilpert, Joseph, *Die gottgeweihten Jungfrauen in den Ersten drei Jahrhunderten,* Freiburg im Breisgau, 1892.

PERIODICALS

L'Ami du Clergé, Paris, 1878—

Analecta Ecclesiastica, Romae, 1893-1911.

Analecta Juris Pontificii, Romae, 1852-1868; Parisiis, 1869-1891.

Apollinaris, Romae, 1928—

Archiv für katholisches Kirchenrecht, Innsbruck, 1857-1861; Mainz, 1862—

Australasian Catholic Record, The, Manly, N. S. W., 1924—

Canoniste Contemporain, Le, Paris, 1897-1923 (later, *Le Canoniste*, Paris, 1924-1926).

Ciencia Thomistica, La, Madrid, 1910—

Commentarium pro Religiosis (later, [1935] *Commentarium pro Religiosis et Missionariis*), Romae, 1920—

Ecclesiastical Review, The (originally *The American Ecclesiastical Review*), Philadelphia, 1889—

Ephemerides Theologicae Lovanienses, Brugis, 1924—

Homiletic and Pastoral Review, The, New York, 1900—

Irish Ecclesiastical Record, The, Dublin, 1864—

Jahrbuch für Philosophie und speculative Theologie, Paderborn und Münster, 1887-1912.

Jus Pontificium, Romae, 1921—

Monitore Ecclesiastico, Il, Romae, 1876—

Nouvelle Revue Théologique, Paris, 1869—

Perfice Munus, Torino, 1926—

Periodica de Re Canonica et Morali utili praesertim Religiosis et Missionariis, Brugis, 1905—

Revue des Communautés Religieuses, Louvain, 1925—

ARTICLES

[Anonymous], "L'union Romaine des Ursulines"—*RCR*, V (1929), 35-40.

[Anonymous], "Questioni"—*Il Monitore Ecclesiastico*, Series IV, V (1923), 57, 58. (Vol. XXXV of the whole set.)

[Anonymous,] "Annotazioni"—*Il Monitore Ecclesiastico*, Series IV, VII (1925), 73-75. (Vol. XXXVII of the whole set.)

Ballay, Fred., "De votis simplicibus, quae votis solemnibus praemittuntur"—*AKKR*, XVII (1867), 1-42.

Beijersbergen, Hubert, "De transitu religiosi de una classe ad alteram eiusdem religiosi instituti"—*Periodica*, XXVI (1937), 33-37; 148-154.

Bergh, E., "Elements et nature de la profession religieuse"—*ETL*, XIV (1934), 5-32.

Boudinhon, A., "Les instituts des voeux simples"—*Le Canoniste Contemporain*, Vols. XXV (1902); XXVI (1903); XXVII (1904); XXVIII (1905).

Bouuaert, F. Claeys, "De metus influxu quoad valorem actus et quoad delictum et poenas secundum codicem juris canonici"—*Jus Pontificium*, VI (1926), 105-111; 138-144.

Coronata, Matthaeus Conte a, "Professione temporanea dei novizi"—*Perfice Munus,* IX (1934), 98.

Creusen, J., "Profès des voeux temporaires atteints d'alienation mental"—*NRT,* LII (1925), 330-333.

———, "Rôle du confesseur dans l'admission en Religion"—*NRT,* LV (1928), 444-447.

———, "De prorogatione professionis temporariae"—*Periodica,* XII (1924), (57)-(58).

———, "Nominatio canonicorum"—*Periodica,* XII (1924), (6)-(9).

———, "De perseverantia in instituto post vota temporaria"—*Periodica,* XII (1924), (17)-(18).

———, "De dimissione monialis votis temporariis astrictae"—*Periodica,* XII (1924), (63)-(64).

———, "Restitution d'une dot"—*RCR,* I (1925), 151, 152.

———, "Profession en danger de mort"—*RCR,* III (1927), 123, 124.

———, "Renvoi brusqué d'un profès des voeux perpetuels"—*RCR,* II (1926), 178, 179.

———, "Admission au renouvellement des voeux"—*RCR,* V (1929), 167.

———, "Relations entre les Vicaires ou Préfets Apostoliques et les supérieurs religieux"—*RCR,* VI (1930), 113-120.

———, "Admission déférée ou renvoi"—*RCR,* XI (1935), 194.

———, "Consultations"—*RCR,* XIV (1938), 28, 29; 33-37; 155, 156.

———, "Esquisse Historique: Les instituts religieux à voeux simples"—*RCR,* XV (1939), 52-63.

D'Ambrosio, F. X., "De causis exclusionis religiosi a renovatione professionis in institutis votorum temporariorum"—*Apollinaris,* I (1928), 173-176; 297-299; IV (1931), 124-128.

Damen, C. A., "De irritatione et suspensione votorum spectato jure naturali atque ecclesiastico antiquo et novo"—*Apollinaris,* I (1928), 469-476; II (1929), 53-61; 306-318; 495-509; III (1930), 109-119; 274-295.

Ellis, Adamus, "De transitu ad alium eiusdem religionis classem"—*Periodica,* XXV (1936), 102*-104*.

———, "De religiosi minoristae saecularizati incardinatione"—*Periodica,* XXV (1936), 53*-55*.

Fallon, M. J., "Consequence of failure to consult diocesan consultors collegialiter"—*IER,* LIII (1939), 297-300.

Gomez, D. Maurus, "De abbatum potestate tonsuram minoresque ordines conferendi"—*CpR,* IX (1928), 434-446.

Goyeneche, Servus, "Annotatio"—*CpR,* IV (1923), 257-264.

———, "Consultationes"—*CpR,* I (1920), 51, 52; 231-236.

———, "Consultatio"—*CpR,* II (1921), 148-153.

———, "Consultationes"—*CpR,* III (1922), 10-15; 52-54; 78-81; 82-84; 170; 215, 216; 217; 220, 221; 265; 329-335.

———, "Consultatio"—*CpR,* IV (1923), 146, 147.

———, "Consultationes"—*CpR,* V (1924), 26-28; 163, 164; 165, 166; 390-393.

———, "Consultationes"—*CpR,* VI (1925), 24; 90, 91.

———, "Consultatio"—*CpR,* VII (1926), 449, 450.

———, "Consultatio"—*CpR,* VIII (1927), 34, 35.

———, "Consultationes"—*CpR,* XI (1930), 80, 81; 437, 438; 440, 441.

———, "Consultatio"—*CpR,* XII (1931), 131, 132.

———, "Consultationes"—*CpR,* XIII (1932), 39, 40; 100, 101.

———, "Consultationes"—*CpR,* XIV (1933), 49, 50; 183, 184; 257-259; 351-354.

———, "Consultationes"—*CpRM,* XVI (1935), 122-126; 233, 234; 315, 316.

———, "Consultatio"—*CpRM,* XVII (1936), 347-350.

———, "Consultatio"—*CpRM,* XVIII (1937), 158-160.

———, "Consultationes"—*CpRM,* XIX (1938), 8-12; 163, 164.

———, "Quaestio Canonica"—*CpR,* IV (1923), 368-372.

———, "Quaestio Canonica"—*CpR,* V (1924), 21-25.

———, "De transitu ad aliam religionem"—*CpR,* I (1920), 22-30; 73-77; 107-111.

———, "De egressu a religione"—*CpR,* V (1924), 50-55; 86-93; 211-216; 335-341.

———, "De votis simplicibus in fontibus et in doctrina in ordine ad statum religiosum constituendum"—*Acta Congressus Iuridici Internationalis,* IV, 301-315.

Hanssen, Antonius, "De sanctione nullitatis in processu canonico"—*Apollinaris,* XI (1938), 71-109; 215-263; 381-403; XII (1939), 198-251.

Jombart, E., "De dimissione ex mutuo consensu"—*Periodica,* XII (1924), (58)-(60).

———, "L'Essence de l'état religieux—*RCR,* I (1925), 172-182.

———, "Congrégations de droit pontifical"—*RCR,* III (1927), 19-23; 42-46; 78-82.

———, "Les dots"—*RCR,* III (1927), 55-58.

———, "La sortie de religion a l'expiration des voeux temporaires"—*RCR,* V (1929), 158-164.

———, "Le renvoi au cours des voeux temporaires"—*RCR,* V (1929), 195-203.

———, "Restitution de trousseau"—*RCR,* VI (1930), 190, 191.

———, "Maladie de volonté"—*RCR,* VII (1931), 189-191.

———, "Autonomie et centralization"—*RCR,* X (1934), 125-134; 146-161.

———, "Conseil de quitter l'institut"—*RCR,* XI (1935), 197-199.

———, "Intention de persévérer"—*RCR,* XII (1936), 103, 104.

Koch, Hugo, "Virgines Christi. Die Gelübde der gottgeweihten Jungfrauen in den ersten drei Jahrhunderten"—*Texte und Untersuchungen,* XXXI (1907), n. 2.

Langogne, Pie de, "Le decret *'Auctis Admodum'* "—*Analecta Ecclesiastica,* I (1893), 92-96.

La Puma, Vincenzo, Cardinale, "Evoluzione del diritto dei religiose da Pio IX a Pio XI"—*Acta Congressus Iuridici Internationalis,* IV, 193-203.

———, "Annotatio"—*CpR,* XIV (1933), 164.

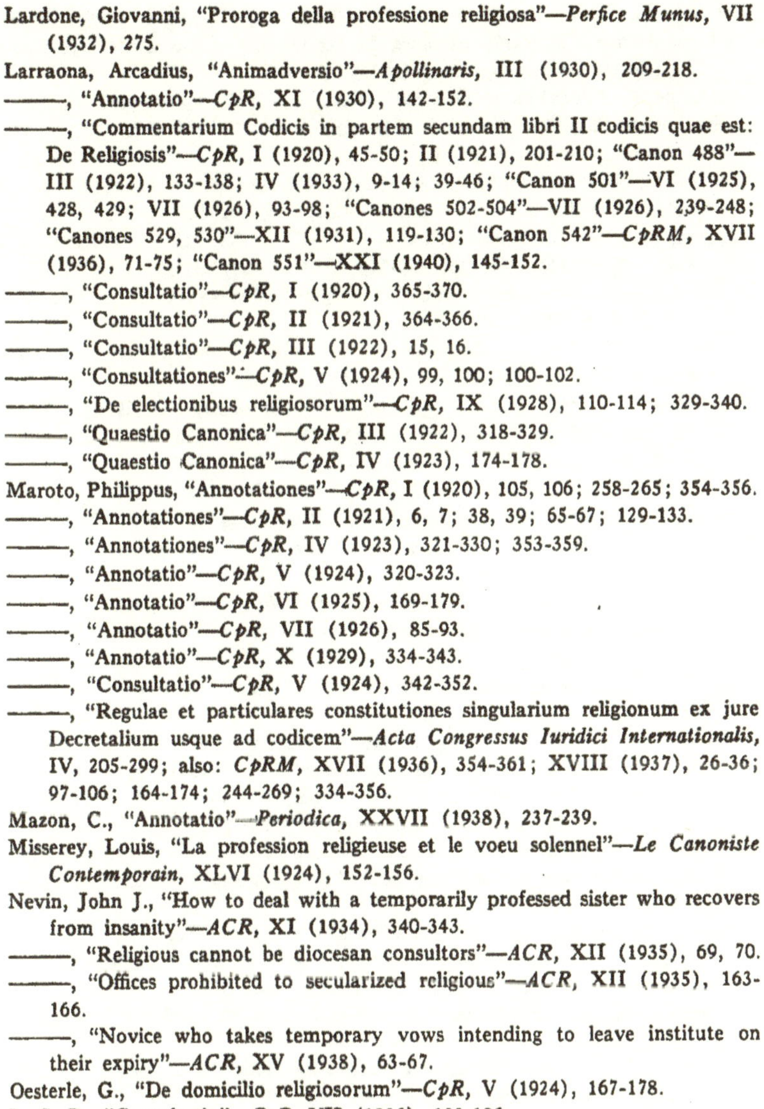

Lardone, Giovanni, "Proroga della professione religiosa"—*Perfice Munus,* VII (1932), 275.

Larraona, Arcadius, "Animadversio"—*Apollinaris,* III (1930), 209-218.

———, "Annotatio"—*CpR,* XI (1930), 142-152.

———, "Commentarium Codicis in partem secundam libri II codicis quae est: De Religiosis"—*CpR,* I (1920), 45-50; II (1921), 201-210; "Canon 488"—III (1922), 133-138; IV (1933), 9-14; 39-46; "Canon 501"—VI (1925), 428, 429; VII (1926), 93-98; "Canones 502-504"—VII (1926), 239-248; "Canones 529, 530"—XII (1931), 119-130; "Canon 542"—*CpRM,* XVII (1936), 71-75; "Canon 551"—XXI (1940), 145-152.

———, "Consultatio"—*CpR,* I (1920), 365-370.

———, "Consultatio"—*CpR,* II (1921), 364-366.

———, "Consultatio"—*CpR,* III (1922), 15, 16.

———, "Consultationes"—*CpR,* V (1924), 99, 100; 100-102.

———, "De electionibus religiosorum"—*CpR,* IX (1928), 110-114; 329-340.

———, "Quaestio Canonica"—*CpR,* III (1922), 318-329.

———, "Quaestio Canonica"—*CpR,* IV (1923), 174-178.

Maroto, Philippus, "Annotationes"—*CpR,* I (1920), 105, 106; 258-265; 354-356.

———, "Annotationes"—*CpR,* II (1921), 6, 7; 38, 39; 65-67; 129-133.

———, "Annotationes"—*CpR,* IV (1923), 321-330; 353-359.

———, "Annotatio"—*CpR,* V (1924), 320-323.

———, "Annotatio"—*CpR,* VI (1925), 169-179.

———, "Annotatio"—*CpR,* VII (1926), 85-93.

———, "Annotatio"—*CpR,* X (1929), 334-343.

———, "Consultatio"—*CpR,* V (1924), 342-352.

———, "Regulae et particulares constitutiones singularium religionum ex jure Decretalium usque ad codicem"—*Acta Congressus Iuridici Internationalis,* IV, 205-299; also: *CpRM,* XVII (1936), 354-361; XVIII (1937), 26-36; 97-106; 164-174; 244-269; 334-356.

Mazon, C., "Annotatio"—*Periodica,* XXVII (1938), 237-239.

Misserey, Louis, "La profession religieuse et le voeu solennel"—*Le Canoniste Contemporain,* XLVI (1924), 152-156.

Nevin, John J., "How to deal with a temporarily professed sister who recovers from insanity"—*ACR,* XI (1934), 340-343.

———, "Religious cannot be diocesan consultors"—*ACR,* XII (1935), 69, 70.

———, "Offices prohibited to secularized religious"—*ACR,* XII (1935), 163-166.

———, "Novice who takes temporary vows intending to leave institute on their expiry"—*ACR,* XV (1938), 63-67.

Oesterle, G., "De domicilio religiosorum"—*CpR,* V (1924), 167-178.

P. G. R., "Consultatio"—*CpR,* VII (1926), 103-106.

Prümmer, Dominicus, "Kann der Papst in den feierlichen Ordensgelübden dispensieren?"—*Jahrbuch für Philosophie und spekulative Theologie,* XXII (1908), 55-79.

Roberti, F., "De recursu ob reiectionem libelli"—*Apollinaris*, I (1928), 73, 74.

Sabino, Alonso, "Situación canónica de las monjas sujetas a los regulares"—*La Ciencia Tomistica*, XXX (1924), 120.

Salsmans, J., "Vocation et chasteté"—*NRT*, LX (1933), 401-403.

Schaaf, Valentine, "Can ex-religious become pastors?"—*ER*, LXXXIX (1933), 431, 432.

Schiewietz, S., "Vorgeschichte des Mönchtums oder das Ascetentum der drei ersten christlichen Jahrhunderte"—*AKKR*, LXXVIII (1898), 3-23.

Tabera, A., "De dimissione religiosorum"—*CpR*, XI (1930), 277-285; 411-420; XII (1931), 140-148; 369-375; XIV (1933), 53-59; 266-274.

———, "De dissolutione votorum in religiosis dimissis—Excursus historicus" —*CpR*, XII (1931), 455-458.

Steiger, A. P., "De propagatione et diffusione vitae religiosae"—*Periodica*, XIII (1924), (170)-(181).

Vermeersch, A., "De domicilio religiosorum"—*Periodica*, IX (1919), (7)-(8).

———, "Annotationes"—*Periodica*, X (1922), 71, 73, 253, 325; XII (1924), 39-42, 100-104, (143); XIII (1925), 69; XIX (1930), 260-265.

———, "De monasteriis seu domibus sui iuris"—*Periodica*, X (1922), (7)-(9).

———, "De superioribus maioribus"—*Periodica*, X (1922), (9)-(10).

———, "De professione novicii vel probandi in articulo mortis"—*Periodica*, XII (1924), (159)-(162).

———, "De dotis quantitate definienda"—*Periodica*, XII (1924), (162).

———, "De exclusione a renovandis votis a Canon 637"—*Periodica*, XIII (1925), (70)-(71).

———, "De status religiosi essentia et interpretatione can. 487 et 488, 1°"—*Periodica*, XV (1927), (1)-(13).

———, "De conscribendis constitutionibus congregationis votorum simplicium vel de iisdem ad codicem aptandis"—*Periodica*, XVI (1927), 154*-172*.

———, "De accidentali causa cur vota temporaria nunquam in perpetua convertantur"—*Periodica*, XVII (1928), 222*-223*.

———, "A quonam momento estne professo a votis temporariis integrum religionem desere ad normam can. 637?"—*Periodica*, XXII (1933), 34*-39*.

Vindex, "Domicilium et quasi-domicilium eorumque effectus in codice juris canonici"—*Jus Pontificium*, VI (1926), 34-55; 112-126; 154-158.

Voltas, Petrus, "Consultatio"—*CpR*, I (1920), 300, 301.

Vromant, "De actibus personae moralis collegialis ac superioris"—*ETL*, VII (1930), 676-688.

Weckesser, Paul, "Das feierliche Keuschheitsgelübde in der alten Kirche"—*AKKR*, LXXVI (1896), 83-104; 187-211; 321-351.

Woywod, Stanislaus, "Answers to Questions"—*HPR*, XXXV (1934-1935), 1062-1064; XXXVII (1936-1937), 417-420; 855, 856.

———, "Novitiate and profession of religious who have permission to leave their community and join another"—*HPR*, XXIV (1923-1924), 75, 76.

ABBREVIATIONS

AAS—*Acta Apostolicae Sedis.*

ACR—*Australasian Catholic Record, The.*

AKKR—*Archiv für katholisches Kirchenrecht.*

ASS—*Acta Sanctae Sedis.*

Bull. Rom.—*Bullarium Romanum.*

Bull. Rom. Cont.—*Bullarii Romani Continuatio.*

Coll. Lac.—*Acta et Decreta Sacrorum Conciliorum Recentiorum, Collectio Lacensis.*

Coll. S. C. Ep. et Reg.—*Collectanea in usum Secretariae S. C. Episcoporum et Regularium.*

CpR—*Commentarium pro Religiosis.*

CpRM—*Commentarium pro Religiosis et Missionariis.*

ER—*Ecclesiastical Review, The.*

ETL—*Ephemerides Theologicae Lovanienses.*

Fontes—*Codicis Iuris Canonici Fontes cura . . . Gasparri editi.*

HPR—*Homiletic and Pastoral Review, The.*

IER—*Irish Ecclesiastical Record, The.*

Mansi—*Sacrorum Conciliorum Nova et Amplissima Collectio.*

MPG—Migne *Patrologia, Series Graeca.*

MPL—Migne *Patrologia, Series Latina.*

NRT—*Nouvelle Revue Théologique.*

PCI—*Pontificia Commissio ad Codicis Canones authentice interpretandos.*

Periodica—*Periodica de Re Canonica et Morali utili praesertim Religiosis et Missionariis.*

RCR—*Revue des Communautés Religieuses.*

ALPHABETICAL INDEX

BIOGRAPHICAL NOTE

Francis Joseph O'Neill was born in Windsor, Canada, September 14, 1912. He received his primary education in the parochial schools of St. Vincent and of the Most Holy Redeemer in Detroit, Michigan. In 1932 he graduated from Saint Joseph's College, Kirkwood, Missouri, the Juvenate of the Redemptorist Fathers of the St. Louis Province. In August, 1933, he made his profession as a member of the Congregation of the Most Holy Redeemer. After his course of studies made at the Redemptorist Seminary, Oconomowoc, Wisconsin, he was ordained to the priesthood, June 29, 1938. In September, 1939, he was sent by his superiors to the Catholic University of America to pursue a course of graduate studies in the School of Canon Law. In June, 1940, he received there the degree of Baccalaureate in Canon Law, and in June, 1941, the degree of Licentiate in Canon Law.

CANON LAW STUDIES

1. Freriks, Rev. Celestine A., C.PP.S., J.C.D., Religious Congregations in Their External Relations, 121 pp., 1916.
2. Galliher, Rev. Daniel M., O.P., J.C.D., Canonical Elections, 117 pp., 1917.
3. Borkowski, Rev. Aurelius L., O.F.M., J.C.D., De Confraternitatibus Ecclesiasticis, 136 pp., 1918.
4. Castillo, Rev. Cayo, J.C.D.,. Disertacion Historico-Canonica sobre la Potestad del Cabildo en Sede Vacante o Impedida del Vicario Capitular, 99 pp., 1919 (1918).
5. Kubelbeck, Rev. William J., S.T.B., J.C.D., The Sacred Penitentiaria and Its Relation to Faculties of Ordinaries and Priests, 129 pp., 1918.
6. Petrovits, Rev. Joseph, J.C., S.T.D., J.C.D., The New Church Law on Matrimony, X-461 pp., 1919.
7. Hickey, Rev. John J., S.T.B., J.C.D., Irregularities and Simple Impediments in the New Code of Canon Law, 100 pp., 1920.
8. Klekotka, Rev. Peter J., S.T.B., J.C.D., Diocesan Consultors, 179 pp., 1920.
9. Wanenmacher, Rev. Francis, J.C.D., The Evidence in Ecclesiastical Procedure Affecting the Marriage Bond, 1920 (Printed 1935).
10. Golden, Rev. Henry Francis, J.C.D., Parochial Benefices in the New Code, IV-119 pp., 1921 (Printed 1925).
11. Koudelka, Rev. Charles J., J.C.D., Pastors, Their Rights and Duties According to the New Code of Canon Law, 211 pp., 1921.
12. Melo, Rev. Antonius, O.F.M., J.C.D., De Exemptione Regularium, X-188 pp., 1921.
13. Schaaf, Rev. Valentine Theodore, O.F.M., S.T.B., J.C.D., The Cloister, X-180 pp., 1921.
14. Burke, Rev. Thomas Joseph, S.T.D., J.C.D., Competence in Ecclesiastical Tribunals, IV-117 pp., 1922.
15. Leech, Rev. George Leo, J.C.D., A Comparative Study of the Constitution "Apostolicae Sedis" and the "Codex Juris Canonici," 179 pp., 1922.
16. Motry, Rev. Hubert Louis, S.T.D., J.C.D., Diocesan Faculties According to the Code of Canon Law, II-167 pp., 1922.
17. Murphy, Rev. George Lawrence, J.C.D., Delinquencies and Penalties in the Administration and the Reception of the Sacraments, IV-121 pp., 1923.
18. O'Reilly, Rev. John Anthony, S.T.B., J.C.D., Ecclesiastical Sepulture in the New Code of Canon Law, II-129 pp., 1923.
19. Michalicka, Rev. Wenceslas Cyrill, O.S.B., J.C.D., Judicial Procedure in Dismissal of Clerical Exempt Religious, 107 pp., 1923.

20. Dargin, Rev. Edward Vincent, S.T.B., J.C.D., Reserved Cases According to the Code of Canon Law, IV-103 pp., 1924.

21. Godfrey, Rev. John A., S.T.B., J.C.D., The Right of Patronage According to the Code of Canon Law, 153 pp., 1924.

22. Hagedorn, Rev. Francis Edward, J.C.D., General Legislation on Indulgences, II-154 pp., 1924.

23. King, Rev. James Ignatius, J.C.D., The Administration of the Sacraments to Dying Non-Catholics, V-141 pp., 1924.

24. Winslow, Rev. Francis Joseph, O.F.M., J.C.D., Vicars and Prefects Apostolic, IV-149 pp., 1924.

25. Correa, Rev. Jose Servelion, S.T.L., J.C.D., La Potestad Legislativa de la Iglesia Catolica, IV-127 pp., 1925.

26. Dugan, Rev. Henry Francis, A.M., J.C.D., The Judiciary Department of the Diocesan Curia, 87 pp., 1925.

27. Keller, Rev. Charles Frederick, S.T.B., J.C.D., Mass Stipends, 167 pp., 1925.

28. Paschang, Rev. John Linus, J.C.D., The Sacramentals According to the Code of Canon Law, 129 pp., 1925.

29. Piontek, Rev. Cyrillus, O.F.M., S.T.B., J.C.D., De Indulto Exclaustrationis necnon Saecularizationis, XIII-289 pp., 1925.

30. Kearney, Rev. Richard Joseph, S.T.B., J.C.D., Sponsors at Baptism According to the Code of Canon Law, IV-127 pp., 1925.

31. Bartlett, Rev. Chester Joseph, A.M., LL.B., J.C.D., The Tenure of Parochial Property in the United States of America, V-108 pp., 1926.

32. Kilker, Rev. Adrian Jerome, J.C.D., Extreme Unction, V-425 pp., 1926.

33. McCormick, Rev. Robert Emmett, J.C.D., Confessors of Religious, VIII-266 pp., 1926.

34. Miller, Rev. Newton Thomas, J.C.D., Founded Masses According to the Code of Canon Law, VII-93 pp., 1926.

35. Roelker, Rev. Edward G., S.T.D., J.C.D., Principles of Privilege According to the Code of Canon Law, XI-166 pp., 1926.

36. Bakalarczyk, Rev. Richardus, M.I.C., J.U.D., De Novitiatu, VIII-208 pp., 1927.

37. Pizzuti, Rev. Lawrence, O.F.M., J.U.L., De Parochis Religiosis, 1927. (Not Printed.)

38. Bliley, Rev. Nicholas Martin, O.S.B., J.C.D., Altars According to the Code of Canon Law, XIX-132 pp., 1927.

39. Brown, Mr. Brendan Francis, A.B., LL.M., J.U.D., The Canonical Juristic Personality with Special Reference to its Status in the United States of America, V-212 pp., 1927.

40. Cavanaugh, Rev. William Thomas, C.P., J.U.D., The Reservation of the Blessed Sacrament, VIII-101 pp., 1927.

41. Doheny, Rev. William J., C.S.C., A.B., J.U.D., Church Property: Modes of Acquisition, X-118 pp., 1927.

42. Feldhaus, Rev. Aloysius H., C.PP.S., J.C.D., Oratories, IX-141 pp., 1927.
43. Kelly, Rev. James Patrick, A.B., J.C.D., The Jurisdiction of the Simple Confessor, X-208 pp., 1927.
44. Neuberger, Rev. Nicholas J., J.C.D., Canon 6 or the Relation of the Codex Juris Canonici to the Preceding Legislation, V-95 pp., 1927.
45. O'Keefe, Rev. Gerald Michael, J.C.D., Matrimonial Dispensations, Powers of Bishops, Priests, and Confessors, VIII-232 pp., 1927.
46. Quigley, Rev. Joseph A. M., A.B., J.C.D., Condemned Societies, 139 pp., 1927.
47. Zaplotnik, Rev. Johannes Leo, J.C.D., De Vicariis Foraneis, X-142 pp., 1927.
48. Duskie, Rev. John Aloysius, A.B., J.C.D., The Canonical Status of the Orientals in the United States, VIII-196 pp., 1928.
49. Hyland, Rev. Francis Edward, J.C.D., Excommunciation, Its Nature, Historical Development and Effects, VIII-181 pp., 1928.
50. Reinmann, Rev. Gerald Joseph, O.M.C., J.C.D., The Third Order Secular of Saint Francis, 201 pp., 1928.
51. Schenk, Rev. Francis J., J.C.D., The Matrimonial Impediments of Mixed Religion and Disparity of Cult, XVI-318 pp., 1929.
52. Coady, Rev. John Joseph, S.T.D., J.U.D., A.M., The Appointment of Pastors, VIII-150 pp., 1929.
53. Kay, Rev. Thomas Henry, J.C.D., Competence in Matrimonial Procedure, VIII-164 pp., 1929.
54. Turner, Rev. Sidney Joseph, C.P., J.U.D., The Vow of Poverty, XLIX-217 pp., 1929.
55. Kearney, Rev. Raymond A., A.B., S.T.D., J.C.D., The Principles of Delegation, VII-149 pp., 1929.
56. Conran, Rev. Edward James, A.B., J.C.D., The Interdict, V-163 pp., 1930.
57. O'Neill, Rev. William H., J.C.D., Papal Rescripts of Favor, VII-218 pp., 1930.
58. Bastnagel, Rev. Clement Vincent, J.U.D., The Appointment of Parochial Adjutants and Assistants, XV-257 pp., 1930.
59. Ferry, Rev. William A., A.B., J.C.D., Stole Fees, V-136 pp., 1930.
60. Costello, Rev. John Michael, A.B., J.C.D., Domicile and Quasi-Domicile, VII-201 pp., 1930.
61. Kremer, Rev. Michael Nicholas, A.B., S.T.B., J.C.D., Church Support in the United States, VI-136 pp., 1930.
62. Angulo, Rev. Luis, C.M., J.C.D., Legislation de la Iglesia sobre la intencion en la application de la Santa Misa, VII-104 pp., 1931.
63. Frey, Rev. Wolfgang Norbert, O.S.B., A.B., J.C.D., The Act of Religious Profession, VIII-174 pp., 1931.
64. Roberts, Rev. James Brendan, A.B., J.C.D., The Banns of Marriage, XIV-140 pp., 1931.

65. Ryder, Rev. Raymond Aloysius, A.B., J.C.D., Simony, IX-151 pp., 1931.
66. Campagna, Rev. Angelo, Ph.D., J.U.D., Il Vicario Generale del Vescovo, VII-205 pp., 1931.
67. Cox, Rev. Joseph Godfrey, A.B., J.C.D., The Administration of Seminaries, VI-124 pp., 1931.
68. Gregory, Rev. Donald J., J.U.D., The Pauline Privilege, XV-165 pp., 1931.
69. Donohue, Rev. John F., J.C.D., The Impediment of Crime, VII-110 pp., 1931.
70. Dooley, Rev. Eugene A., O.M.I., J.C.D., Church Law on Sacred Relics, IX-143 pp., 1931.
71. Orth, Rev. Clement Raymond, O.M.C., J.C.D., The Approbation of Religious Institutes, 171 pp., 1931.
72. Pernicone, Rev. Joseph M., A.B., J.C.D., The Ecclesiastical Prohibition of Books, XII-267 pp., 1932.
73. Clinton, Rev. Connell, A.B., J.C.D., The Paschal Precept, IX-108 pp., 1932.
74. Donnelly, Rev. Francis B., A.M., S.T.L., J.C.D., The Diocesan Synod, VIII-125 pp., 1932.
75. Torrente, Rev. Camilo, C.M.F., J.C.D., Las Processiones Sagradas, V-145 pp., 1932.
76. Murphy, Rev. Edwin J., C.PP.S., J.C.D., Suspension Ex Informata Conscientia, XI-122 pp., 1932.
77. MacKenzie, Rev. Eric F., A.M., S.T.L., J.C.D., The Delict of Heresy in its Commission, Penalization, Absolution, VII-124 pp., 1932.
78. Lyons, Rev. Avitus E., S.T.B., J.C.D., The Collegiate Tribunal of First Instance, XI-147 pp., 1932.
79. Connolly, Rev. Thomas A., J.C.D., Appeals, XI-195 pp., 1932.
80. Sangmeister, Rev. Joseph V., A.B., J.C.D., Force and Fear as Precluding Matrimonial Consent, V-211 pp., 1932.
81. Jaeger, Rev. Leo A., A.B., J.C.D., The Administration of Vacant and Quasi-Vacant Episcopal Sees in the United States, IX-229 pp., 1932.
82. Rimlinger, Rev. Herbert T., J.C.D., Error Invalidating Matrimonial Consent, VII-79 pp., 1932.
83. Barrett, Rev. John D. M., S.S., J.C.D., A Comparative Study of the Third Plenary Council of Baltimore and the Code, IX-221 pp., 1932.
84. Carberry, Rev. John J., Ph.D., S.T.D., J.C.D., The Juridical Form of Marriage, X-177 pp., 1934.
85. Dolan, Rev. John L., A.B., J.C.D., The Defensor Vinculi, XII-157 pp., 1934.
86. Hannan, Rev. Jerome D., A.M., S.T.D., LL.B., J.C.D., The Canon Law of Wills, IX-517 pp., 1934.
87. Lemieux, Rev. Delise A., A.M., J.C.D., The Sentence in Ecclesiastical Procedure, IX-131 pp., 1934.

88. O'ROURKE, REV. JAMES J., A.B., J.C.D., Parish Registers, VII-109 pp., 1934.
89. TIMLIN, REV. BARTHOLOMEW, O.F.M., A.M., J.C.D., Conditional Matrimonial Consent, X-381 pp., 1934.
90. WAHL, REV. FRANCIS X., A.B., J.C.D., The Matrimonial Impediments of Consanguinity and Affinity, VI-125 pp., 1934.
91. WHITE, REV. ROBERT J., A.B., LL.B., S.T.B., J.C.D., Canonical Ante-Nuptial Promises and the Civil Law, VI-152 pp., 1934.
92. HERRERA, REV. ANTONIO PARRA, O.C.D., J.C.D., Legislacion Ecclesiastica sobra el Ayuno y la Abstinencia, XI-191 pp., 1935.
93. KENNEDY, REV. EDWIN J., J.C.D., The Special Matrimonial Process in Cases of Evident Nullity, X-165 pp., 1935.
94. MANNING, REV. JOHN J., A.B., J.C.D., Presumption of Law in Matrimonial Procedure, XI-111 pp., 1935.
95. MOEDER, REV. JOHN M., J.C.D., The Proper Bishop for Ordination and Dimissorial Letters, VII-135 pp., 1935.
96. O'MARA, REV. WILLIAM A., A.B., J.C.D., Canonical Causes for Matrimonial Dispensations, IX-155 pp., 1935.
97. REILLY, REV. PETER, J.C.D., Residence of Pastors, IX-81 pp., 1935.
98. SMITH, REV. MARINER T., O.P., S.T.Lr., J.C.D., The Penal Law for Religious, VII-169 pp., 1935.
99. WHALEN, REV. DONALD W., A.M., J.C.D., The Value of Testimonial Evidence in Matrimonial Procedure, XIII-297 pp., 1935.
100. CLEARY, REV. JOSEPH F., J.C.D., Canonical Limitations on the Alienation of Church Property, VIII-141 pp., 1936.
101. GLYNN, REV. JOHN C., J.C.D., The Promoter of Justice, XX-337 pp., 1936.
102. BRENNAN, REV. JAMES H., S.S., M.A., S.T.B., J.C.D., The Simple Convalidation of Marriage, VI-135 pp., 1937.
103. BRUNINI, REV. JOSEPH BERNARD, J.C.D., The Clerical Obligations of Canons 139 and 142, X-121 pp., 1937.
104. CONNOR, REV. MAURICE, A.B., J.C.D., The Administrative Removal of Pastors, VIII-159 pp., 1937.
105. GUILFOYLE, REV. MERLIN JOSEPH, J.C.D., Custom, XI-144 pp., 1937.
106. HUGHES, REV. JAMES AUSTIN, A.B., A.M., J.C.D., Witnesses in Criminal Trials of Clerics, IX-140 pp., 1937.
107. JANSEN, REV. RAYMOND J., A.B., S.T.L., J.C.D., Canonical Provisions for Catechetical Instruction, VII-153 pp., 1937.
108. KEALY, REV. JOHN JAMES, A.B., J.C.D., The Introductory Libellus in Church Court Procedure, XI-121 pp., 1937.
109. MCMANUS, REV. JAMES EDWARD, C.SS.R., J.C.D., The Administration of Temporal Goods in Religious Institutes, XVI-196 pp., 1937.
110. MORIARTY, REV. EUGENE JAMES, J.C.D., Oaths in Ecclesiastical Courts, X-115 pp., 1937.

111. RAINER, REV. ELIGIUS GEORGE, C.SS.R., J.C.D., Suspension of Clerics, XVII-249 pp., 1937.
112. REILLY, REV. THOMAS F., C.SS.R., J.C.D., Visitation of Religious, VI-195 pp., 1938.
113. MORIARTY, RFV. FRANCIS E., C.SS.R., J.C.D., The Extraordinary Absolution from Censures, XV-334 pp., 1938.
114. CONNOLLY, REV. NICHOLAS P., J.C.D., The Canonical Erection of Parishes, X-132 pp., 1938.
115. DONOVAN, REV. JAMES JOSEPH, J.C.D., The Pastor's Obligation in Prenuptial Investigation, XII-322 pp., 1938.
116. HARRIGAN, REV. ROBERT J., M.A., S.T.B., J.C.D., The Radical Sanation of Invalid Marriages, VIII-208 pp., 1938.
117. BOFFA, REV. CONRAD HUMBERT, J.C.D., Canonical Provisions for Catholic Schools, VII-211 pp., 1939.
118. PARSONS, REV. ANSCAR JOHN, O.M.Cap., J.C.D., Canonical Elections, XII-236 pp., 1939.
119. REILLY, REV. EDWARD MICHAEL, A.B., J.C.D., The General Norms of Dispensation, XII-156 pp., 1939.
120. RYAN, REV. GERALD ALOYSIUS, A.B., J.C.D., Principles of Episcopal Jurisdiction, XII-172 pp., 1939.
121. BURTON, REV. FRANCIS JAMES, C.S.C., A.B., J.C.D., A Commentary on Canon 1125, X-222 pp., 1940.
122. MIASKIEWICZ, REV. FRANCIS SIGISMUND, J.C.D., Supplied Jurisdiction According to Canon 209, XII-340 pp., 1940.
123. RICE, REV. PATRICK WILLIAM, A.B., J.C.D., Proof of Death in Prenuptial Investigation, VIII-156 pp., 1940.
124. ANGLIN, REV. THOMAS FRANCIS, M.S., J.C.D., The Eucharistic Fast, VIII-183 pp., 1941.
125. COLEMAN, REV. JOHN JEROME, J.C.D., The Minister of Confirmation, VI-153 pp., 1941.
126. DOWNS, REV. JOSEPH EMMANUEL, A.B., J.C.D., The Concept of Clerical Immunity, XI-163 pp., 1941.
127. ESSWEIN, REV. ANTHONY ALBERT, J.C.D., Extrajudicial Penal Powers of Ecclesiastical Superiors, X-144 pp., 1941.
128. FARRELL, REV. BENJAMIN FRANCIS, M.A., S.T.L., J.C.D., The Rights and Duties of the Local Ordinary Regarding Congregations of Women Religious of Pontifical Approval, V-195 pp., 1941.
129. FEENEY, REV. THOMAS JOHN, A.B., S.T.L., J.C.D., Restitutio in Integrum, VI-169 pp., 1941.
130. FINDLAY, REV. STEPHEN WILLIAM, O.S.B., A.B., J.C.D., Canonical Norms Governing the Deposition and Degradation of Clerics, XVII-279 pp., 1941.
131. GOODWINE, REV. JOHN, A.B., S.T.L., J.C.D., The Right of the Church to Acquire Property, VIII-119 pp., 1941.

132. Heston, Rev. Edward Louis, C.S.C., Ph.D., S.T.D., J.C.D., The Alienation of Church Property in the United States, XII-222 pp., 1941.
133. Hogan, Rev. James John, A.B., S.T.L., J.C.D., Judicial Advocates and Procurators, XIII-200 pp., 1941.
134. Kealy, Rev. Thomas M., A.B., Litt.B., J.C.D., Dowry of Women Religious, IX-152 pp., 1941.
135. Keene, Rev. Michael James, O.S.B., J.C.D., Religious Ordinaries and Canon 198, V-164 pp., 1942.
136. Kerin, Rev. Charles A., S.S., M.A., S.T.B., J.C.D., The Privation of Christian Burial, XVI-279 pp., 1941.
137. Louis, Rev. William Francis, M.A., J.C.D., Diocesan Archives, X-101 pp., 1941.
138. McDevitt, Rev. Gilbert Joseph, A.B., J.C.D., Legitimacy and Legitimation, X-247 pp., 1941.
139. McDonough, Rev. Thomas Joseph, A.B., J.C.D., Apostolic Administrators, X-217 pp., 1941.
140. Meier, Rev. Carl Anthony, A.B., J.C.D., Penal Administration Procedure Against Negligent Pastors, XI-240 pp., 1941.
141. Schmidt, Rev. John Rogg, A.B., J.C.D., The Principles of Authentic Interpretation in Canon 17 of the Code of Canon Law, XII-331 pp., 1941.
142. Slafkosky, Rev. Andrew Leonard, A.B., J.C.D., The Canonical Episcopal Visitation of the Diocese, X-197 pp., 1941.
143. Swoboda, Rev. Innocent Robert, O.F.M., J.C.D., Ignorance in Relation to the Imputability of Delicts, IX-271 pp., 1941.
144. Dubé, Rev. Arthur Joseph, A.B., J.C.D., The General Principles for the Reckoning of Time in Canon Law, VIII-299 pp., 1941.
145. McBride, Rev. James T., A.B., J.C.D., Incardination and Excardination of Seculars, XX-585 pp., 1941.
146. Król, Rev. John T., J.C.D., The Defendant in Ecclesiastical Trials, XII-207 pp., 1942.
147. Comyns, Rev. Joseph J., C.SS.R., A.B., J.C.D., Papal and Episcopal Administration of Church Property, XIV-155 pp., 1942.
148. Barry, Rev. Garrett Francis, O.M.I., J.C.L., Violation of the Cloister.
149. Bolduc, Rev. Gatien, C.S.V., A.B., S.T.L., J.C.L., Les études dans les religions cléricales.
150. Boyle, Rev. David John, M.A., J.C.L., The Juridic Effects of Moral Certitude on Pre-Nuptial Guarantees.
151. Canavan, Rev. Walter Joseph, M.A., Litt.D., J.C.L., The Profession of Faith.
152. Desrochers, Rev. Bruno, A.B., Ph.L., S.T.B., J.C.L., Le Premier Concile Plénier de Québec et le Code de Droit Canonique.
153. Dillon, Rev. Robert Edward, A.B., J.C.L., Common Law Marriage.
154. Dodwell, Rev. Edward John, Ph.D., S.T.B., J.C.L., The Time and Place for the Celebration of Marriage.

155. DONNELLAN, REV. THOMAS ANDREW, A.B., J.C.L., The Obligation of the Missa pro Populo.
156. ELTZ, REV. LOUIS ANTHONY, A.B., J.C.L., Cooperators in Crimes According to Canon 2209.
157. GASS, REV. SYLVESTER FRANCIS, M.A., J.C.L., Ecclesiastical Pensions.
158. GUINIVEN, REV. JOHN JOSEPH, C.SS.R., J.C.L., The Precept of Hearing Mass.
159. GULCZYNSKI, REV. JOHN THEOPHILUS, J.C.L., The Desecration and Violation of Churches.
160. HAMMILL, REV. JOHN LEO, M.A., J.C.L., The Obligations of the Traveler According to Canon 14.
161. HAYDT, REV. JOHN JOSEPH, A.B., J.C.L., Reserved Benefices.
162. HUSER, REV. ROGER JOHN, O.F.M., A.B., J.C.L., The Canonical Crime of Abortion.
163. KEARNEY, REV. FRANCIS PATRICK, A.B., S.T.L., J.C.L., The Principles of Canon 1127.
164. LINAHEN, REV. LEO JAMES, S.T.L., J.C.L., De Absolutione Complicis In Peccato Turpi.
165. MCCLOSKEY, REV. JOSEPH ALOYSIUS, A.B., J.C.L., The Subject of Ecclesiastical Law According to Canon 12.
166. O'NEILL, REV. FRANCIS JOSEPH, C.SS.R., J.C.L., The Dismissal of Religious in Temporary Vows.
167. PRINCE, REV. JOHN EDWARD, A.B., S.T.B., J.C.L., The Diocesan Chancellor.
168. RIESNER, REV. ALBERT JOSEPH, C.SS.R., J.C.L., Apostates and Fugitives from Religious Institutes.
169. STENGER, REV. JOSEPH BERNARD, J.C.L., The Mortgaging of Church Property.
170. WALDRON, REV. JOSEPH FRANCIS, A.B., J.C.L., The Minister of Baptism.
171. WILLETT, REV. ROBERT ALBERT, J.C.L., The Probative Value of Documents in Ecclesiastical Trials.
172. WOEBER, REV. EDWARD MARTIN, M.A., J.C.L., The Interpellations.

www.ingramcontent.com/pod-product-compliance
Lightning Source LLC
LaVergne TN
LVHW050246080826
844660LV00012B/602

* 9 7 8 0 8 1 3 2 2 3 5 5 1 *